Engineering and Scientific
Computations Using MATLAB®

Engineering and Scientific Computations Using MATLAB®

Sergey E. Lyshevski

Rochester Institute of Technology

A JOHN WILEY & SONS, INC., PUBLICATION

Library of Congress Cataloging-in-Publication Data is available.

ISBN 0-471-46200-4

Printed in the United States of America.

10 9 8 7 6 5 4 3 2 1

Contents

Preface   vii

About the Author   x

1. Matlab Basics   **1**
    1.1.   Introduction   1
    1.2.   Matlab Start   5
    1.3.   Matlab Help and Demo   9
    References   26

2. Matlab Functions, Operators, and Commands   **27**
    2.1.   Mathematical Functions   27
    2.2.   Matlab Characters and Operators   31
    2.3.   Matlab Commands   32
    References   41

3. Matlab and Problem Solving   **42**
    3.1.   Starting Matlab   42
    3.2.   Basic Arithmetic   42
    3.3.   How to Use Some Basic Matlab Features   49
         3.3.1.   Scalars and Basic Operations with Scalars   50
         3.3.2.   Arrays, Vectors, and Basic Operations   51
    3.4.   Matrices and Basic Operations with Matrices   53
    3.5.   Conditions and Loops   73
    3.6.   Illustrative Examples   80
    References   98

4. Matlab Graphics   **99**
    4.1.   Plotting   99
    4.2.   Two- and Three-Dimensional Graphics   113
    4.3.   Illustrative Examples   125
    References   132

5. Matlab Applications: Numerical Simulations of Differential Equations and Introduction to Dynamic Systems   **133**
    5.1.   Solution of Differential Equations and Dynamic Systems Fundamentals   133
    5.2.   Mathematical Model Developments and Matlab Applications   141

5.3.   Modeling and Computing Using MATLAB   152
References   171

6.   SIMULINK   **172**
6.1.   Introduction to SIMULINK   172
6.2.   Engineering and Scientific Computations Using SIMULINK
       with Examples   185
References   206

**APPENDIX: MATLAB Functions, Operators, Characters,
Commands, and Solvers**   **207**
References   225

Index   **226**

PREFACE

I would like to welcome the reader to this MATLAB® book, which is the companion to the high-performance MATLAB environment and outstanding MathWorks users manuals. I sincerely feel that I have written a very practical problem-solving type of book that provides a synergetic, informative, and entertaining learning experience. Having used MATLAB for almost 20 years, I have been challenged to write a coherent book that assist readers in discovering MATLAB from its power and efficiency to its advantages and superiority. Many books and outstanding MATLAB reference manuals are available. The MathWorks user manuals provide an excellent collection of the MATLAB features for professional users [1], while textbooks [2 - 9] have been used to introduce the MATLAB environment for students. Having used the referenced manuals and books with different levels of user and student satisfaction, accomplishment, and success, the critical need to write a focused (companion) book became evident. This is the reason that I have embarked upon project.

This book, in addition to being an excellent companion and self-study textbook, can be used in science and engineering courses in MATLAB as well as a complementary book. In addition to covering MATLAB, the author has strived to build and develop engineering and scientific competence, presenting the material visually, numerically, and analytically. Visualization, numerical and analytical delivery features, fully supported by the MATLAB environment, are documented and emphasized in this book. Real-world examples and problems introduce, motivate, and illustrate the application of MATLAB.

MATLAB books and user manuals have been written, published, and distributed. Unfortunately, the MATLAB environment is usually introduced in the introductory freshman (or sophomore) course with very limited time allocated to cover MATLAB during the allocated modules. This does not allow the instructors to comprehensively cover MATLAB, and inclusive books which cover the material in details and depth cannot be effectively used. Furthermore, there are many engineers and scientists who did not have the chance to study MATLAB at colleges, but would like to master it in the every-day practice MATLAB environment. Therefore, this book covers introductory example-oriented problems. This book is written with the ultimate goal of offering a far-reaching, high-quality, stand-alone and companion-type user-friendly educational textbook which can be efficiently used in introductory MATLAB courses in undergraduate/graduate courses or course modules, and as a self-study or supplementary book.

There are increasing demands for further development in high-performance computing environments, and hundreds of high-level languages exist including C, FORTRAN, PASCAL, etc. This book covers the MATLAB environment, which is uniquely suited to perform heterogeneous simulations, data-intensive analysis, optimization, modeling, code generation, visualization, etc. These features are extremely important in engineering, science, and technology. To avoid possible obstacles, the material is presented in sufficient detail. MATLAB basics are covered to help the reader to fully understand, appreciate, apply, and develop the skills and confidence to work in the MATLAB environment. A wide range of worked-out examples and qualitative illustrations, which are treated in depth, bridge the gap between theoretical knowledge and practice. Step-by-step, *Engineering and Scientific Computations Using MATLAB* guides the reader through the most important aspects and basics in

MATLAB programming and problem-solving: form fundamentals to applications. In this book, many practical real-world problems and examples are solved in MATLAB, which promotes enormous gains in productivity and creativity.

Analysis (analytical and numerical) and simulation are critical and urgently important aspects in design, optimization, development and prototyping of different systems, e.g., from living organisms and systems to man-made devices and systems. This book illustrates that MATLAB can be efficiently used to speed up analysis and design, facilitate enormous gains in productivity and creativity, generate real-time C code, and visualize the results. MATLAB is a computational environment that integrates a great number of toolboxes (e.g., SIMULINK®, Real-Time Workshop, Optimization, Signal Processing, Symbolic Math, etc.). A flexible high-performance simulation, analysis, and design environment, MATLAB has become a standard cost-effective tool within the engineering, science, and technology communities. The book demonstrates the MATLAB capabilities and helps one to master this user-friendly environment in order to attack and solve distinct problems of different complexity. The application of MATLAB increases designer productivity and shows how to use the advanced software. The MATLAB environment offers a rich set of capabilities to efficiently solve a variety of complex analysis, simulation, and optimization problems that require high-level language, robust numeric computations, interactive graphical user interface (GUI), interoperability, data visualization capabilities, etc. The MATLAB files, scripts, statements, and SIMULINK models that are documented in the book can be easily modified to study application-specific problems encountered in practice. A wide spectrum of practical real-world problems are simulated and analyzed in this book. A variety of complex systems described by nonlinear differential equations are thoroughly studied, and SIMULINK diagrams to simulate dynamic systems and numerical results are reported. Users can easily apply these results as well as develop new MATLAB files and SIMULINK block diagrams using the enterprise-wide practical examples. The developed scripts and models are easily assessed, and can be straightforwardly modified.

The major objectives of this readable and user-friendly book are to establish in students, engineers, and scientists confidence in their ability to apply advanced concepts, enhance learning, improve problem-solving abilities, as well as to provide a gradual progression from versatile theoretical to practical topics in order to effectively apply MATLAB accomplishing the desired objectives and milestones. This book is written for engineers, scientists and students interested in the application of the MATLAB environment to solve real-world problems. Students and engineers are not primarily interested in theoretical encyclopedic studies, and engineering and scientific results need to be covered and demonstrated. This book presents well-defined MATLAB basics with step-by-step instructions on how to apply the results by thoroughly studying and solving a great number of practical real-world problems and examples. These worked-out examples prepare one to effectively use the MATLAB environment in practice.

Wiley FTP Web Site

For more information on this book and for the MATLAB files and SIMULINK diagrams please visit the following site ftp://ftp.wiley.com/public/sci_tech_med/matlab/.

Acknowledgments

Many people contributed to this book. First thanks go to my beloved family - my father Edward, mother Adel, wife Marina, daughter Lydia, and son Alexander. I would like to express my sincere acknowledgments to many colleagues and students. It gives me great pleasure to acknowledge the help I received from many people in the preparation of this book. The outstanding John Wiley & Sons team assisted me by providing valuable and deeply treasured feedback. Many thanks to Math-Works, Inc. for supplying the MATLAB environment and encouraging this project.

MathWorks, Inc., 24 Prime Park Way, Natick, MA 01760-15000 http://www.mathworks.com.

Sergey Edward Lyshevski
Department of Electrical Engineering
Rochester Institute of Technology
Rochester, New York 14623
E-mail: *seleee@rit.edu*
Web: *www.rit.edu/~seleee*

REFERENCES

1. *MATLAB 6.5 Release 13,* CD-ROM, MathWorks Inc., 2002.
2. Biran, A. and Breiner, M., *MATLAB For Engineers,* Addison-Wesley, Reading, MA, 1995.
3. Dabney, J. B. and Harman, T. L., *Mastering SIMULINK 2,* Prentice Hall, Upper Saddle River, NJ, 1998.
4. Etter, D. M., *Engineering Problem Solving with MATLAB,* Prentice Hall, Upper Saddle River, NJ, 1993.
5. Hanselman, D. and Littlefield, B., *The Student Edition of MATLAB,* Prentice Hall, Upper Saddle River, NJ, 1997.
6. Hanselman, D. and Littlefield, B., *Mastering MATLAB 5,* Prentice Hall, Upper Saddle River, NJ, 1998.
7. Palm, W. J., *Introduction to MATLAB for Engineers,* McGraw-Hill, Boston, MA, 2001.
8. Recktenwald, G., *Numerical Methods with MATLAB: Implementations and Applications,* Prentice Hall, Upper Saddle River, NJ, 2000.
9. *User's Guide. The Student Edition of MATLAB: The Ultimate Computing Environment for Technical Education,* MathWorks, Prentice Hall, NJ, 1995.

ABOUT THE AUTHOR

Sergey Edward Lyshevski was born in Kiev, Ukraine. He received M.S. (1980) and Ph.D. (1987) degrees from Kiev Polytechnic Institute, both in Electrical Engineering. From 1980 to 1993 Dr. Lyshevski held faculty positions at the Department of Electrical Engineering at Kiev Polytechnic Institute and the Academy of Sciences of Ukraine. From 1989 to 1993 he was the Microelectronic and Electromechanical Systems Division Head at the Academy of Sciences of Ukraine. From 1993 to 2002 he was with Purdue School of Engineering as an Associate Professor of Electrical and Computer Engineering. In 2002, Dr. Lyshevski joined Rochester Institute of Technology as a professor of Electrical Engineering, professor of Microsystems Engineering, and Gleason Chair.

Dr. Lyshevski serves as the Senior Faculty Fellow at the US Surface and Undersea Naval Warfare Centers. He is the author of 8 books (including *Nano- and Micro-Electromechanical Systems: Fundamentals of Micro- and Nanoengineering,* CRC Press, 2000; *MEMS and NEMS: Systems, Devices, and Structures,* CRC Press, 2002), and author and co-author of more than 250 journal articles, handbook chapters, and regular conference papers. His current teaching and research activities are in the areas of MEMS and NEMS (CAD, design, high-fidelity modeling, data-intensive analysis, heterogeneous simulation, fabrication), micro- and nanoengineering, intelligent large-scale microsystems, learning configurations, novel architectures, self-organization, micro- and nanoscale devices (actuators, sensors, logics, switches, memories, etc.), nanocomputers and their components, reconfigureable (adaptive) defect-tolerant computer architectures, systems informatics, etc. Dr. Lyshevski has made significant contribution in design, application, verification, and implementation of advanced aerospace, automotive, electromechanical, and naval systems.

Dr. Lyshevski made 29 invited presentations (nationally and internationally). He serves as the CRC Books Series Editor in *Nano- and Microscience, Engineering, Technology, and Medicine.* Dr. Lyshevski has taught undergraduate and graduate courses in NEMS, MEMS, microsystems, computer architecture, microelectromechanical motion devices, integrated circuits, signals and systems, etc.

Chapter 1

MATLAB Basics

1.1. Introduction

I (and probably many engineers and researchers) remember the difficulties that we had solving even simple engineering and scientific problems in the 1970s and 1980s. These problems have been solved through viable mathematical methods and algorithms to simplify and reduce the complexity of problems enhancing the robustness and stability. However, many problems can be approached and solved only through high-fidelity modeling, heterogeneous simulation, parallel computing, and data-intensive analysis. Even in those days, many used to apply Basic, C, FORTRAN, PL, and Pascal in numerical analysis and simulations. Though I cannot regret the great experience I had exploring many high-performance languages, revolutionary improvements were made in the middle 1980s with the development of the meaningful high-performance application-specific software environments (e.g., MATEMATICA, MATLAB®, MATRIX$_X$, etc.). These developments, which date back at least to the mid 1960s when FORTRAN and other languages were used to develop the application-specific toolboxes, were partially unsuccessful due to limited software capabilities, flexibility, and straightforwardness. MATLAB, introduced in the middle 1980s, is one of the most important and profound advances in computational and applied engineering and science.

MATLAB (MATrix LABoratory) is a high-performance interacting data-intensive software environment for high-efficiency engineering and scientific numerical calculations [1]. Applications include: heterogeneous simulations and data-intensive analysis of very complex systems and signals, comprehensive matrix and arrays manipulations in numerical analysis, finding roots of polynomials, two- and three-dimensional plotting and graphics for different coordinate systems, integration and differentiation, signal processing, control, identification, symbolic calculus, optimization, etc. The goal of MATLAB is to enable the users to solve a wide spectrum of analytical and numerical problems using matrix-based methods, attain excellent interfacing and interactive capabilities, compile with high-level programming languages, ensure robustness in data-intensive analysis and heterogeneous simulations, provide easy access to and straightforward implementation of state-of-the-art numerical algorithms, guarantee powerful graphical features, etc. Due to high flexibility and versatility, the MATLAB environment has been significantly enhanced and developed during recent years. This provides users with advanced cutting-edge algorithms, enormous data-handling abilities, and powerful programming tools. MATLAB is based on a high-level matrix/array language with control flow statements, functions, data structures, input/output, and object-oriented programming features.

MATLAB was originally developed to provide easy access to matrix software developed by the LINPACK and EISPACK matrix computation software. MATLAB has evolved over the last 20 years and become the standard instructional tool for introductory and advanced courses in science, engineering, and technology. The MATLAB environment allows one to integrate user-friendly tools with superior computational capabilities. As a result, MATLAB is one of the most useful tools for scientific and engineering calculations and computing. Users practice and appreciate the MATLAB environment interactively, enjoy the flexibility and completeness, analyze and verify the results by applying the range of build-in commands and functions, expand MATLAB by developing their own application-specific files, etc. Users quickly access data files, programs, and graphics using MATLAB help. A family of application-specific toolboxes, with a specialized collection of m-files for solving problems commonly encountered in practice, ensures comprehensiveness and effectiveness. SIMULINK is a companion graphical mouse-driven interactive environment enhancing MATLAB. SIMULINK® is used for simulating linear and nonlinear continuous- and discrete-time dynamic systems. The MATLAB features are illustrated in Figure 1.1.

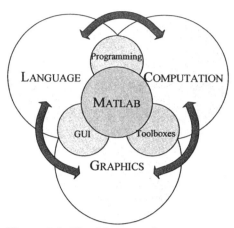

Figure 1.1. The MATLAB features

A great number of books and MathWorks user manuals in MATLAB, SIMULINK and different MATLAB toolboxes are available. In addition to demonstrations (demos) and viable help available, the MathWorks Inc. educational web site can be used as references (e.g., http://education.mathworks.com and http://www.mathworks.com). This book is intended to help students and engineers to use MATLAB efficiently and professionally, showing and demonstrating how MATLAB and SIMULINK can be applied. The MATLAB environment (MATLAB 6.5, release 13) is covered in this book, and the website http://www.mathworks.com/access/helpdesk/help/helpdesk.shtml can assist users to master the MATLAB features. It should be emphasized that all MATLAB documentation and user manuals are available in the Portable Document Format (PDF) using the Help Desk. For example, the MATLAB `help` folder includes all user manuals (C:\MATLAB6p5\help\pdf_doc). The subfolders are illustrated in Figure 1.2.

aeroblks	ccslink	cdma	combuilder	comm	commblks	compiler	control	curvefit	daq
database	datafeed	dials	dspblks	ecoder	exlink	filterdesign	finance	finderiv	fixpoint
ftseries	fuzzy	garch	ident	images	instrument	map	matlab	matlabxl	mbc
mpc	mpc555dk	mutools	ncd	nnet	optim	otherdocs	pde	physmod	powersys
reqmgt	robust	rptgen	rtw	rtwin	runtime	sb2sl	signal	simulink	splines
stateflow	stats	symbolic	tic6000	vr	wavelet	webserver	xpc		

Figure 1.2. Subfolders in the MATLAB `help` folder

The matlab subfolders have 18 MATLAB user manuals as reported in Figure 1.3.

apiext.pdf Adobe Acrobat Document 3,125 KB	apiref.pdf Adobe Acrobat Document 3,290 KB	buildgui.pdf Adobe Acrobat Document 2,027 KB
getstart.pdf Adobe Acrobat Document 2,687 KB	graphg.pdf Adobe Acrobat Document 13,245 KB	ins_pcmc.pdf Adobe Acrobat Document 1,120 KB
ins_unix.pdf Adobe Acrobat Document 658 KB	mac_install_using_book.pdf Adobe Acrobat Document 587 KB	matfile_format.pdf Adobe Acrobat Document 400 KB
newfeat_r11.pdf Adobe Acrobat Document 1,418 KB	newfeat_r11p1.pdf Adobe Acrobat Document 178 KB	programming_tips.pdf Adobe Acrobat Document 515 KB
refbook2.pdf Adobe Acrobat Document 6,013 KB	refbook3.pdf Adobe Acrobat Document 7,686 KB	refbook.pdf Adobe Acrobat Document 6,002 KB
relnotes.pdf Adobe Acrobat Document 329 KB	rn.pdf Adobe Acrobat Document 1,204 KB	using_ml.pdf Adobe Acrobat Document 10,069 KB

Figure 1.3. MATLAB user manuals in the matlab subfolder

These user manuals can be accessed and printed using the Adobe Acrobat Reader. Correspondingly, this book does not attempt to rewrite these available thousand-page MATLAB user manuals. For example, the outstanding *MATLAB The Language of Technical Computing* manual, available as the ml.pdf file, consists of 1188 pages. The front page of the *MATLAB The Language of Technical Computing* user manual is shown in Figure 1.4.

The Language of Technical Computing

Computation
Visualization
Programming

Using MATLAB   The MathWorks
Version 6

Figure 1.4. Front page of the *MATLAB The Language of Technical Computing* user manual

This book focuses on MATLAB applications and educates the reader on how to solve practical problems using step-by-step instructions.

The MATLAB environment consists of the following five major ingredients: (1) MATLAB Language, (2) MATLAB Working Environment, (3) Handle Graphics®, (4) MATLAB Mathematical Function Library, and (5) MATLAB Application Program Interface.

The MATLAB Language is a high-level matrix/array language with control flow statements, functions, data structures, input/output, and object-oriented programming features. It allows the user to program in the small (creating throw-away programs) and program in the large (creating complete large and complex application-specific programs).

The MATLAB Working Environment is a set of tools and facilities. It includes facilities for managing the variables in workspace, manipulation of variables and data, importing and exporting data, etc. Tools for developing, managing, debugging, and profiling m-files for different applications are available.

Handle Graphics is the MATLAB graphics system. It includes high-level commands for two- and three-dimensional data visualization, image processing, animation, and presentation. It also includes low-level commands that allow the user to fully customize the appearance of graphics and build complete graphical user interfaces (GUIs).

The MATLAB Mathematical Function Library is a collection of computationally efficient and robust algorithms and functions ranging from elementary functions (sine, cosine, tangent, cotangent, etc.) to specialized functions (eigenvalues, Bessel functions, Fourier and Laplace transforms, etc.) commonly used in scientific and engineering practice.

The MATLAB Application Program Interface (API) is a library that allows the user to write C and FORTRAN programs that interact within the MATLAB environment. It includes facilities for calling routines from MATLAB (dynamic linking), calling MATLAB for computing and processing, reading and writing m-files, etc. Real-Time Workshop® allows the user to generate C code from block diagrams and to run it for real-time systems.

MATLAB 6.5 is supported by the following platforms: Microsoft Windows, Windows Millennium, Windows NT, Compaq Alpha, Linux, SGI, and Sun Solaris.

In this introduction, before giving in the MATLAB description, the application of MATLAB should be justified through familiar examples. This will provide the reasoning for MATLAB applications. This book is intended as an introductory MATLAB textbook though advanced application-specific problems are solved to illustrate the applicability and versatility of the MATLAB environment. Therefore familiar examples will be covered. In multivariable calculus, students study parametric and polar equations, vectors, coordinate systems (Cartesian, cylindrical, and spherical), vector-valued functions, derivatives, partial derivatives, directional derivatives, gradient, optimization problems, multiple integration, integration in vector fields, and other topics. In contrast, linear algebra emphasizes matrix techniques for solving systems of linear and nonlinear equations covering matrices and operations with matrices, determinants, vector spaces, independent and dependent sets of vectors, bases for vector spaces, linear transformations, eigenvalues and eigenvectors, orthogonal sets, least squares approximation, interpolation, etc. The MATLAB environment is uniquely suitable to solving a variety of problems in engineering and science. Using the calculus and physics background, a variety of real-world engineering problems can be attacked and resolved. This book illustrates the application of MATLAB in order to solve of this class of problems.

MATLAB integrates computation, visualization, and programming in an easy-to-use systematic, robust and computationally efficient environment where problems and solutions are expressed in familiar (commonly used) mathematical notation. The user can perform mathematic computation, algorithm development, simulation, prototyping, data analysis, visualization, interactive graphics, and application-specific developments including graphical user interface features. In MATLAB, the data is manipulated in the array form, allowing the user to solve complex problems. It was emphasized that the MATLAB environment was originally developed using data-intensive matrix computation methods.

MATLAB is a high-performance environment for engineering, scientific and technical computing, visualization, and programming. It will be illustrated that in MATLAB, the user straightforwardly performs numerical computations, analytical and numerical analysis, algorithm developments, heterogeneous simulations, data-intensive analysis, visualization, graphics, etc. Compared with other computational environments, in MATLAB, the data analysis, manipulation, processing, and computing do not require arrays dimensioning, allowing one to very efficiently perform matrix computations. The MATLAB environment features a family of application-specific toolboxes which integrate specialized m-files that extend MATLAB in order to approach and solve particular application-specific problems. It was mentioned that the MATLAB system environment consists of five main parts: the MATLAB language (high-level matrix-array language with control flow statements, functions, data structures, input/output, and object-oriented programming features), the MATLAB Working Environment (set of tools to manage the variables in the workspace, import and export the data, as well as tools for developing, managing, debugging, and profiling m-files), the Handle Graphics (high-performance graphic system that includes high-level commands for two- and three-dimensional data visualization, image processing, animation, graphics presentation, and low-level commands allowing the user to customize the appearance of graphics and build graphical user interfaces), the MATLAB Mathematical Function Library (collection of computational algorithms ranging from elementary to complex and specialized functions as well as transforms), and the MATLAB application program interface (library that allows one to write C and FORTRAN programs that interact with MATLAB).

1.2. MATLAB Start

MATLAB is a high-performance language for technical computing. It integrates computation, visualization and programming within an easy-to-use environment where problems and solutions are represented in familiar notation. Mathematics, computation, algorithm development, simulation, data analysis, visualization, graphics and graphical user interface building can be performed. One of the most important features, compared with Basic, C, FORTRAN, PL, Pascal, and other high-performance languages, is that MATLAB does not require dimensioning. MATLAB features application-specific toolboxes which utilize specific and well-defined methods. To start MATLAB, double-click the MATLAB icon (illustrated below),

MATLAB 6.5.lnk

and the MATLAB Command and Workspace windows appear on the screen - see Figure 1.5.

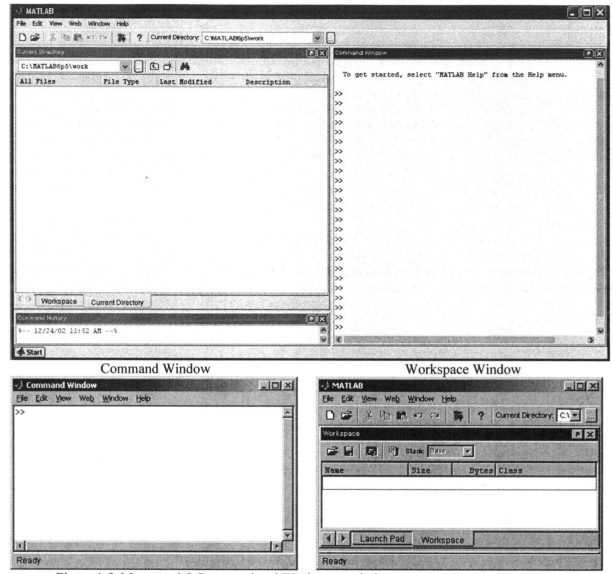

Command Window　　　　　　　　　　　　　　　Workspace Window

Figure 1.5. MATLAB 6.5 Command and Workspace windows

For all MATLAB versions, the line

>>

is the MATLAB prompt.

For the UNIX platform, to start MATLAB, type MATLAB at the operating system prompt.

To end MATLAB, select Exit MATLAB (Ctrl+Q) from the File menu, or type

>> quit

in the Command Window.

After each MATLAB command, the Enter (Return) key must be pressed. One interacts with MATLAB using the Command Window. The MATLAB prompt >> is displayed in the Command Window, and a blinking cursor appears to the right of the prompt when the Command Window is active. Typing ver, we have the information regarding the MATLAB version and the MATLAB toolboxes that are available (see Figure 1.6 for MATLAB versions 6.5, 6.1, and 6.0).

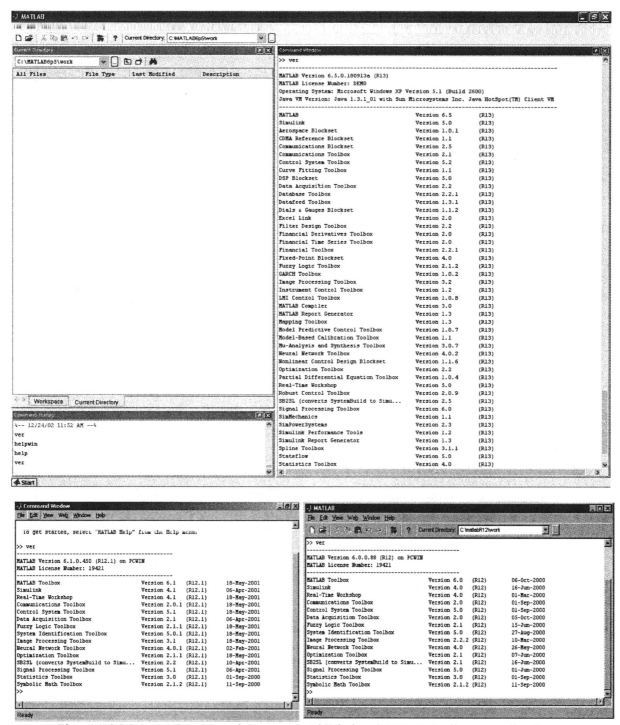

Figure 1.6. MATLAB 6.5, 6.1, and 6.0 Command Window (MATLAB toolboxes are listed)

MATLAB Command Window. The MATLAB Command Window is where the user interacts with MATLAB. We illustrate the MATLAB application through a simple example. To find the sum 1+2 type

```
>> 1+3
```

and press the Enter key. The result displayed is

```
4
```

Typing
```
>> a=1+2
```
and pressing the Enter (Return) key, we have the value for a. In particular,
```
a =

    3
```
The MATLAB statement (which uses `ones` function)
```
>> a=ones(3)
```
gives the following three-by-three matrix:
```
a =

    1    1    1
    1    1    1
    1    1    1
```

This represents a three-by-three matrix of ones, e.g., $a = \begin{bmatrix} 1 & 1 & 1 \\ 1 & 1 & 1 \\ 1 & 1 & 1 \end{bmatrix}$.

The Command and Workspace windows are documented in Figure 1.7.

Command Window   Workspace Window

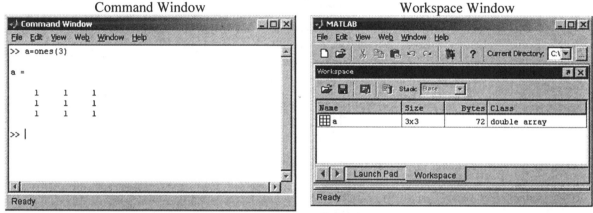

Figure 1.7. Command and Workspace windows for `a=ones(3)`

As soon the prompt line appears, the user is in the MATLAB environment. Online help is available.

Thus, MATLAB has Command, Workspace, File (edit) and Figure windows. To illustrate these features, Figures 1.8 and 1.9 show the above-mentioned windows with the data displayed.

Command Window   Workspace Window

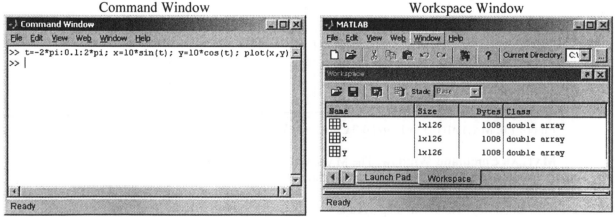

Figure 1.8. Command and Workspace windows

File Window

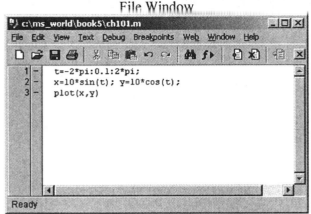

Figure Window

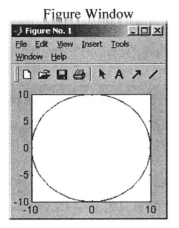

Figure 1.9. File (edit) and Figure windows

1.3. MATLAB Help and Demo

MathWorks offers an extensive set of online and printed documentation. The online MATLAB Function Reference is a compendium of all MATLAB commands, functions, solvers, operators, and characters. You may access this documentation from the MATLAB Help Desk. Microsoft Windows and Macintosh users can also access the Help Desk with the **Help** menu or the **?** icon on the Command Window toolbar. From the Help Desk main menu, one chooses "MATLAB Functions" to display the Function Reference. The online resources are augmented with printed documentation that includes *Getting Started with MATLAB* (covers basic fundamentals) getstart.pdf, *Using MATLAB* (describes how to use MATLAB as both a programming language and a command-line application) using_ml.pdf, *Using MATLAB Graphics* (how to use graphics and visualization tools), *Building GUIs with MATLAB* (covers the construction of graphical user interfaces and introduces the Guide GUI building tool), *MATLAB Application Programmer's Interface Guide* (describes how to write C or FORTRAN programs that interact with MATLAB), *MATLAB New Features Guide* (covers recent and previous MATLAB releases), *MATLAB Release Notes* (explicitly describes features of specific releases), and others as illustrated in Figure 1.3.

MATLAB includes the Command Window, Command History, Launch Pad, Workspace Browser, Array Editor, and other tools to assist the user. The Launch Pad tool displays a list of all the products installed. From the Launch Pad, we view demos, access help, find examples, and obtain interactive tools. For example, the user can get the MATLAB Demos screen to see the MATLAB features. MATLAB 6.5 (as well as earlier MATLAB versions) contains documentation for all the products that are installed.

We can type

```
>> helpwin
>> helpdesk
```
or
```
>> demo
```
and press the Enter key. For example, typing
```
>> helpwin
```
and pressing the Enter key, we have the MATLAB widow shown in Figure 1.10.

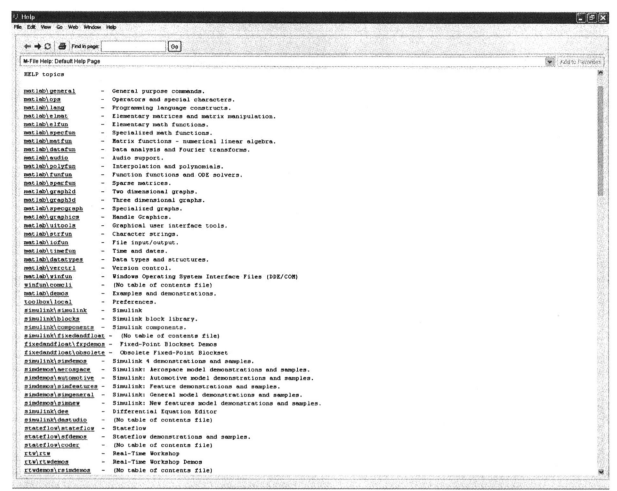

Figure 1.10. MATLAB `helpwin` window

The complete list of the HELP topics is available by typing `help`. In particular, we have

```
>> help

HELP topics:
matlab\general     -  General purpose commands.
matlab\ops         -  Operators and special characters.
matlab\lang        -  Programming language constructs.
matlab\elmat       -  Elementary matrices and matrix manipulation.
matlab\elfun       -  Elementary math functions.
matlab\specfun     -  Specialized math functions.
matlab\matfun      -  Matrix functions - numerical linear algebra.
matlab\datafun     -  Data analysis and Fourier transforms.
matlab\audio       -  Audio support.
matlab\polyfun     -  Interpolation and polynomials.
matlab\funfun      -  Function functions and ODE solvers.
matlab\sparfun     -  Sparse matrices.
matlab\graph2d     -  Two dimensional graphs.
matlab\graph3d     -  Three dimensional graphs.
matlab\specgraph   -  Specialized graphs.
matlab\graphics    -  Handle Graphics.
matlab\uitools     -  Graphical user interface tools.
matlab\strfun      -  Character strings.
matlab\iofun       -  File input/output.
```

```
matlab\timefun        -   Time and dates.
matlab\datatypes      -   Data types and structures.
matlab\verctrl        -   Version control.
matlab\winfun         -   Windows Operating System Interface Files (DDE/COM)
winfun\comcli         -   (No table of contents file)
matlab\demos          -   Examples and demonstrations.
toolbox\local         -   Preferences.
simulink\simulink     -   Simulink
simulink\blocks       -   Simulink block library.
simulink\components   -   Simulink components.
simulink\fixedandfloat -  (No table of contents file)
fixedandfloat\fxpdemos -  Fixed-Point Blockset Demos
fixedandfloat\obsolete -  Obsolete Fixed-Point Blockset
simulink\simdemos     -   Simulink 4 demonstrations and samples.
simdemos\aerospace    -   Simulink: Aerospace model demonstrations and samples.
simdemos\automotive   -   Simulink: Automotive model demonstrations and samples.
simdemos\simfeatures  -   Simulink: Feature demonstrations and samples.
simdemos\simgeneral   -   Simulink: General model demonstrations and samples.
simdemos\simnew       -   Simulink: New features model demonstrations and samples.
simulink\dee          -   Differential Equation Editor
simulink\dastudio     -   (No table of contents file)
stateflow\stateflow   -   Stateflow
stateflow\sfdemos     -   Stateflow demonstrations and samples.
stateflow\coder       -   (No table of contents file)
rtw\rtw               -   Real-Time Workshop
rtw\rtwdemos          -   Real-Time Workshop Demos
rtwdemos\rsimdemos    -   (No table of contents file)
asap2\asap2           -   (No table of contents file)
asap2\user            -   (No table of contents file)
aeroblks\aeroblks     -   Aerospace Blockset
aeroblks\aerodemos    -   Aerospace Blockset demonstrations and examples.
cdma\cdma             -   CDMA Reference Blockset.
cdma\cdmamasks        -   CDMA Reference Blockset mask helper functions.
cdma\cdmamex          -   CDMA Reference Blockset S-Functions.
cdma\cdmademos        -   CDMA Reference Blockset demonstrations and examples.
comm\comm             -   Communications Toolbox.
comm\commdemos        -   Communications Toolbox Demonstrations.
comm\commobsolete     -   Archived MATLAB Files from Communications Toolbox Version 1.5.
commblks\commblks     -   Communications Blockset.
commblks\commmasks    -   Communications Blockset mask helper functions.
commblks\commmex      -   Communications Blockset S-functions.
commblks\commblksdemos -  Communications Blockset Demos.
commblksobsolete\commblksobsolete - Archived Simulink Files from Communications
Toolbox Version 1.5.
toolbox\compiler      -   MATLAB Compiler
control\control       -   Control System Toolbox.
control\ctrlguis      -   Control System Toolbox -- GUI support functions.
control\ctrlobsolete  -   Control System Toolbox -- obsolete commands.
control\ctrlutil      -   (No table of contents file)
control\ctrldemos     -   Control System Toolbox -- Demos.
curvefit\curvefit     -   Curve Fitting Toolbox
curvefit\cftoolgui    -   (No table of contents file)
daq\daq               -   Data Acquisition Toolbox.
daq\daqguis           -   Data Acquisition Toolbox - Data Acquisition Soft Instruments.
daq\daqdemos          -   Data Acquisition Toolbox - Data Acquisition Demos.
database\database     -   Database Toolbox.
database\dbdemos      -   Database Toolbox Demonstration Functions.
database\vqb          -   Visual Query Builder functions.
datafeed\datafeed     -   Datafeed Toolbox.
datafeed\dfgui        -   Datafeed Toolbox Graphical User Interface
toolbox\dials         -   Dials & Gauges Blockset
dspblks\dspblks       -   DSP Blockset
dspblks\dspmasks      -   DSP Blockset mask helper functions.
```

```
dspblks\dspmex        -  DSP Blockset S-Function MEX-files.
dspblks\dspdemos      -  DSP Blockset demonstrations and examples.
toolbox\exlink        -  Excel Link.
filterdesign\filterdesign -  Filter Design Toolbox
filterdesign\quantization -  (No table of contents file)
filterdesign\filtdesdemos -  Filter Design Toolbox Demonstrations.
finance\finance       -  Financial Toolbox.
finance\calendar      -  Financial Toolbox calendar functions.
finance\findemos      -  Financial Toolbox demonstration functions.
finance\finsupport    -  (No table of contents file)
finderiv\finderiv     -  Financial Derivatives Toolbox.
toolbox\fixpoint      -  Fixed-Point Blockset
ftseries\ftseries     -  Financial Time Series Toolbox
ftseries\ftsdemos     -  (No table of contents file)
ftseries\ftsdata      -  (No table of contents file)
ftseries\ftstutorials -  (No table of contents file)
fuzzy\fuzzy           -  Fuzzy Logic Toolbox.
fuzzy\fuzdemos        -  Fuzzy Logic Toolbox Demos.
garch\garch           -  GARCH Toolbox.
garch\garchdemos      -  (No table of contents file)
ident\ident           -  System Identification Toolbox.
ident\idobsolete      -  (No table of contents file)
ident\idguis          -  (No table of contents file)
ident\idutils         -  (No table of contents file)
ident\iddemos         -  (No table of contents file)
ident\idhelp          -  (No table of contents file)
images\images         -  Image Processing Toolbox.
images\imdemos        -  Image Processing Toolbox --- demos and sample images
instrument\instrument -  Instrument Control Toolbox.
instrument\instrumentdemos -  (No table of contents file)
lmi\lmictrl           -  LMI Control Toolbox: Control Applications
lmi\lmilab            -  LMI Control Toolbox
map\map               -  Mapping Toolbox
map\mapdisp           -  Mapping Toolbox Map Definition and Display.
map\mapproj           -  Mapping Toolbox Projections.
mbc\mbc               -  Model-Based Calibration Toolbox
mbc\mbcdata           -  Model-Based Calibration Toolbox.
mbc\mbcdesign         -  Model-Based Calibration Toolbox.
mbc\mbcexpr           -  Model-Based Calibration Toolbox.
mbc\mbcguitools       -  Model-Based Calibration Toolbox.
mbc\mbclayouts        -  (No table of contents file)
mbc\mbcmodels         -  Model-Based Calibration Toolbox.
mbc\mbcsimulink       -  Model-Based Calibration Toolbox.
mbc\mbctools          -  Model-Based Calibration Toolbox.
mbc\mbcview           -  Model-Based Calibration Toolbox.
mech\mech             -  SimMechanics
mech\mechdemos        -  SimMechanics Demos.
mpc\mpccmds           -  Model Predictive Control Toolbox.
mpc\mpcdemos          -  Model Predictive Control Toolbox
mutools\commands      -  Mu-Analysis and Synthesis Toolbox.
mutools\subs          -  Mu-Analysis and Synthesis Toolbox.
toolbox\ncd           -  Nonlinear Control Design Blockset
nnet\nnet             -  Neural Network Toolbox.
nnet\nnutils          -  (No table of contents file)
nnet\nncontrol        -  Neural Network Toolbox Control System Functions.
nnet\nndemos          -  Neural Network Demonstrations.
nnet\nnobsolete       -  (No table of contents file)
toolbox\optim         -  Optimization Toolbox
toolbox\pde           -  Partial Differential Equation Toolbox.
simulink\perftools    -  Simulink Performance Tools
simulink\mdldiff      -  Simulink Graphical Merge
simulink\simcoverage  -  Simulink Model Coverage Tool
rtw\accel             -  Simulink Accelerator
```

```
powersys\powersys      -   SimPowerSystems
powersys\powerdemo     -   SimPowerSystems Demos.
toolbox\robust         -   Robust Control Toolbox.
toolbox\rptgen         -   MATLAB Report Generator
toolbox\rptgenext      -   Simulink Report Generator
toolbox\sb2sl          -   SB2SL (converts SystemBuild to Simulink)
signal\signal          -   Signal Processing Toolbox
signal\sigtools        -   Filter Design & Analysis Tool (GUI)
signal\sptoolgui       -   Signal Processing Toolbox GUI
signal\sigdemos        -   Signal Processing Toolbox Demonstrations.
toolbox\splines        -   Spline Toolbox.
toolbox\stats          -   Statistics Toolbox
toolbox\symbolic       -   Symbolic Math Toolbox.
vr\vr                  -   Virtual Reality Toolbox
vr\vrdemos             -   Virtual Reality Toolbox examples.
wavelet\wavelet        -   Wavelet Toolbox
wavelet\wavedemo       -   Wavelet Toolbox Demonstrations.
MATLAB6p5\work         -   (No table of contents file)


For more help on directory/topic, type "help topic".
For command syntax information, type "help syntax".
```

By clicking MATLAB\general, we have the Help Window illustrated in Figure 1.11 and a complete description is given as well.

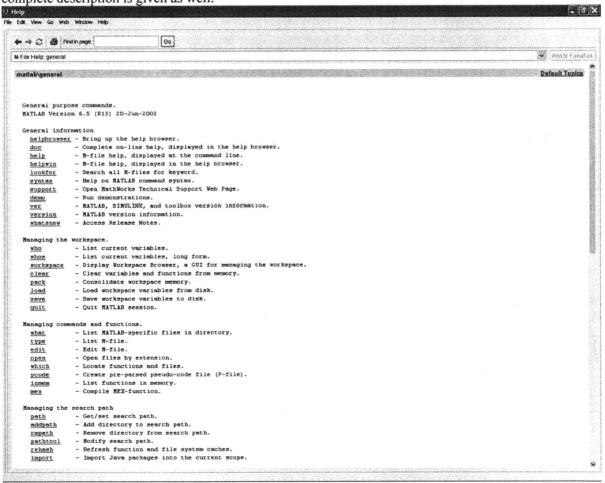

Figure 1.11. Help Window

General purpose commands.

General purpose commands.
MATLAB Version 6.5 (R13) 20-Jun-2002

General information
```
  helpbrowser  - Bring up the help browser.
  doc          - Complete on-line help, displayed in the help browser.
  help         - M-file help, displayed at the command line.
  helpwin      - M-file help, displayed in the help browser.
  lookfor      - Search all M-files for keyword.
  syntax       - Help on MATLAB command syntax.
  support      - Open MathWorks Technical Support Web Page.
  demo         - Run demonstrations.
  ver          - MATLAB, SIMULINK, and toolbox version information.
  version      - MATLAB version information.
  whatsnew     - Access Release Notes.
```

Managing the workspace.
```
  who          - List current variables.
  whos         - List current variables, long form.
  workspace    - Display Workspace Browser, a GUI for managing the workspace.
  clear        - Clear variables and functions from memory.
  pack         - Consolidate workspace memory.
  load         - Load workspace variables from disk.
  save         - Save workspace variables to disk.
  quit         - Quit MATLAB session.
```

Managing commands and functions.
```
  what         - List MATLAB-specific files in directory.
  type         - List M-file.
  edit         - Edit M-file.
  open         - Open files by extension.
  which        - Locate functions and files.
  pcode        - Create pre-parsed pseudo-code file (P-file).
  inmem        - List functions in memory.
  mex          - Compile MEX-function.
```

Managing the search path
```
  path         - Get/set search path.
  addpath      - Add directory to search path.
  rmpath       - Remove directory from search path.
  pathtool     - Modify search path.
  rehash       - Refresh function and file system caches.
  import       - Import Java packages into the current scope.
```

Controlling the command window.
```
  echo         - Echo commands in M-files.
  more         - Control paged output in command window.
  diary        - Save text of MATLAB session.
  format       - Set output format.
  beep         - Produce beep sound.
```

Operating system commands
```
  cd           - Change current working directory.
  copyfile     - Copy a file or directory.
  movefile     - Move a file or directory.
```

```
    delete        - Delete file.
    pwd           - Show (print) current working directory.
    dir           - List directory.
    fileattrib    - Get or set attributes of files and directories.
    isdir         - True if argument is a directory.
    mkdir         - Make directory.
    rmdir         - Remove directory.
    getenv        - Get environment variable.
    !             - Execute operating system command (see PUNCT).
    dos           - Execute DOS command and return result.
    unix          - Execute UNIX command and return result.
    system        - Execute system command and return result.
    perl          - Execute Perl command and return result.
    web           - Open Web browser on site or files.
    computer      - Computer type.
    isunix        - True for the UNIX version of MATLAB.
    ispc          - True for the PC (Windows) version of MATLAB.

Debugging M-files.
    debug         - List debugging commands.
    dbstop        - Set breakpoint.
    dbclear       - Remove breakpoint.
    dbcont        - Continue execution.
    dbdown        - Change local workspace context.
    dbstack       - Display function call stack.
    dbstatus      - List all breakpoints.
    dbstep        - Execute one or more lines.
    dbtype        - List M-file with line numbers.
    dbup          - Change local workspace context.
    dbquit        - Quit debug mode.
    dbmex         - Debug MEX-files (UNIX only).

Profiling M-files.
    profile       - Profile function execution time.
    profreport    - Generate profile report.

Tools to locate dependent functions of an M-file.
    depfun        - Locate dependent functions of an m-file.
    depdir        - Locate dependent directories of an m-file.
    inmem         - List functions in memory.

See also punct.
```

When we type

```
>> helpdesk
```

the MATLAB Help Window is displayed for all MATLAB versions. For example, for MATLAB 6.1, see Figure 1.12.

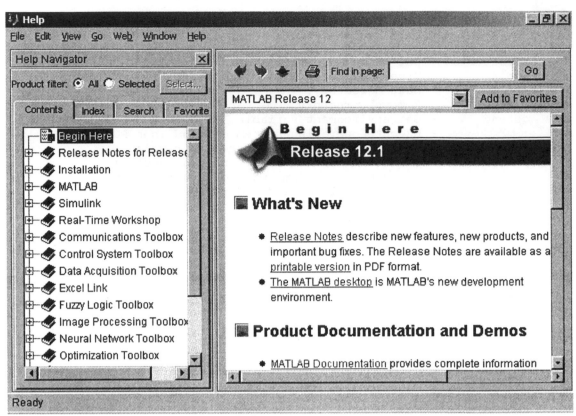

Figure 1.12. MATLAB 6.1 `helpdesk` window

The complete MATLAB documentation is available for users. In general, the use of the `help` and `demo` commands is the simplest way to find the needed information. Typing

```
>> help log
```

and pressing the Enter key, the following information is displayed:

```
LOG    Natural logarithm.
   LOG(X) is the natural logarithm of the elements of X.
   Complex results are produced if X is not positive.
   See also LOG2, LOG10, EXP, LOGM.
 Overloaded methods
   help sym/log.m
```

Typing

```
>> help sym/log.m
```

and pressing the Enter key, the following is displayed:

```
LOG     Symbolic matrix element-wise natural logarithm.
```

The Help System will be also covered in the next section.

If the user has never used MATLAB, the `demo` command provides very useful tutorial features. Typing

```
>> demo
```

and pressing the Enter key guides us into the MATLAB Demos Window as illustrated in Figure 1.13 for MATLAB 6.5 and 6.1.

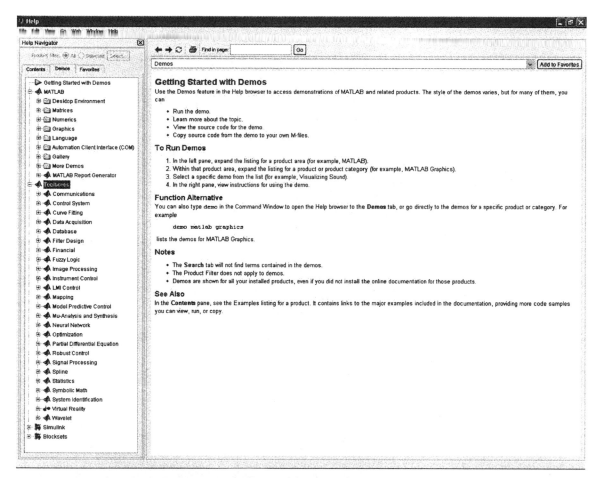

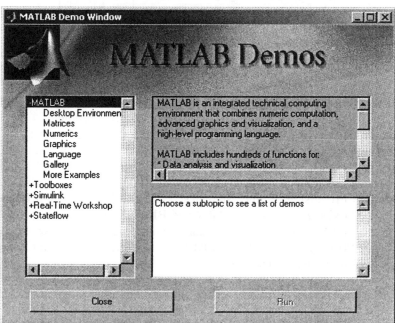

Figure 1.13. MATLAB 6.5 and 6.1 Demos Windows

A list of topics which have demonstrations appears in the left-hand window, while the information on these topics appears in the upper right-hand window. In order to expand a topic in the left window, double-click on it and subtopics will appear below. When the user clicks on one of these, a list of possible demonstrations to run in the lower right-hand window appears. The button below this window changes to run demonstration. Choosing the subtopics (Matrices, Numerics, Visualization, Language/Graphics, Gallery, Games, Miscellaneous and To learn more), different topics will be explained and thoroughly covered. For example, clicking the subtopic Matrices, we have the Matrices MATLAB Demos (demonstrations) Window, as documented in Figure 1.14.

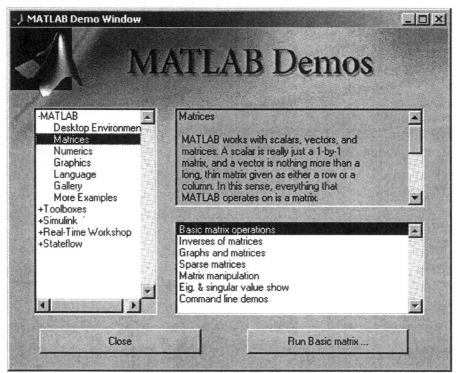

Figure 1.14. Matrices MATLAB 6.1 Demos Window

By double clicking Basic matrix operations, Inverse of matrices, Graphs and matrices, Sparse matrices, Matrix multiplication, Eigenvalues and singular value show, and Command line demos, illustrative example are available to demonstrate, examine, and explore different problems.

Newest MATLAB releases provide the user with the full capabilities of the MATLAB environment. As illustrated, MATLAB 6.5 integrates Communication, Control System, Curve Fitting, Data Acquisition, Database, Filter Design, Financial, Fuzzy Logic, Image Processing, Instrument Control, LMI, Mapping, Model Predictive Control, Mu-Analysis and Synthesis, Neural Network, Optimization, Partial Differential Equations, Robust Control, Signal Processing, Spline, Statistics, Symbolic Math, System Identification, Virtual Reality, and Wavelet Toolboxes, as well as SIMULINK and Blocksets environments and libraries. The demonstration capabilities of MATLAB 6.5 were significantly enhanced, and Figures 1.15 and 1.16 illustrate the application of the MATLAB environment and SIMULINK to perform simulations for the F-14 and three-degrees-of-freedom guided missile models.

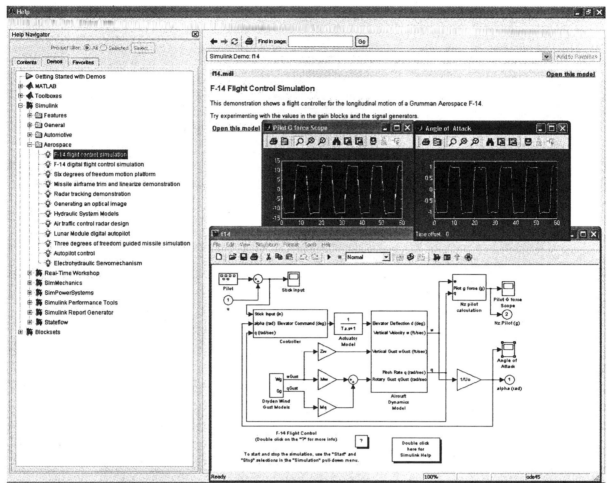

Figure 1.15. MATLAB 6.5 Demos Window running F-14 flight control simulation

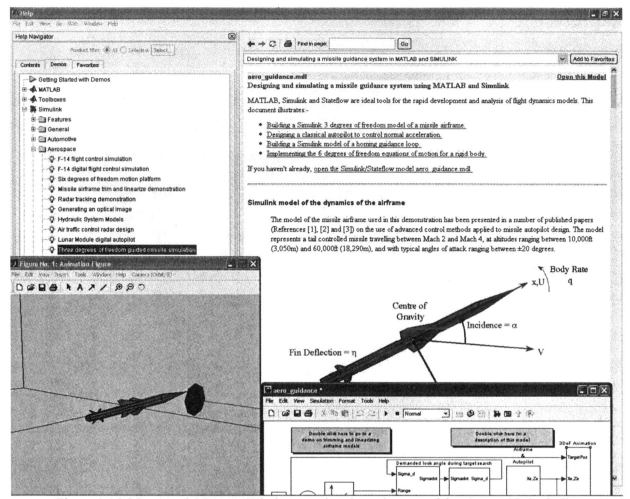

Figure 1.16. MATLAB 6.5 Demos Window running three-degrees-of-freedom guided missile simulation with animation in SIMULINK

The M-file Editor/Debugger enables one to view, develop, edit, and debug MATLAB programs. Using the menu, the user can select a code segment for evaluation in the Command Window. Many MATLAB routines are developed and supplied as readable m-files, allowing one to examine the source code, learn from it, and modify it for specific applications and problems. New functions can be written and added, and links to external software and data sources can be created.

Access to History is performed through the Command History tool in order to maintain a running record of all commands that the user has executed in the MATLAB Command Window. The user can refer back to these commands and execute code directly from the Command History menu.

Access to Files is performed through the Current Directory window and allows one to select a directory to work in. The user can browse, run, and modify files in the directory.

Access to Data is performed through the Workspace Browser, allowing one to view the variables in the MATLAB workspace as well as access the Array Editor to view and edit data.

The commonly used toolboxes are Statistics, Symbolic Math, Partial Differential Equations, etc. An incomplete list of toolboxes, including the application-specific toolboxes, is as follows (see http://www.mathworks.com/access/helpdesk/help/helpdesk.shtml for details):

1. Communication Toolbox
2. Control System Toolbox
3. Data Acquisition Toolbox
4. Database Toolbox
5. Datafeed Toolbox
6. Filter Design Toolbox
7. Financial Toolbox
8. Financial Derivatives Toolbox
9. Fuzzy Logic Toolbox
10. GARCH Toolbox
11. Image Processing Toolbox
12. Instrument Control Toolbox
13. Mapping Toolbox
14. Model Predictive Control Toolbox
15. Mu-Analysis and Synthesis Toolbox
16. Neural Network Toolbox
17. Optimization Toolbox
18. Partial Differential Equations Toolbox
19. Robust Control Toolbox
20. Signal Processing Toolbox
21. Spline Toolbox
22. Statistics Toolbox
23. Symbolic Math Toolbox
24. System Identification Toolbox
25. Wavelet Toolbox

However, the user must purchase and install the toolboxes needed, and different MATLAB versions and configurations might have different toolboxes available, see Figure 1.17. The user can practice examples to quickly learn how to efficiently use MATLAB to solve a wide variety of scientific and engineering problems. Toolboxes are comprehensive collections of MATLAB functions, commands and solvers that expand the MATLAB environment to solve particular classes of problems.

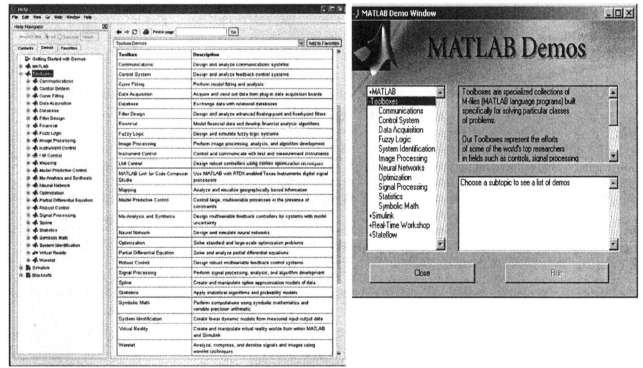

Figure 1.17. MATLAB 6.5. and 6.1 Demos Window with Toolboxes

All MATLAB toolboxes have demonstration features. Figure 1.18 illustrates the MATLAB Demos Window for the Optimization Toolbox.

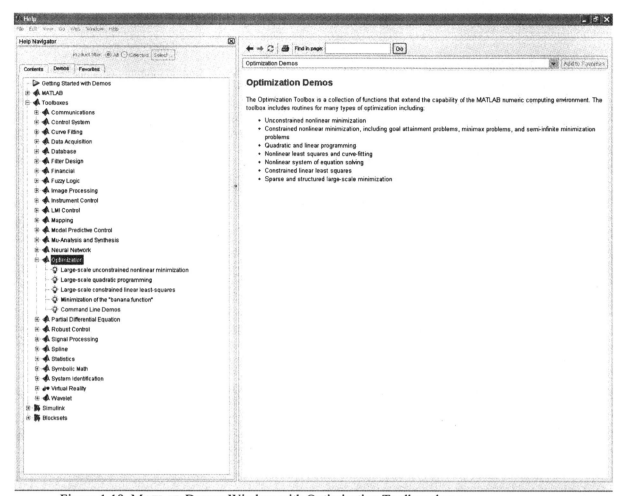

Figure 1.18. MATLAB Demos Window with Optimization Toolbox demo

    The use of the toolboxes allows the user to quickly and efficiently learn the MATLAB capabilities for general and application-specific problems. Click on the Communication, Control Systems, Curve Fitting or other toolboxes for meaningful demonstrations (see Figure 1.18). Hence, the MATLAB environment provides access to different toolboxes and supplies help and demonstrations needed to efficiently use the MATLAB environment.

    It is evident to the reader by now that MATLAB has demonstration programs. One should use

```
» help demos
```

to gain more information, and the number of demos will depend on the version of MATLAB installed.

    MATLAB Exit. To exit MATLAB, type at the MATLAB prompt

```
>> quit
```

or

```
>> exit
```

Close MATLAB using the Exit MATLAB (Ctrl+Q) command in the MATLAB Command Window (File menu).

    MATLAB Menu Bar and Toolbar. Figure 1.19 illustrates the MATLAB menu bar and toolbar in the Command and Workspace windows.

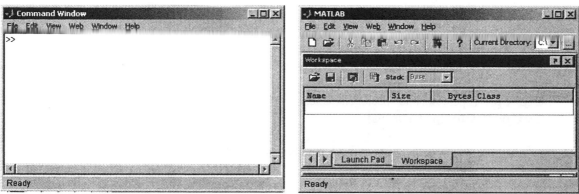

Figure 1.19. MATLAB menu bar and toolbar

The menu bar has File, Edit, View, Window, and Help options. The File Window allows the user to open and close files, create new files (m-files, figures, and model), load and save workspace, print, view recently used files, exit MATLAB, etc. Window allows the user to switch between demo windows. The Help Window offers a set of help features, such as Help Desk, Examples and Demos, About MATLAB, etc. The buttons and the corresponding functions are given in Table 1.1.

Table 1.1. MATLAB buttons

Icon	Description
New file and open file
Cut, copy, and paste
Undo last action
Workspace browser (used for graphically edit variables)
Path browser (used to edit the paths that MATLAB will look in for functions)
SIMULINK library browser
Open help window

MATLAB Help System. The user has easy access to the MathWorks "help desk" http://www.mathworks.com/access/helpdesk, which opens the MATLAB web page. It appears that the MATLAB environment features a most powerful built-in help system. If the name of a MATLAB command, function or solver is known, type

```
>> help [command, function, or solver name]
```
for example
```
>> help sin
```
and press the Enter key.

As shown, the search can be effectively performed using the `helpwin` command. We can receive the needed information using the following help topics:

- `help datafun` (data analysis);
- `help demo` (demonstration);
- `help funfun` (differential equations solvers);

- help general (general-purpose command);
- help graph2d and help graph3d (two- and three-dimensional graphics);
- help elmat and help matfun (matrices and linear algebra);
- help elfun and help specfun (mathematical functions);
- help lang (programming language);
- help ops (operators and special characters);
- help polyfun (polynomials).

Saving. You can save the files and information needed. Making use of the help command, we have

```
>> help save
 SAVE Save workspace variables to disk.
    SAVE FILENAME saves all workspace variables to the binary "MAT-file"
    named FILENAME.mat.  The data may be retrieved with LOAD.  If FILENAME
    has no extension, .mat is assumed.

    SAVE, by itself, creates the binary "MAT-file" named 'matlab.mat'.  It is
    an error if 'matlab.mat' is not writable.

    SAVE FILENAME X  saves only X.
    SAVE FILENAME X Y Z  saves X, Y, and Z. The wildcard '*' can be used to
    save only those variables that match a pattern.

    ASCII Options:
    SAVE ...   -ASCII  uses 8-digit ASCII form instead of binary regardless
                       of file extension.
    SAVE ...   -ASCII -DOUBLE  uses 16-digit ASCII form.
    SAVE ...   -ASCII -TABS  delimits with tabs.
    SAVE ...   -ASCII -DOUBLE -TABS  16-digit, tab delimited.

    MAT Options:
    SAVE ...   -MAT     saves in MAT format regardless of extension.
    SAVE ...   -V4      saves a MAT-file that MATLAB 4 can LOAD.
    SAVE ...   -APPEND  adds the variables to an existing file (MAT-file only).

    When using the -V4 option, variables that incompatible with MATLAB 4 are
    not saved to the MAT-file. For example, ND arrays, structs, cells, etc.
    cannot be saved to a MATLAB 4 MAT-file. Also, variables with names that
    are longer than 19 characters cannot be saved to a MATLAB 4 MAT-file.

    Use the functional form of SAVE, such as SAVE('filename','var1','var2'),
    when the filename or variable names are stored in strings.

    See also LOAD, DIARY, FWRITE, FPRINTF, UISAVE, FILEFORMATS.
 Overloaded methods
    help mdevproject/save.m
    help cgproject/save.m
    help vrworld/save.m
```

Thus, you can save values in a file by typing save [filename]. This creates a file [filename].mat that contains the values of the variables from your session. If you do not want to save all variables there are two options. First is to clear unneeded variables using the command clear. For example,

```
>> clear a b c d e
```

removes the variables a, b, c, d, and e. The second option is to use the save command

```
>> save x y
```

which will save only variables x and y in the file [filename].mat. The saved variables can be reloaded by typing load [filename].

MATLAB variables can be numerical (real and complex) and string values. Strings (matrices with character elements) are used for labeling, referring to the names of the user-defined functions, etc. An example of a string is given below:

```
>> class='MATLAB'; section='Introduction'; students='25'; data=[class,' ',section,' ',students]
data =
MATLAB Introduction 25
```

We defined three string variables, and then created a new string variable `data` using other strings. Substrings can be extracted using the index and colon notations. In particular, we have

```
>> class='MATLAB'; section='Introduction'; students='25'; data=[class,' ',section,' ',students]
data =
MATLAB Introduction 25
>> course=data(1:6), number=data(22:24)
course =
MATLAB
number =
 25
```

and the string variables are documented in the Workspace Window as illustrated in Figure 1.20.

Name	Size	Bytes	Class
abc class	1x6	12	char array
abc course	1x6	12	char array
abc data	1x24	48	char array
abc number	1x3	6	char array
abc section	1x12	24	char array
abc students	1x2	4	char array

Figure 1.20. Workspace Window with string variables used

The various toolboxes provide valuable capabilities. For example, the application of the Image Processing Toolbox will be briefly covered [2]. The user can perform different image processing tasks (e.g., image transformations, filtering, transforms, image analysis and enhancement, etc.). Different image formats (bmp, hdf, jpeg, pcx, png, tiff, and xwd) are supported. For example, let us restore the image UUV.jpg. To solve this problem, using the `imread` and `imadd` functions (to read and to add the contrast to the image), we type in the Command Window

```
>> IMAGE=imread('UUV.jpg'); IMAGE_contrast=imadd(IMAGE,25);
>> imshow(IMAGE);
>> imshow(IMAGE_contrast);
```

and the resulting images are documented in Figure 1.21.

Figure 1.21. Original and updated images of the underwater vehicle with the animation results

The size of the images can be displayed. In particular,

```
>> clear all; IMAGE=imread('UUV.jpg'); IMAGE_contrast=imadd(IMAGE,25); whos
   Name                    Size                        Bytes  Class
   IMAGE                   149x231x3                  103257  uint8 array
   IMAGE_contrast          149x231x3                  103257  uint8 array
Grand total is 206514 elements using 206514 bytes
```

Another example illustrates the application of the Image Processing Toolbox. In the Command Window, we type

```
>> IMAGE=imread('im.jpg'); IMAGE_N=imadd(IMAGE,60); imshow(IMAGE);
>> imshow(IMAGE_N);
```

and the original image is shown in Figure 1.22.

Figure 1.22. Original and updated parrot images

The size of the images is found using the whos command that lists the current variables, e.g.,

```
>> clear all; IMAGE=imread('im.jpg'); IMAGE_N=imadd(IMAGE,60); whos
   Name          Size               Bytes  Class
   IMAGE         110x170x3          56100  uint8 array
   IMAGE_N       110x170x3          56100  uint8 array
Grand total is 112200 elements using 112200 bytes
```

REFERENCES

1. *MATLAB 6.5 Release 13,* CD-ROM, MathWorks, Inc., Naick, MA, 2002.
2. *Image Processing Toolbox for Use with MATLAB, User's Guide Version 3*, MathWorks, Inc., Natick, MA, 2001.

Chapter 2

MATLAB Functions, Operators, and Commands

2.1. Mathematical Functions

Many mathematical functions, operators, special characters, and commands are available in the MATLAB standard libraries that enable us to perform mathematical calculations, string and character manipulations, input/output, and other needed functional operations and capabilities [1 - 4].

Let us start with simple examples. For example, one would like to find the values of the function $y = \sin(x)$ if $x = 0$ and $x = 1$. To find the values, the built-in `sin` function can be straightforwardly used. In particular, to solve the problem, we type the following statements in the Command Window, and the corresponding results are documented:

```
>> y=sin(0)

y =
    0

>> y=sin(1)

y =
    0.8415

>> x0=0; x1=1; y0=sin(x0), y1=sin(x1)

y0 =
    0

y1 =
    0.8415
```

To plot the function $y = \sin(t+1)$ if t varies from 1 to 30 with increment 0.01, we should use the built-in `sin` function, + operator, and `plot` function. In particular we have

```
>> t=1:0.01:30; y=sin(t+1); plot(t,y)
```

and the resulting plot is illustrated in Figure 2.1.

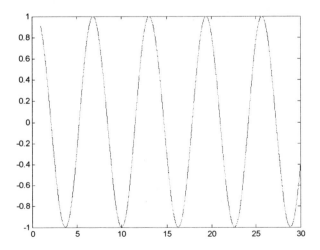

Figure 2.1. Plot of the function $y = \sin(t+1)$ if t varies from 1 to 30

These simple examples illustrate the need to use the MATLAB functions and operators. Elementary math functions supported in the MATLAB environment are listed below.

Trigonometric Functions:

sin	- sine
sinh	- hyperbolic sine
asin	- inverse sine
asinh	- inverse hyperbolic sine
cos	- cosine
cosh	- hyperbolic cosine
acos	- inverse cosine
acosh	- inverse hyperbolic cosine
tan	- tangent
tanh	- hyperbolic tangent
atan	- inverse tangent
atan2	- four quadrant inverse tangent
atanh	- inverse hyperbolic tangent
sec	- secant
sech	- hyperbolic secant
asec	- inverse secant
asech	- inverse hyperbolic secant
csc	- cosecant
csch	- hyperbolic cosecant
acsc	- inverse cosecant
acsch	- inverse hyperbolic cosecant
cot	- cotangent
coth	- hyperbolic cotangent
acot	- inverse cotangent.
acoth	- inverse hyperbolic cotangent.

Exponential Functions:

exp	– exponential
log	– natural logarithm
log10	– common logarithm
sqrt	– square root

Complex Functions:

abs	– absolute value
angle	– phase angle
conj	– complex conjugate
imag	– complex imaginary part
real	– complex real part

Various mathematical library functions allow one to perform needed mathematical calculations. The elementary mathematical functions supported by MATLAB are summarized in Table 2.1.

Table 2.1. Mathematics: Elementary Mathematical Functions

abs	Absolute value and complex magnitude
acos, acosh	Inverse cosine and inverse hyperbolic cosine
acot, acoth	Inverse cotangent and inverse hyperbolic cotangent
acsc, acsch	Inverse cosecant and inverse hyperbolic cosecant
angle	Phase angle
asec, asech	Inverse secant and inverse hyperbolic secant
asin, asinh	Inverse sine and inverse hyperbolic sine
atan, atanh	Inverse tangent and inverse hyperbolic tangent
atan2	Four-quadrant inverse tangent
ceil	Round toward infinity
complex	Construct complex data from real and imaginary components
conj	Complex conjugate
cos, cosh	Cosine and hyperbolic cosine
cot, coth	Cotangent and hyperbolic cotangent
csc, csch	Cosecant and hyperbolic cosecant
exp	Exponential function
fix	Round toward zero
floor	Round toward minus infinity
gcd	Greatest common divisor
imag	Imaginary part of a complex number
lcm	Least common multiple
log	Natural logarithm
log2	Base 2 logarithm and dissect floating-point numbers into exponent and mantissa
log10	Common (base 10) logarithm
mod	Modulus (signed remainder after division)
nchoosek	Binomial coefficient or all combinations
real	Real part of complex number
rem	Remainder after division
round	Round to nearest integer
sec, sech	Secant and hyperbolic secant
sign	Signum function
sin, sinh	Sine and hyperbolic sine
sqrt	Square root
tan, tanh	Tangent and hyperbolic tangent

Function arguments can be constants, variables, or expressions. Some mathematical library functions with simple examples are documented in Table 2.2.

Table 2.2. Elementary Mathematical Functions with Illustrative Examples

Function	Description	Example	MATLAB Statement and Results in the Command Window
cos	Cosine	cos(0)	>> cos(0) ans = 1
		c=cos([0, 1, pi, 2*pi])	>> c=cos([0, 1, pi, 2*pi]) c = 1.0000 0.5403 -1.0000 1.0000
exp	Exponential function	exp(1)	>> exp(1) ans = 2.7183
		e=exp([0, 1, 2, 3])	>> e=exp([0, 1, 2, 3]) e = 1.0000 2.7183 7.3891 20.0855
log	Natural logarithm	log(10)	>> log(10) ans = 2.3026
		l=log([1, 2, 5, 10])	>> l=log([1, 2, 5, 10]) l = 0 0.6931 1.6094 2.3026
real	Real part of complex number	real(10+10*i)	>> real(10+10*i) ans = 10
		r=real([-1+i,-5-5*i,10])	>> r=real([-1+i, -5-5*i, 10]) r = -1 -5 10
sin	Sine	sin(0)	>> sin(0) ans = 0
		s=sin([0, 1, pi, 2*pi])	>> s=sin([0, 1, pi, 2*pi]) s = 0 0.8415 0.0000 -0.0000
sqrt	Square root	sqrt(2)	>> sqrt(2) ans = 1.4142
		sq=sqrt([-9, 0, 3, 25])	>> sq=sqrt([-9, 0, 3, 25]) sq = 0+3.0000i 0 1.7321 5.0000

The user can either type the commands, functions or solvers in the MATLAB prompt (Command Window) or create m-files integrating the commands and functions needed.

2.2. MATLAB Characters and Operators

The commonly used MATLAB operators and special characters used to solve many engineering and science problems are given below.

Operators and Special Characters:

+	plus
–	minus
*	matrix multiplication
.*	array multiplication
^	matrix power
.^	array power
kron	Kronecker tensor product
\	backslash (left division)
/	slash (right division)
./ and .\	right and left array division
:	colon
( )	parentheses
[ ]	brackets
{}	curly braces
.	decimal point
...	continuation
,	comma
;	semicolon
%	comment
!	exclamation point
'	transpose and quote
.'	nonconjugated transpose
=	assignment
==	equality
< >	relational operators
&	logical AND
|	logical OR
~	logical NOT
xor	logical exclusive OR

The MATLAB operators, functions, and commands can be represented as tables. For example, the scalar and array arithmetic operators and characters are reported in Table 2.3.

Table 2.3. Scalar and Array Arithmetic with Operators and Characters

Symbol	MATLAB Statement	Arithmetic Operation
+	a+b+c	addition
–	a–b–c	subtraction
* and .*	a*b*c and a.*b.*c	multiplication
/ and ./	a/b and a./b	right division
\ and .\	b\a (equivalent to a/b) and b.\a	left division
^ and .^	a^b and a.^b	exponentiation

2.3. MATLAB Commands

In order to introduce MATLAB through examples and illustrations, let us document and implement several commonly used commands listed in Table 2.4.

Table 2.4. MATLAB Commands

Command	MATLAB Help	Description
clear	help clear	Clear variables and functions from memory (removes all variables from the workspace)
clc	help clc	Clear Command Window
help	Help	On-line help, display text at command line
quit	help quit	Quits MATLAB session (terminates MATLAB after running the script finish.m, if it exists. The workspace information will not be saved unless finish.m calls save)
who	help who	Lists current variables (lists the variables in the current workspace)
whos	help whos	Lists current variables in the expanded form (lists all the variables in the current workspace, together with information about their size, bytes, class, etc.)

Bellow are some examples to illustrate the scalar and array arithmetic operators as well as commands:

```
>> clear all
>> a=10; b=2; c=a+b, d=a/b, e=b\a, i=a^b
c =
    12
d =
     5
e =
     5
i =
   100
>> a=[10 5]; b=[2 4]; c=a+b, d=a./b, e=b.\a, i=a.^b
c =
    12     9
d =
    5.0000    1.2500
e =
    5.0000    1.2500
i =
   100   625
>> whos
  Name      Size        Bytes  Class
    a        1x2            16  double array
    b        1x2            16  double array
    c        1x2            16  double array
    d        1x2            16  double array
    e        1x2            16  double array
    i        1x2            16  double array
Grand total is 12 elements using 96 bytes
```

The MATLAB environment contains documentation for all the products that are installed. In particular, typing

```
>> helpwin
```
und pressing the Enter key, we have the Window shown in Figure 2.2. The user has access to the general-purpose commands, operators, special characters, elementary, specialized mathematical functions, etc.

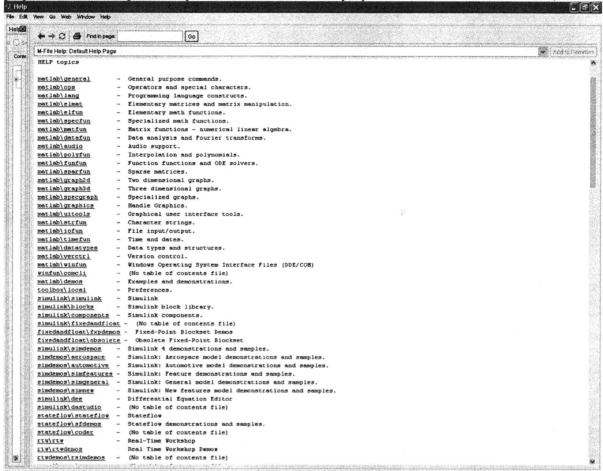

```
HELP topics

matlab\general      -  General purpose commands.
matlab\ops          -  Operators and special characters.
matlab\lang         -  Programming language constructs.
matlab\elmat        -  Elementary matrices and matrix manipulation.
matlab\elfun        -  Elementary math functions.
matlab\specfun      -  Specialized math functions.
matlab\matfun       -  Matrix functions - numerical linear algebra.
matlab\datafun      -  Data analysis and Fourier transforms.
matlab\audio        -  Audio support.
matlab\polyfun      -  Interpolation and polynomials.
matlab\funfun       -  Function functions and ODE solvers.
matlab\sparfun      -  Sparse matrices.
matlab\graph2d      -  Two dimensional graphs.
matlab\graph3d      -  Three dimensional graphs.
matlab\specgraph    -  Specialized graphs.
matlab\graphics     -  Handle Graphics.
matlab\uitools      -  Graphical user interface tools.
matlab\strfun       -  Character strings.
matlab\iofun        -  File input/output.
matlab\timefun      -  Time and dates.
matlab\datatypes    -  Data types and structures.
matlab\verctrl      -  Version control.
matlab\winfun       -  Windows Operating System Interface Files (DDE/COM)
winfun\comcli       -  (No table of contents file)
matlab\demos        -  Examples and demonstrations.
toolbox\local       -  Preferences.
simulink\simulink   -  Simulink
simulink\blocks     -  Simulink block library.
simulink\components -  Simulink components.
simulink\fixedandfloat -  (No table of contents file)
fixedandfloat\fxpdemos -  Fixed-Point Blockset Demos
fixedandfloat\obsolete -  Obsolete Fixed-Point Blockset
simulink\simdemos   -  Simulink 4 demonstrations and samples.
simdemos\aerospace  -  Simulink: Aerospace model demonstrations and samples.
simdemos\automotive -  Simulink: Automotive model demonstrations and samples.
simdemos\simfeatures -  Simulink: Feature demonstrations and samples.
simdemos\simgeneral -  Simulink: General model demonstrations and samples.
simdemos\simnew     -  Simulink: New features model demonstrations and samples.
simulink\dee        -  Differential Equation Editor
simulink\dastudio   -  (No table of contents file)
stateflow\stateflow -  Stateflow
stateflow\sfdemos   -  Stateflow demonstrations and samples.
stateflow\coder     -  (No table of contents file)
rtw\rtw             -  Real-Time Workshop
rtw\rtwdemos        -  Real Time Workshop Demos
rtwdemos\rsimdemos  -  (No table of contents file)
```

Figure 2.2. MATLAB `helpwin` Window

The complete list of the help topics is available by typing `help`:

```
>> help

HELP topics:
matlab\general      -  General purpose commands.
matlab\ops          -  Operators and special characters.
matlab\lang         -  Programming language constructs.
matlab\elmat        -  Elementary matrices and matrix manipulation.
matlab\elfun        -  Elementary math functions.
matlab\specfun      -  Specialized math functions.
matlab\matfun       -  Matrix functions - numerical linear algebra.
matlab\datafun      -  Data analysis and Fourier transforms.
matlab\audio        -  Audio support.
matlab\polyfun      -  Interpolation and polynomials.
matlab\funfun       -  Function functions and ODE solvers.
matlab\sparfun      -  Sparse matrices.
matlab\graph2d      -  Two dimensional graphs.
matlab\graph3d      -  Three dimensional graphs.
matlab\specgraph    -  Specialized graphs.
matlab\graphics     -  Handle Graphics.
```

```
matlab\uitools        -  Graphical user interface tools.
matlab\strfun         -  Character strings.
matlab\iofun          -  File input/output.
matlab\timefun        -  Time and dates.
matlab\datatypes      -  Data types and structures.
matlab\verctrl        -  Version control.
matlab\winfun         -  Windows Operating System Interface Files (DDE/COM)
winfun\comcli         -  (No table of contents file)
matlab\demos          -  Examples and demonstrations.
toolbox\local         -  Preferences.
simulink\simulink     -  Simulink
simulink\blocks       -  Simulink block library.
simulink\components   -  Simulink components.
simulink\fixedandfloat -  (No table of contents file)
fixedandfloat\fxpdemos -  Fixed-Point Blockset Demos
fixedandfloat\obsolete -  Obsolete Fixed-Point Blockset
simulink\simdemos     -  Simulink 4 demonstrations and samples.
simdemos\aerospace    -  Simulink: Aerospace model demonstrations and samples.
simdemos\automotive   -  Simulink: Automotive model demonstrations and samples.
simdemos\simfeatures  -  Simulink: Feature demonstrations and samples.
simdemos\simgeneral   -  Simulink: General model demonstrations and samples.
simdemos\simnew       -  Simulink: New features model demonstrations and samples.
simulink\dee          -  Differential Equation Editor
simulink\dastudio     -  (No table of contents file)
stateflow\stateflow   -  Stateflow
stateflow\sfdemos     -  Stateflow demonstrations and samples.
stateflow\coder       -  (No table of contents file)
rtw\rtw               -  Real-Time Workshop
rtw\rtwdemos          -  Real-Time Workshop Demos
rtwdemos\rsimdemos    -  (No table of contents file)
asap2\asap2           -  (No table of contents file)
asap2\user            -  (No table of contents file)
aeroblks\aeroblks     -  Aerospace Blockset
aeroblks\aerodemos    -  Aerospace Blockset demonstrations and examples.
cdma\cdma             -  CDMA Reference Blockset.
cdma\cdmamasks        -  CDMA Reference Blockset mask helper functions.
cdma\cdmamex          -  CDMA Reference Blockset S-Functions.
cdma\cdmademos        -  CDMA Reference Blockset demonstrations and examples.
comm\comm             -  Communications Toolbox.
comm\commdemos        -  Communications Toolbox Demonstrations.
comm\commobsolete     -  Archived MATLAB Files from Communications Toolbox Version 1.5.
commblks\commblks     -  Communications Blockset.
commblks\commmasks    -  Communications Blockset mask helper functions.
commblks\commmex      -  Communications Blockset S-functions.
commblks\commblksdemos -  Communications Blockset Demos.
commblksobsolete\commblksobsolete -  Archived Simulink Files from Communications
Toolbox Version 1.5.
toolbox\compiler      -  MATLAB Compiler
control\control       -  Control System Toolbox.
control\ctrlguis      -  Control System Toolbox -- GUI support functions.
control\ctrlobsolete  -  Control System Toolbox -- obsolete commands.
control\ctrlutil      -  (No table of contents file)
control\ctrldemos     -  Control System Toolbox -- Demos.
curvefit\curvefit     -  Curve Fitting Toolbox
curvefit\cftoolgui    -  (No table of contents file)
daq\daq               -  Data Acquisition Toolbox.
daq\daqguis           -  Data Acquisition Toolbox - Data Acquisition Soft Instruments.
daq\daqdemos          -  Data Acquisition Toolbox - Data Acquisition Demos.
database\database     -  Database Toolbox.
database\dbdemos      -  Database Toolbox Demonstration Functions.
database\vqb          -  Visual Query Builder functions.
datafeed\datafeed     -  Datafeed Toolbox.
datafeed\dfgui        -  Datafeed Toolbox Graphical User Interface
```

```
toolbox\dials            -  Dials & Gauges Blockset
dspblks\dspblks          -  DSP Blockset
dspblks\dspmasks         -  DSP Blockset mask helper functions.
dspblks\dspmex           -  DSP Blockset S-Function MEX-files.
dspblks\dspdemos         -  DSP Blockset demonstrations and examples.
toolbox\exlink           -  Excel Link.
filterdesign\filterdesign -  Filter Design Toolbox
filterdesign\quantization -  (No table of contents file)
filterdesign\filtdesdemos -  Filter Design Toolbox Demonstrations.
finance\finance          -  Financial Toolbox.
finance\calendar         -  Financial Toolbox calendar functions.
finance\findemos         -  Financial Toolbox demonstration functions.
finance\finsupport       -  (No table of contents file)
finderiv\finderiv        -  Financial Derivatives Toolbox.
toolbox\fixpoint         -  Fixed-Point Blockset
ftseries\ftseries        -  Financial Time Series Toolbox
ftseries\ftsdemos        -  (No table of contents file)
ftseries\ftsdata         -  (No table of contents file)
ftseries\ftstutorials    -  (No table of contents file)
fuzzy\fuzzy              -  Fuzzy Logic Toolbox.
fuzzy\fuzdemos           -  Fuzzy Logic Toolbox Demos.
garch\garch              -  GARCH Toolbox.
garch\garchdemos         -  (No table of contents file)
ident\ident              -  System Identification Toolbox.
ident\idobsolete         -  (No table of contents file)
ident\idguis             -  (No table of contents file)
ident\idutils            -  (No table of contents file)
ident\iddemos            -  (No table of contents file)
ident\idhelp             -  (No table of contents file)
images\images            -  Image Processing Toolbox.
images\imdemos           -  Image Processing Toolbox --- demos and sample images
instrument\instrument    -  Instrument Control Toolbox.
instrument\instrumentdemos -  (No table of contents file)
lmi\lmictrl              -  LMI Control Toolbox: Control Applications
lmi\lmilab               -  LMI Control Toolbox
map\map                  -  Mapping Toolbox
map\mapdisp              -  Mapping Toolbox Map Definition and Display.
map\mapproj              -  Mapping Toolbox Projections.
mbc\mbc                  -  Model-Based Calibration Toolbox
mbc\mbcdata              -  Model-Based Calibration Toolbox.
mbc\mbcdesign            -  Model-Based Calibration Toolbox.
mbc\mbcexpr              -  Model-Based Calibration Toolbox.
mbc\mbcguitools          -  Model-Based Calibration Toolbox.
mbc\mbclayouts           -  (No table of contents file)
mbc\mbcmodels            -  Model-Based Calibration Toolbox.
mbc\mbcsimulink          -  Model-Based Calibration Toolbox.
mbc\mbctools             -  Model-Based Calibration Toolbox.
mbc\mbcview              -  Model-Based Calibration Toolbox.
mech\mech                -  SimMechanics
mech\mechdemos           -  SimMechanics Demos.
mpc\mpccmds              -  Model Predictive Control Toolbox.
mpc\mpcdemos             -  Model Predictive Control Toolbox
mutools\commands         -  Mu-Analysis and Synthesis Toolbox.
mutools\subs             -  Mu-Analysis and Synthesis Toolbox.
toolbox\ncd              -  Nonlinear Control Design Blockset
nnet\nnet                -  Neural Network Toolbox.
nnet\nnutils             -  (No table of contents file)
nnet\nncontrol           -  Neural Network Toolbox Control System Functions.
nnet\nndemos             -  Neural Network Demonstrations.
nnet\nnobsolete          -  (No table of contents file)
toolbox\optim            -  Optimization Toolbox
toolbox\pde              -  Partial Differential Equation Toolbox.
simulink\perftools       -  Simulink Performance Tools
```

```
simulink\mdldiff        -   Simulink Graphical Merge
simulink\simcoverage -   Simulink Model Coverage Tool
rtw\accel               -   Simulink Accelerator
powersys\powersys       -   SimPowerSystems
powersys\powerdemo      -   SimPowerSystems Demos.
toolbox\robust          -   Robust Control Toolbox.
toolbox\rptgen          -   MATLAB Report Generator
toolbox\rptgenext       -   Simulink Report Generator
toolbox\sb2sl           -   SB2SL (converts SystemBuild to Simulink)
signal\signal           -   Signal Processing Toolbox
signal\sigtools         -   Filter Design & Analysis Tool (GUI)
signal\sptoolgui        -   Signal Processing Toolbox GUI
signal\sigdemos         -   Signal Processing Toolbox Demonstrations.
toolbox\splines         -   Spline Toolbox.
toolbox\stats           -   Statistics Toolbox
toolbox\symbolic        -   Symbolic Math Toolbox.
vr\vr                   -   Virtual Reality Toolbox
vr\vrdemos              -   Virtual Reality Toolbox examples.
wavelet\wavelet         -   Wavelet Toolbox
wavelet\wavedemo        -   Wavelet Toolbox Demonstrations.
MATLAB6p5\work          -   (No table of contents file)

For more help on directory/topic, type "help topic".
For command syntax information, type "help syntax".
```

By clicking MATLAB\general, we have the Help Window illustrated in Figure 2.3, and a complete description of the general-purpose commands can be easily accessed.

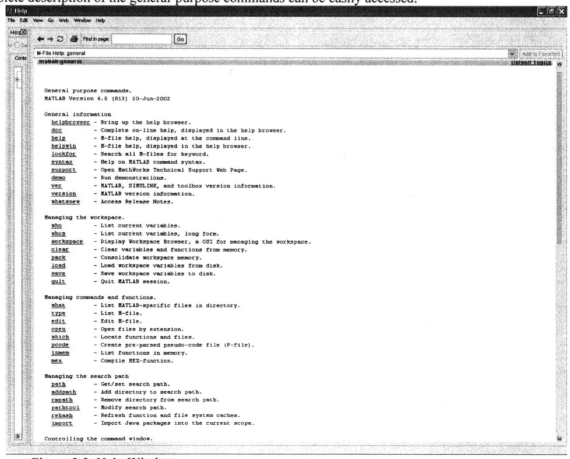

Figure 2.3. Help Window

In particular, we have

```
General purpose commands
MATLAB Version 6.5 (R13) 20-Jun-2002

General information
  helpbrowser - Bring up the help browser.
  doc         - Complete on-line help, displayed in the help browser.
  help        - M-file help, displayed at the command line.
  helpwin     - M-file help, displayed in the help browser.
  lookfor     - Search all M-files for keyword.
  syntax      - Help on MATLAB command syntax.
  support     - Open MathWorks Technical Support Web Page.
  demo        - Run demonstrations.
  ver         - MATLAB, SIMULINK, and toolbox version information.
  version     - MATLAB version information.
  whatsnew    - Access Release Notes.

Managing the workspace.
  who         - List current variables.
  whos        - List current variables, long form.
  workspace   - Display Workspace Browser, a GUI for managing the workspace.
  clear       - Clear variables and functions from memory.
  pack        - Consolidate workspace memory.
  load        - Load workspace variables from disk.
  save        - Save workspace variables to disk.
  quit        - Quit MATLAB session.

Managing commands and functions.
  what        - List MATLAB-specific files in directory.
  type        - List M-file.
  edit        - Edit M-file.
  open        - Open files by extension.
  which       - Locate functions and files.
  pcode       - Create pre-parsed pseudo-code file (P-file).
  inmem       - List functions in memory.
  mex         - Compile MEX-function.

Managing the search path
  path        - Get/set search path.
  addpath     - Add directory to search path.
  rmpath      - Remove directory from search path.
  pathtool    - Modify search path.
  rehash      - Refresh function and file system caches.
  import      - Import Java packages into the current scope.

Controlling the command window.
  echo        - Echo commands in M-files.
  more        - Control paged output in command window.
  diary       - Save text of MATLAB session.
  format      - Set output format.
  beep        - Produce beep sound.

Operating system commands
  cd          - Change current working directory.
  copyfile    - Copy a file or directory.
  movefile    - Move a file or directory.
  delete      - Delete file.
  pwd         - Show (print) current working directory.
  dir         - List directory.
  fileattrib  - Get or set attributes of files and directories.
  isdir       - True if argument is a directory.
  mkdir       - Make directory.
  rmdir       - Remove directory.
```

```
getenv      - Get environment variable.
!           - Execute operating system command (see PUNCT).
dos         - Execute DOS command and return result.
unix        - Execute UNIX command and return result.
system      - Execute system command and return result.
perl        - Execute Perl command and return result.
web         - Open Web browser on site or files.
computer    - Computer type.
isunix      - True for the UNIX version of MATLAB.
ispc        - True for the PC (Windows) version of MATLAB.

Debugging M-files.
debug       - List debugging commands.
dbstop      - Set breakpoint.
dbclear     - Remove breakpoint.
dbcont      - Continue execution.
dbdown      - Change local workspace context.
dbstack     - Display function call stack.
dbstatus    - List all breakpoints.
dbstep      - Execute one or more lines.
dbtype      - List M-file with line numbers.
dbup        - Change local workspace context.
dbquit      - Quit debug mode.
dbmex       - Debug MEX-files (UNIX only).

Profiling M-files.
profile     - Profile function execution time.
profreport  - Generate profile report.

Tools to locate dependent functions of an M-file.
depfun      - Locate dependent functions of an m-file.
depdir      - Locate dependent directories of an m-file.
inmem       - List functions in memory.

See also punct.
```

In addition to the general-purpose commands, specialized commands and functions are used. As illustrated in Figure 2.4, the MATLAB environment integrates the toolboxes. In particular, Communication Toolbox, Control System Toolbox, Data Acquisition Toolbox, Database Toolbox, Datafeed Toolbox, Filter Design Toolbox, Financial Toolbox, Financial Derivatives Toolbox, Fuzzy Logic Toolbox, GARCH Toolbox, Image Processing Toolbox, Instrument Control Toolbox, Mapping Toolbox, Model Predictive Control Toolbox, Mu-Analysis and Synthesis Toolbox, Neural Network Toolbox, Optimization Toolbox, Partial Differential Equations Toolbox, Robust Control Toolbox, Signal Processing Toolbox, Spline Toolbox, Statistics Toolbox, Symbolic Math Toolbox, System Identification Toolbox, Wavelet Toolbox, etc.

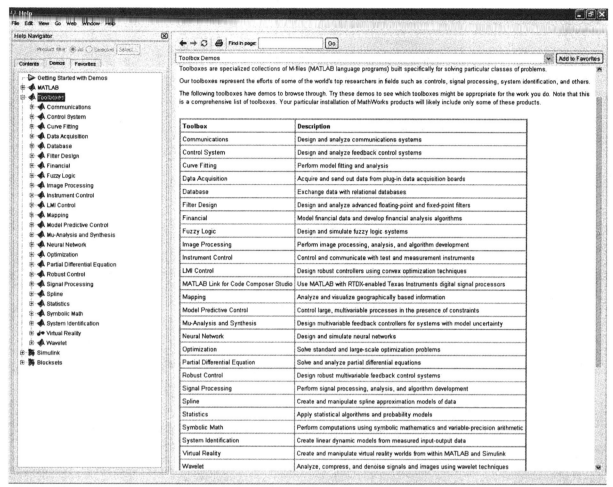

Figure 2.4. MATLAB `demo` window with toolboxes available

Having accessed the general-purpose commands, the user should consult the MATLAB user manuals or specialized books for specific toolboxes. Throughout this book, we will apply and emphasize other commonly used commands needed in engineering and scientific computations. As was shown, the search can be effectively performed using the `helpwin` command. One can obtain the information needed using the following help topics:

- `help datafun` (data analysis);
- `help demo` (demonstration);
- `help funfun` (differential equations solvers);
- `help general` (general purpose command);
- `help graph2d` and `help graph3d` two- and three-dimensional graphics);
- `help elmat` and `help matfun` (matrices and linear algebra);
- `help elfun` and `help specfun` (mathematical functions);
- `help lang` (programming language);
- `help ops` (operators and special characters);
- `help polyfun` (polynomials).

In this book, we will concentrate on numerical solutions of equations. The list of MATLAB specialized functions and commands involved is given below.

```
>> help funfun
```

Function functions and ODE solvers.

Optimization and root finding.
```
  fminbnd    - Scalar bounded nonlinear function minimization.
  fminsearch - Multidimensional unconstrained nonlinear minimization,
                 by Nelder-Mead direct search method.
  fzero      - Scalar nonlinear zero finding.
```

Optimization Option handling
```
  optimset   - Create or alter optimization OPTIONS structure.
  optimget   - Get optimization parameters from OPTIONS structure.
```

Numerical integration (quadrature).
```
  quad       - Numerically evaluate integral, low order method.
  quadl      - Numerically evaluate integral, higher order method.
  dblquad    - Numerically evaluate double integral.
  triplequad - Numerically evaluate triple integral.
```

Plotting.
```
  ezplot     - Easy to use function plotter.
  ezplot3    - Easy to use 3-D parametric curve plotter.
  ezpolar    - Easy to use polar coordinate plotter.
  ezcontour  - Easy to use contour plotter.
  ezcontourf - Easy to use filled contour plotter.
  ezmesh     - Easy to use 3-D mesh plotter.
  ezmeshc    - Easy to use combination mesh/contour plotter.
  ezsurf     - Easy to use 3-D colored surface plotter.
  ezsurfc    - Easy to use combination surf/contour plotter.
  fplot      - Plot function.
```

Inline function object.
```
  inline     - Construct INLINE function object.
  argnames   - Argument names.
  formula    - Function formula.
  char       - Convert INLINE object to character array.
```

Differential equation solvers.
Initial value problem solvers for ODEs. (If unsure about stiffness, try ODE45
first, then ODE15S.)
```
  ode45      - Solve non-stiff differential equations, medium order method.
  ode23      - Solve non-stiff differential equations, low order method.
  ode113     - Solve non-stiff differential equations, variable order method.
  ode23t     - Solve moderately stiff ODEs and DAEs Index 1, trapezoidal rule.
  ode15s     - Solve stiff ODEs and DAEs Index 1, variable order method.
  ode23s     - Solve stiff differential equations, low order method.
  ode23tb    - Solve stiff differential equations, low order method.
```

Initial value problem solvers for delay differential equations (DDEs).
```
  dde23      - Solve delay differential equations (DDEs) with constant delays.
```

Boundary value problem solver for ODEs.
```
  bvp4c      - Solve two-point boundary value problems for ODEs by collocation.
```

1D Partial differential equation solver.
```
  pdepe      - Solve initial-boundary value problems for parabolic-elliptic PDEs.
```

Option handling.
```
  odeset     - Create/alter ODE OPTIONS structure.
  odeget     - Get ODE OPTIONS parameters.
  ddeset     - Create/alter DDE OPTIONS structure.
  ddeget     - Get DDE OPTIONS parameters.
  bvpset     - Create/alter BVP OPTIONS structure.
```

```
    bvpget    - Get BVP OPTIONS parameters.

Input and Output functions.
    deval     - Evaluates the solution of a differential equation problem.
    odeplot   - Time series ODE output function.
    odephas2  - 2-D phase plane ODE output function.
    odephas3  - 3-D phase plane ODE output function.
    odeprint  - Command window printing ODE output function.
    bvpinit   - Forms the initial guess for BVP4C.
    pdeval    - Evaluates by interpolation the solution computed by PDEPE.
    odefile   - MATLAB v5 ODE file syntax (obsolete).
```

Distinct functions that can be straightforwardly used in optimization, plotting, numerical integration, as well as in ordinary and partial differential equations solvers, are reported in [1 - 4]. The application of many of these functions and solvers will be thoroughly illustrated in this book.

REFERENCES

1. *MATLAB 6.5 Release 13,* CD-ROM, MathWorks, Inc., 2002.
2. Dabney, J. B. and Harman, T. L., *Mastering SIMULINK 2*, Prentice Hall, Upper Saddle River, NJ, 1998.
3. Hanselman, D. and Littlefield, B., *Mastering MATLAB 5*, Prentice Hall, Upper Saddle River, NJ, 1998.
4. *User's Guide. The Student Edition of MATLAB: The Ultimate Computing Environment for Technical Education*, MathWorks, Inc., Prentice Hall, Upper Saddle River, NJ, 1995.

Chapter 3

MATLAB and Problem Solving

3.1. Starting MATLAB

As we saw in Chapter 1, we start MATLAB by double-clicking the MATLAB icon:

MATLAB 6.5.lnk

The MATLAB Command and Workspace windows appear as shown in Figure 3.1.

Command Window   Workspace Window

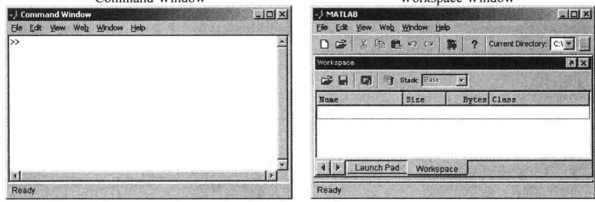

Figure 3.1. MATLAB Command and Workspace windows

The line
```
>>
```
is the MATLAB prompt in the Command Window.

3.2. Basic Arithmetic

MATLAB uses conventional notations for basic scalar arithmetic to be applied [1 - 5]. The simplest MATLAB notations (arithmetic operators) for real and complex numbers, vectors, and matrices are:

```
+      addition
-      subtraction
*      multiplication
/      division
^      exponentiation
```

Let us illustrate the addition. Using the number a=1, we find aa=a+1 as
```
>> a=1; aa=a+1
aa =
     2
```
Thus, aa=2, and Figure 3.2 illustrates the answer displayed.

Command Window   Workspace Window

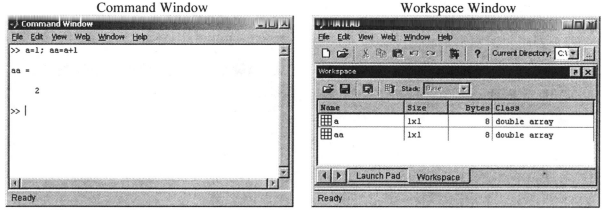

Figure 3.2. Solution of aa=a+1 if a=1: Command and Workspace windows

For the vector a=[1 2 3], to find aa=a+1, we have
```
>> a=[1 2 3]; aa=a+1
aa =
        2             3             4
```
Variables, arrays, and matrices occupy the memory. For the example considered, we have the MATLAB statement a=[1 2 3]; aa=a+1 (typed in the Command Window). Executing this statement, the data displayed in the Workspace Window is documented in Figure 3.3.

Command Window   Workspace Window

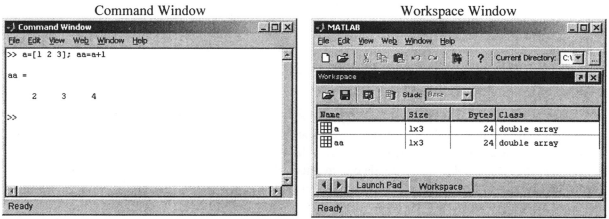

Figure 3.3. Solution of aa=a+1 if a=[1 2 3]: Command and Workspace windows

For a three-by-three matrix a (assigning all entries to be equal to 1 using the ones function, e.g., a=ones(3)), adding 1 to all entries, the following statement must be typed in the Command Window to obtain the resulting matrix aa:
```
>> a=ones(3); aa=a+1
aa =
        2             2             2
        2             2             2
        2             2             2
```
Specifically, as shown in Figure 3.4, we have $aa = \begin{bmatrix} 2 & 2 & 2 \\ 2 & 2 & 2 \\ 2 & 2 & 2 \end{bmatrix}$.

Command Window

Workspace Window

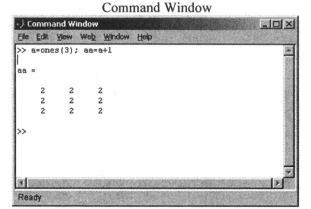 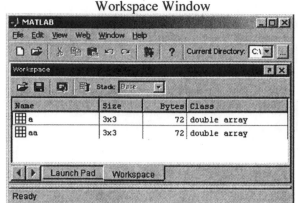

Figure 3.4. Solution of `aa=a+1` if `a=ones(3)`: Command and Workspace windows

Here, the `once` function was used. It is obvious that this function was called by reference from the MATLAB functions library. Call commands, functions, operators, and variables by reference should be used whenever necessary.

The element-wise operations allow us to perform operations on each element of a vector. For example, let us add, multiply, and divide two vectors by adding, multiplying, and dividing the corresponding elements. We have:

```
>> A=[1 2 3 4]; B=[5 6 7 8]; AA=A+B, AB=A.*B, BB=A./B, BA=A.\B
AA =
        6           8          10          12
AB =
        5          12          21          32
BB =
      1/5         1/3         3/7         1/2
BA =
        5           3         7/3           2
```

It was illustrated that the multiplication and division of two matrices (element by element) can be performed. The symbol `*` represents the multiplication of matrices (matrices can be multiplied if the number of rows is equal to the number of columns). In contrast, the symbol `.*` specifies the element-wise multiplication. We cannot use `/` to divide two matrices element-wise, since `/` and `\` are used for left and right matrix division. Therefore, `./` and `.\` were illustrated.

Typing `A.^3`, we cube each element of the vector. In particular,

```
>> A=[1 2 3 4]; A3=A.^3
A3 =
        1           8          27          64
```

The `abs` operator returns the magnitude of its argument. If applied to a vector, it returns a vector of the magnitudes of the elements. For example, if `A=[1+1i 2-2i 3+3i 4-4i]`, we have

```
>> format short e; A=[1+1i 2-2i 3+3i 4-4i]; AA=abs(A)
AA =
  1.4142e+000  2.8284e+000  4.2426e+000  5.6569e+000
```

The `angle` operator returns the phase angle (argument) of its operand in radians. As an illustration, we have

```
>> format short e; A=[1+1i 2-2i 3+3i 4-4i]; AA=angle(A)
AA =
  7.8540e-001 -7.8540e-001  7.8540e-001 -7.8540e-001
```

MATLAB has operators for taking the real part, imaginary part, or complex conjugate of a complex number. These operators are real, imag and conj. They are defined to work element-wise on any matrix or vector. For example,

```
>> format short
>> A=[1+1i 2-2i 3+3i 4-4i]; RA=real(A), IA=imag(A), CA=conj(A)
RA =
    1    2    3    4
IA =
    1   -2    3   -4
CA =
   1.0000-1.0000i  2.0000+2.0000i 3.0000-3.0000i 4.0000+4.0000i
```

MATLAB has operators that round fractional numbers to integers. The round operator rounds its elements to the nearest integer, the fix rounds its elements to the nearest integer toward zero (rounds down for positive numbers and up for negative numbers), the floor rounds its elements to the nearest integer towards negative infinity, and the ceil rounds its elements to the nearest integer towards positive infinity.

The standard trigonometric operators are all defined as element-wise operators. For example, sin and cos calculate the sine and cosine of their arguments. The arguments to these functions are angles given in radians.

Let us calculate the vector x and plot the function $x(t) = \sin(2t)$ if t varies from 0 to 10π sec. We type in the Command Window the following statement

```
>> t=0:0.1:10*pi; x=sin(2*t); plot(t,x)
```

using the sin and plot functions. The corresponding Command and Workspace windows are documented in Figure 3.5.

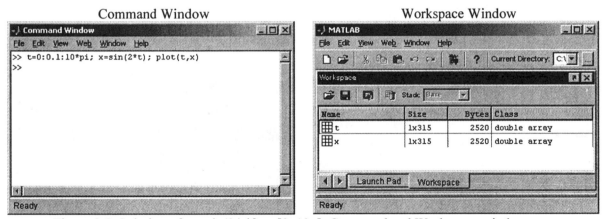

Command Window   Workspace Window

Figure 3.5. Solution of $x = \sin(2t)$ if $t = [0 \quad 10\pi]$: Command and Workspace windows

It is obvious that the size of vectors x and t is 315 (see the Workspace Window in Figure 3.5). The plot of $x(t) = \sin(2t)$ if $t=[0 \quad 10\pi]$ sec is illustrated in Figure 3.6.

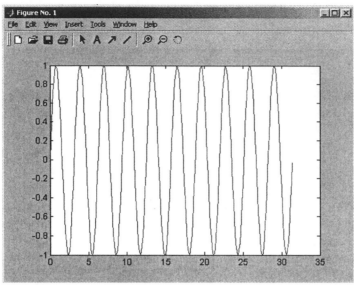

Figure 3.6. Plot of $x = \sin(2t)$ if $t=[0 \quad 10\pi]$ sec

MATLAB does not require any type declarations or dimension statements for variables (as was shown in the previous example). When MATLAB encounters a new variable name, it automatically creates the variable and allocates the appropriate memory. For example,

```
>> Grade_A=4.0
```

creates a one-by-one matrix (variable) named `Grade_A` and stores the value 4.0 in its single element. We have

```
>> Grade_A=4.0
Grade_A =
    4
```

The Command and Workspace windows are illustrated in Figure 3.7.

Command Window   Workspace Window

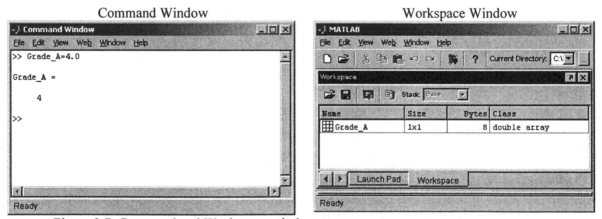

Figure 3.7. Command and Workspace windows

Variable names can have letters, digits, or underscores (only the first 31 characters of a variable name are used). One must distinguish uppercase and lowercase letters because A and a are not the same variable.

Conventional decimal notation is used (e.g., -1, 0, 1, 1.11, 1.11e11, etc.). All numbers are stored internally using the long format specified by the IEEE floating-point standard. Floating-point numbers have a finite precision of 16 significant decimal digits and a finite range of 10^{-308} to 10^{+308}.

As was illustrated, MATLAB provides a large number of standard elementary mathematical functions (e.g., abs, sqrt, exp, log, sin, cos, etc.). Many advanced and specialized mathematical functions (e.g., Bessel and gamma functions) are available. Most of these functions accept complex arguments. For a list of the elementary mathematical functions, use `help elfun` (the MATLAB functions are listed in the Appendix):

```
>> help elfun
   Elementary math functions
Trigonometric
     sin         - Sine
     sinh        - Hyperbolic sine
     asin        - Inverse sine
     asinh       - Inverse hyperbolic sine
     cos         - Cosine
     cosh        - Hyperbolic cosine
     acos        - Inverse cosine
     acosh       - Inverse hyperbolic cosine
     tan         - Tangent
     tanh        - Hyperbolic tangent
     atan        - Inverse tangent
     atan2       - Four quadrant inverse tangent
     atanh       - Inverse hyperbolic tangent
     sec         - Secant
     sech        - Hyperbolic secant
     asec        - Inverse secant
     asech       - Inverse hyperbolic secant
     csc         - Cosecant
     csch        - Hyperbolic cosecant
     acsc        - Inverse cosecant
     acsch       - Inverse hyperbolic cosecant
     cot         - Cotangent
     coth        - Hyperbolic cotangent
     acot        - Inverse cotangent
     acoth       - Inverse hyperbolic cotangent
Exponential
     exp         - Exponential
     log         - Natural logarithm
     log10       - Common (base 10) logarithm
     log2        - Base 2 logarithm and dissect floating point number
     pow2        - Base 2 power and scale floating point number
     sqrt        - Square root
     nextpow2    - Next higher power of 2
Complex
     abs         - Absolute value
     angle       - Phase angle
     complex     - Construct complex data from real and imaginary parts
     conj        - Complex conjugate
     imag        - Complex imaginary part
     real        - Complex real part
     unwrap      - Unwrap phase angle
     isreal      - True for real array
     cplxpair    - Sort numbers into complex conjugate pairs
Rounding and remainder
     fix         - Round towards zero
     floor       - Round towards minus infinity
     ceil        - Round towards plus infinity
     round       - Round towards nearest integer
```

```
    mod        - Modulus (signed remainder after division)
    rem        - Remainder after division
    sign       - Signum
```

For a list of advanced mathematical and matrix functions, use `help specfun`. In particular,

```
>> help specfun
Specialized math functions
    airy       - Airy functions
    besselj    - Bessel function of the first kind
    bessely    - Bessel function of the second kind
    besselh    - Bessel functions of the third kind (Hankel function)
    besseli    - Modified Bessel function of the first kind
    besselk    - Modified Bessel function of the second kind
    beta       - Beta function
    betainc    - Incomplete beta function
    betaln     - Logarithm of beta function
    ellipj     - Jacobi elliptic functions
    ellipke    - Complete elliptic integral
    erf        - Error function
    erfc       - Complementary error function
    erfcx      - Scaled complementary error function
    erfinv     - Inverse error function
    expint     - Exponential integral function
    gamma      - Gamma function
    gammainc   - Incomplete gamma function
    gammaln    - Logarithm of gamma function
    legendre   - Associated Legendre function
    cross      - Vector cross product
    dot        - Vector dot product
Number theoretic functions
    factor     - Prime factors
    isprime    - True for prime numbers
    primes     - Generate list of prime numbers
    gcd        - Greatest common divisor
    lcm        - Least common multiple
    rat        - Rational approximation
    rats       - Rational output
    perms      - All possible permutations
    nchoosek   - All combinations of N elements taken K at a time
    factorial  - Factorial function
Coordinate transforms
    cart2sph   - Transform Cartesian to spherical coordinates
    cart2pol   - Transform Cartesian to polar coordinates
    pol2cart   - Transform polar to Cartesian coordinates
    sph2cart   - Transform spherical to Cartesian coordinates
    hsv2rgb    - Convert hue-saturation-value colors to red-green-blue
    rgb2hsv    - Convert red-green-blue colors to hue-saturation-value
```

Some of the functions, like `sqrt` and `cos`, are built-in. Other functions, like `gamma` and `cosh`, are implemented using the m-files. You can see the code and modify it if you need to. The examples are:

```
>> a=1; aa=a+1
aa =
     2
```

or

```
>> a=1; aa=sin(a)+sqrt(a+3)+1
aa =
    3.8415
```

3.3. How to Use Some Basic MATLAB Features

MATLAB works by executing the statements you enter (type) in the Command Window, and the MATLAB syntax must be followed. By default, any output is immediately printed to the window.

To illustrate the basic arithmetic operations (addition, subtraction, multiplication, division, and exponentiation), we calculate $\dfrac{1+2-e^{-3}+\sin 5}{\cos 6 - 7^{-8}}$. In the MATLAB Command Window we type the following statement:

```
» (1+2-exp(-3)+sin(5))/(cos(6)-7^(-8))
```

Pressing the Enter key, the following answer appears:

```
ans =
   2.0739
```

As an alternative, we can use variables. In particular, for the example considered, we type

```
»a=1;b=2;c=3;d=5;e=6;f=7;g=8;(a+b-exp(-c)+sin(d))/(cos(e)-f^(-g))
```

then press the Enter key, and the answer is displayed:

```
ans =
   2.0739
```

To display the value of variables used, we should enter the variable name at the prompt and press the Enter key. For example,

```
»f,g
f =
    7
g =
    8
```

A list of the variables used are obtained using the command who. We have

```
»who
Your variables are:
a    ans   b    c    d    e    f    g
```

The clear is the command that clears the memory:

```
>> help clear all

 CLEAR  Clear variables and functions from memory.
    CLEAR removes all variables from the workspace.
    CLEAR VARIABLES does the same thing.
    CLEAR GLOBAL removes all global variables.
    CLEAR FUNCTIONS removes all compiled M- and MEX-functions.

    CLEAR ALL removes all variables, globals, functions and MEX links.
    CLEAR ALL at the command prompt also removes the Java packages
    import list.

    CLEAR IMPORT removes the Java packages import list at the command
    prompt.  It cannot be used in a function.

    CLEAR CLASSES is the same as CLEAR ALL except that class definitions
    are also cleared.  If any objects exist outside the workspace (say in
    userdata or persistent in a locked m-file) a warning will be issued
    and the class definition will not be cleared.  CLEAR CLASSES must be
    used if the number or names of fields in a class are changed.

    CLEAR VAR1 VAR2 ... clears the variables specified.  The wildcard
    character '*' can be used to clear variables that match a pattern.
    For instance, CLEAR X* clears all the variables in the current
    workspace that start with X.

    If X is global, CLEAR X removes X from the current workspace,
    but leaves it accessible to any functions declaring it global.
```

```
CLEAR GLOBAL X completely removes the global variable X.

CLEAR FUN clears the function specified.  If FUN has been locked
by MLOCK it will remain in memory. Use a partial path (see
PARTIALPATH) to distinguish between different overloaded versions of
FUN.  For instance, 'clear inline/display' clears only the INLINE
method for DISPLAY, leaving any other implementations in memory.

CLEAR ALL, CLEAR FUN, or CLEAR FUNCTIONS also have the side effect of
removing debugging breakpoints and reinitializing persistent variables
since the breakpoints for a function and persistent variables are
cleared whenever the m-file changes or is cleared.

Use the functional form of CLEAR, such as CLEAR('name'),  ·
when the variable name or function name is stored in a string.

See also WHO, WHOS, MLOCK, MUNLOCK, PERSISTENT.

ALL   True if all elements of a vector are nonzero.
    For vectors, ALL(V) returns 1 if none of the elements of the
    vector are zero. Otherwise it returns 0. For matrices,
    ALL(X) operates on the columns of X, returning a row vector
    of 1's and 0's. For N-D arrays, ALL(X) operates on the first
    non-singleton dimension.

    ALL(X,DIM) works down the dimension DIM.  For example, ALL(X,1)
    works down the first dimension (the rows) of X.

See also ANY.
```

The whos command allows us to know the variables (that we have in the workspace), their size, and memory used. As an example, we have

```
>> clear all; a=1; A=[1 2;3 4]; whos
  Name       Size          Bytes  Class

  A          2x2              32  double array
  a          1x1               8  double array

Grand total is 5 elements using 40 bytes
```

3.3.1. Scalars and Basic Operations with Scalars

Mastering MATLAB mainly involves learning and practicing how to handle scalars, vectors, matrices, and equations using numerous functions, commands, and computationally efficient algorithms. In MATLAB, a matrix is a rectangular array of numbers. The one-by-one matrices are scalars, and matrices with only one row or column are vectors.

A scalar is a variable with one row and one column (e.g., 1, 20, or 300). Scalars are the simple variables that we use and manipulate in simple algebraic equations. To create a scalar, the user simply introduces it on the left-hand side of a prompt sign. That is,

```
>> a=1;
>> b=20;
>> c=300;
```

The Command and Workspace windows are illustrated in Figure 3.8 (scalars a, b, and c were downloaded in the Command Window, and the size of a, b, and c is given in the Workspace Window).

Command Window   Workspace Window

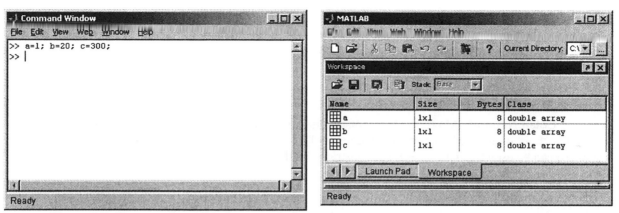

Figure 3.8. Command and Workspace windows

MATLAB fully supports the standard scalar operations using an obvious notation. The following statements demonstrate scalar addition, subtraction, multiplication, and division.

```
>> x=a+b+c; y=a-b-c; z=a*b*c; v=a/b/c;
```

3.3.2. Arrays, Vectors, and Basic Operations

To introduce the vector, let us first define the array. The array is a group of memory locations related by the fact that they have the same name and same type. The array can contain n elements (entries). Any one of these number (entry) has the "array number" specified the particular element (entry) number in the array. The simple array example and the corresponding result are given below:

- array is (MATLAB statement):

```
>> a:1:2:10
```

- corresponding result:

```
a =
     1     3     5     7     9
```

The arrays are used to create (generate) vectors and matrices. For example, to create row and column vectors, we can:

- Introduce the vector by typing the numbers (enter an explicit list of elements or numbers)

```
>> a=[1 20 300];
```

- Use the built-in functions (`ones`, `zeros`, `linspace`, `logspace` and other functions allow the user to explicitly create vectors of a specific size and with a prescribed spacing between the elements), e.g.,

```
>> a=ones(1,10)      % creates a row vector of ones of length 10
>> b=zeros(5,1)      % creates a column vector of ones of length 10
>> c=linspace(1,4,4) % creates the vector x=[1    2    3    4]
>> d=logspace(1,3,3) % creates the vector d=[10   100   1000]
```

- Load using external data files, etc.

Individual elements of a vector can be addressed as

```
>> d=logspace(1,3,3); d1=d(1), d3=d(3)
d1 =
    10
d3 =
    1000
```

MATLAB allocates memory for all variables used (see the Workspace Window). This allows the user to increase the size of a vector by assigning a value to an element that has not been previously used. For example,

```
>> d=logspace(1,3,3); d(6)=1; d
d =
        10         100        1000           0           0           1
```

Colon Notation. MATLAB colon notation is a compact way to refer to ranges of vector and matrix elements. It is often used in copy operations and in the creation of vectors and matrices. The colon notation can be used to create a vector as illustrated by the following example

$$a=a_{initial}:da:a_{final},$$

where $a_{initial}$ and a_{final} are the range of the values covered by elements of the a vector. It should be emphasized that $a_{initial}$, da, and a_{final} are not necessarily integers. For example,

```
>> a=0:1:10
a =
     0     1     2     3     4     5     6     7     8     9    10

>> a=0.5:1:3.5
a =
    0.5000    1.5000    2.5000    3.5000

>> a=0.5:0.5:3.5
a =
    0.5000    1.0000    1.5000    2.0000    2.5000    3.0000    3.5000
```

If da (increment) is omitted, a value of 1 (unit increment) is used by default.

To create the column vectors using the row vectors, the transpose operator at the end of the vector-creating expression is used. In particular,

```
>> a=[0.5:1:3.5]'
a =
    0.5000
    1.5000
    2.5000
    3.5000
```

The application of the colon notation to create a vector requires us to specify the increment, whereas using the `linspace` function requires the user to specify the total number of elements. The following examples show how to create the same vector with both approaches:

```
>> ainitial=1; afinal=10; size=10; da=(afinal-ainitial)/(size-1);
>> a1=linspace(ainitial,afinal,size); a2=ainitial:da:afinal; a1, a2
```

The results are

```
a1 =
     1     2     3     4     5     6     7     8     9    10
a2 =
     1     2     3     4     5     6     7     8     9    10
```

Mathematical operations involving vectors follow the rules of linear algebra. Addition and subtraction, operations with scalars, transpose, multiplication, element-wise vector operations, and other operations can be performed.

3.4. Matrices and Basic Operations with Matrices

Matrices are created in the similar manner as vectors. For example, the statement

```
>> A = [1 2 3; 4 5 6; 7 8 9]
```

creates the three-by-three matrix $A = \begin{bmatrix} 1 & 2 & 3 \\ 4 & 5 & 6 \\ 7 & 8 & 9 \end{bmatrix}$.

Matrix elements are addressed by notation `A(i,j)`. If A is a matrix, then `A(3,2)` is the element (entry) in the third row and second column. In particular,

```
>> A = [1 2 3; 4 5 6; 7 8 9]; A32=A(3,2)
A32 =
    8
```

Thus, the element in row `i` and column `j` of A is denoted by `A(i,j)`. For example, `A(1,2)` is the number in the first row and second column. Therefore, it is possible to compute the sum of the elements. As an example, for the first row, we have

```
>> A = [1 2 3; 4 5 6; 7 8 9]; A1Row=A(1,1)+A(1,2)+A(1,3)
A1Row =
    6
```

The matrix can be modified. For example, let us reassign the entry `A(3,2)` to be 1000. We have

```
>> A = [1 2 3; 4 5 6; 7 8 9]; A(3,2)=1000; A
A =
       1          2          3
       4          5          6
       7       1000          9
```

That is, $A = \begin{bmatrix} 1 & 2 & 3 \\ 4 & 5 & 6 \\ 7 & 1000 & 9 \end{bmatrix}$.

The function `spy` creates a graphic displaying the sparsity pattern of a matrix. For example, for matrix $A = \begin{bmatrix} 0 & 2 & 3 \\ 4 & 5 & 6 \\ 7 & 0 & 9 \end{bmatrix}$, we have

```
>> A = [1 2 3; 4 5 6; 7 8 9]; A(1,1)=0; A(3,2)=0; A, spy(A)
A =
       0          2          3
       4          5          6
       7          0          9
```

and the sparsity pattern of the matrix A is illustrated in Figure 3.9.

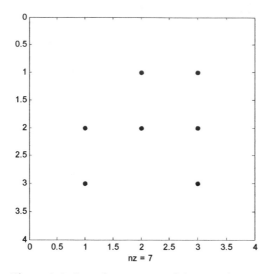

Figure 3.9. Sparsity pattern of the matrix A

Generating Matrices and Working with Matrices. Linear and nonlinear algebraic, differential, and difference equations can be expressed in matrix form. For example, the linear algebraic equations are given as

$$a_{11}x_1 + a_{12}x_2 + ... + a_{1n-1}x_{n-1} + a_{1n}x_n = b_{11},$$

$$a_{21}x_1 + a_{22}x_2 + ... + a_{2n-1}x_{n-1} + a_{2n}x_n = b_{21},$$

$$\vdots$$

$$a_{n-11}x_1 + a_{n-12}x_2 + ... + a_{n-1n-1}x_{n-1} + a_{n-1n}x_n = b_{n-11},$$

$$a_{n1}x_1 + a_{n2}x_2 + ... + a_{nn-1}x_{n-1} + a_{nn}x_n = b_{n1},$$

which in matrix form are expressed by

$$
\begin{bmatrix}
a_{11} & a_{12} & \cdots & a_{1n-1} & a_{1n} \\
a_{21} & a_{22} & \cdots & a_{2n-1} & a_{2n} \\
\vdots & \vdots & \ddots & \vdots & \vdots \\
a_{n-11} & a_{n-12} & \cdots & a_{n-1n-1} & a_{n-1n} \\
a_{n1} & a_{n2} & \cdots & a_{nn-1} & a_{nn}
\end{bmatrix}
\begin{bmatrix}
x_1 \\ x_2 \\ \vdots \\ x_{n-1} \\ x_n
\end{bmatrix}
=
\begin{bmatrix}
b_{11} \\ b_{21} \\ \vdots \\ b_{n-11} \\ b_{n1}
\end{bmatrix}
\text{ or } Ax{=}B,
$$

where x is the vector of variables, $x \in \mathbb{R}^n$, $x = \begin{bmatrix} x_1 \\ x_2 \\ \vdots \\ x_{n-1} \\ x_n \end{bmatrix}$; $A \in \mathbb{R}^{n \times n}$ and $B \in \mathbb{R}^{n \times 1}$ are the matrices of constant coefficients.

To solve linear and nonlinear equations, the matrices are used. These matrices must be downloaded. The most straightforward way to download the matrix is to create it by typing

```
matrix = [value₁₁  value₁₂  .. value₁ₙ₋₁ value₁ₙ;
          value₂₁  value₂₂  .. value₂ₙ₋₁ value₂ₙ],
```

where each value can be a real or complex number. The square brackets are used to form vectors and matrices, and a semicolon is used to end a row. For example,

```
>> matrix=[1 2 3 4 5; 6 7 8 9 10]
matrix =
         1             2             3             4             5
         6             7             8             9            10
```

or

```
>> matrix=[1+1i 2 3 4; 5+5i 6 7 8]
matrix =
     1  +  1i            2             3             4
     5  +  5i            6             7             8
```

It was emphasized that MATLAB indexes matrices in the following manner: (1,1), (1,2), (1,3), (1,4), (2,1), (2,2), (2,3) and (2,4). That is, for the matrix entry (2,3), we have

```
>> entry23=matrix(2,3)
entry23 =
     7
```

The matrix can be generated in many ways. For example,

```
>> A=[-2:1:2; -4:2:4]
A =
        -2            -1             0             1             2
        -4            -2             0             2             4
```

The colon operator : is one of MATLAB's most important and commonly used operators. It occurs in several different forms. The expressions

```
>> A=-5:1:5, B=-5:5
```

give vectors A and B as

```
A =
    -5    -4    -3    -2    -1     0     1     2     3     4     5
B =
    -5    -4    -3    -2    -1     0     1     2     3     4     5
```

That is, we have two identical row vectors containing the integers from − 5 to 5.

The matrix AB is found as

```
>> A=-5:1:5; B=-5:5; AB=[A; B]

AB =
    -5    -4    -3    -2    -1     0     1     2     3     4     5
    -5     4    -3    -2    -1     0     1     2     3     4     5
```

To obtain nonunit spacing, the user specifies an increment. For example,

```
>> C=-50:10:50
C =
  -50   -40   -30   -20   -10     0    10    20    30    40    50
```

The matrix ABC is generated as

```
>> A=-5:1:5; B=-5:5; C=-50:10:50; ABC=[A; A; B; B; C]

ABC =
    -5    -4    -3    -2    -1     0     1     2     3     4     5
    -5    -4    -3    -2    -1     0     1     2     3     4     5
    -5    -4    -3    -2    -1     0     1     2     3     4     5
    -5    -4    -3    -2    -1     0     1     2     3     4     5
   -50   -40   -30   -20   -10     0    10    20    30    40    50
```

Subscript expressions involving colons refer to portions of a matrix. For example, A(1:k,j) represents the first k elements of the jth column of A.

The colon refers to all row and column elements of a matrix, and the keyword end refers to the last row or column. Therefore, sum(A(:,end)) computes the sum of the elements in the last column of A.

As mentioned, MATLAB has a variety of built-in functions, operators, and commands to generate the matrices without having to enumerate all elements. It is easy to illustrate how to use the functions `ones`, `zeros`, `magic`, etc. As an example, we have

```
>> help ones
 ONES   Ones array.
      ONES(N) is an N-by-N matrix of ones.
      ONES(M,N) or ONES([M,N]) is an M-by-N matrix of ones.
      ONES(M,N,P,...) or ONES([M N P ...]) is an M-by-N-by-P-by-...
      array of ones.
      ONES(SIZE(A)) is the same size as A and all ones.
      See also ZEROS.

>> A=ones(4)
A =

      1       1       1       1
      1       1       1       1
      1       1       1       1
      1       1       1       1
>> B=ones(2,4)
B =

      1       1       1       1
      1       1       1       1
```

Hence, the `ones` function allows the user to generate a matrix whose elements are ones. By typing `ones(n,m)`, the user creates an n row by m column matrix of ones. The `zeros` function allows the user to generate a matrix whose elements are zero. By typing `zeros(n,m)`, the user creates an n row by m column matrix of zeros. The `eye` function allows us to generate an identity matrix whose diagonal elements are ones and all other are zeros. Typing `eye(n,n)`, the user creates an n row by n column identity matrix. For example,

```
>> a=eye(4)
a =

      1       0       0       0
      0       1       0       0
      0       0       1       0
      0       0       0       1
```

and

```
>> a=zeros(2,7)
a =

      0       0       0       0       0       0       0
      0       0       0       0       0       0       0
```

The blocked matrices can be generated, and the syntax is straightforward.

For example, let us generate the matrix

$$A = \begin{bmatrix} 1 & 0 & 0 \\ 0 & 1 & 0 \\ 0 & 0 & 1 \\ 1 & 1 & 1 \\ 1 & 1 & 1 \\ 1 & 1 & 1 \\ 0 & 0 & 0 \end{bmatrix}.$$

Then, we have

```
>> a=[eye(3);ones(3);zeros(1,3)]
```

```
     1     0     0
     0     1     0
     0     0     1
     1     1     1
     1     1     1
     1     1     1
     0     0     0
```

Summarizing the matrix building functions, we list some of them [1, 4]:

eye(n)   identity matrix with size n by n
zeros(n,m)   matrix of zeros with size n by m
ones(n,m)   matrix of ones with size n by m
diag(A)   returns diagonal as vector
triu(A)   upper triangular part of a matrix
tril(A)   lower triangular part of a matrix
rand(n,m)   randomly generated matrix with size n by m
hilb(n)   Hilbert matrix with size n by n
magic(n)   magic square with size n by n
toeplitz(n,m) and toeplitz(n)   non-symmetric and symmetric Toeplitz matrices
hankel(n,m) and hankel(n)   non-symmetric and symmetric Hankel matrices

If a is a vector, then diag(a) is the diagonal matrix with the vector a becoming the diagonal. If A is a square matrix, then diag(A) is a vector consisting of the diagonal of A. For example,

```
>> A=-5:1:5, AA=diag(A)
A =
    -5    -4    -3    -2    -1     0     1     2     3     4     5
AA =
    -5     0     0     0     0     0     0     0     0     0     0
     0    -4     0     0     0     0     0     0     0     0     0
     0     0    -3     0     0     0     0     0     0     0     0
     0     0     0    -2     0     0     0     0     0     0     0
     0     0     0     0    -1     0     0     0     0     0     0
     0     0     0     0     0     0     0     0     0     0     0
     0     0     0     0     0     0     1     0     0     0     0
     0     0     0     0     0     0     0     2     0     0     0
     0     0     0     0     0     0     0     0     3     0     0
     0     0     0     0     0     0     0     0     0     4     0
     0     0     0     0     0     0     0     0     0     0     5
```

MATLAB has built-in variables (e.g., pi and ans), and the active variables can be viewed using the command who. For example, we just generated the matrix AA. Thus, typing AA and pressing the Enter key, we have

```
>> AA
AA =
    -5     0     0     0     0     0     0     0     0     0     0
     0    -4     0     0     0     0     0     0     0     0     0
     0     0    -3     0     0     0     0     0     0     0     0
     0     0     0    -2     0     0     0     0     0     0     0
     0     0     0     0    -1     0     0     0     0     0     0
     0     0     0     0     0     0     0     0     0     0     0
     0     0     0     0     0     0     1     0     0     0     0
     0     0     0     0     0     0     0     2     0     0     0
     0     0     0     0     0     0     0     0     3     0     0
     0     0     0     0     0     0     0     0     0     4     0
     0     0     0     0     0     0     0     0     0     0     5
```

because the AA is an active variable. To remove AA from active variables, we type

```
>> clear AA
```

To create other matrices that have the same size as an existing matrix, we can use the `size` operator. For example,

```
>> A=ones(4); D=zeros(size(A))
D =
         0              0              0              0
         0              0              0              0
         0              0              0              0
         0              0              0              0
```

The `max` and `min` operators return the largest and smallest values in matrices and vectors. For example,

```
>> E=magic(4), Maximum=max(E), Minimum=min(E)
E =
        16              2              3             13
         5             11             10              8
         9              7              6             12
         4             14             15              1
Maximum =
        16             14             15             13
Minimum =
         4              2              3              1
```

That is, $E = \begin{bmatrix} 16 & 2 & 3 & 13 \\ 5 & 11 & 10 & 8 \\ 9 & 7 & 6 & 12 \\ 4 & 14 & 15 & 1 \end{bmatrix}$. Thus, MATLAB has a built-in function that creates the magic squares (matrices) of any size.

The `sum` is the sum of all the elements of the vector or sums the columns for matrices, while `prod` is the product of all the elements of the vector or the product down the columns. That is,

```
>> S=sum(E), P=prod(E)
S =
        34             34             34             34
P =
      2880           2156           2700           1248
```

A magic square is a square matrix which has equal sums along all its rows and columns. The matrix can be generated using the `magic` function. For example,

```
>> a=magic(4)
a =
        16      2      3     13
         5     11     10      8
         9      7      6     12
         4     14     15      1
```

The maximum and minimum entries can be found using the `max` and `min` functions. For five rows of the magic matrix a, we have

```
>> a=magic(5), aa=max(a);  aaa=min(a)
a =
        17     24      1      8     15
        23      5      7     14     16
         4      6     13     20     22
        10     12     19     21      3
        11     18     25      2      9
```

```
aa =
    23    24    25    21    22
aaa =
     4     5     1     2     3
```

If we do not specify a variable, MATLAB uses the variable `ans` (answer) to store the results of a calculation. The sums and products of the columns of the magic matrix can be found. We have

```
>> E=magic(4); sum(E), prod(E)
ans =

    34    34    34    34
ans =
         2880       2156       2700       1248
```

The user can summate the rows. To do this, use the transpose operator. In particular, to find the sum of rows, we transpose the matrix E, compute the column sums of the transpose, and then transpose the result. The transpose operation is denoted by an apostrophe or single quote ' . It flips a matrix about its main diagonal. The transpose operation turns a row vector into a column vector. Let us illustrate the results. In particular,

```
>> E=magic(4); ET=E', ST=sum(E')'


ET =
    16     5     9     4
     2    11     7    14
     3    10     6    15
    13     8    12     1

ST =
    34
    34
    34
    34
```

That is, from $E = \begin{bmatrix} 16 & 2 & 3 & 13 \\ 5 & 11 & 10 & 8 \\ 9 & 7 & 6 & 12 \\ 4 & 14 & 15 & 1 \end{bmatrix}$, we have $E^T = \begin{bmatrix} 16 & 5 & 9 & 4 \\ 2 & 11 & 7 & 14 \\ 3 & 10 & 6 & 15 \\ 13 & 8 & 12 & 1 \end{bmatrix}$.

The sum of the elements on the main diagonal is easily obtained using the `diag` function, and we have

```
>> E=magic(4); ED=diag(E), SED=sum(ED)


ED =
    16
    11
     6
     1
SED =
    34
```

The `size` and `length` functions return the size and length of a vector or matrix. For example,

```
>> E=magic(4); SE=size(E), LE=length(E)
SE =
     4     4
LE =
     4
```

Selective Indexing. The user may need to perform operations with certain elements of vectors and matrices. For example, let us change all negative elements of the vector or matrix to be positive. To perform this, we have

```
>> A=[1 2 -3 -4; 5 6 -7 -8]; A(A<0)=-A(A<0)
A =
       1      2      3      4
       5      6      7      8
```

The user can perform operations on a vector or matrix conditionally based on the value of the corresponding element of another vector or matrix. For example, to divide two vectors element-wise, one may face difficulties if the denominator vector has zeros. To overcome this problem, selective indexing is used. The following example illustrates the technique to find the matrix C:

```
>> A=[1 2 3 4 5 6]; B=[1 0 3 0 1 0]; C=zeros(1, length(A)); C(B~=0)=A(B~=0)./B(B~=0)
C =
       1      0      1      0      5      0
```

Solving the linear algebraic equation $Ax = B$, we find that the solution is given as $x = A^{-1}B$.

Let us illustrate the application of MATLAB. Consider the system of two algebraic equations

$$y + 2z = 5,$$

$$3y + 4z = 6.$$

This system is represented in the matrix form $Ax = B$, where

$$x = \begin{bmatrix} y \\ z \end{bmatrix}, A = \begin{bmatrix} 1 & 2 \\ 3 & 4 \end{bmatrix} \text{ and } B = \begin{bmatrix} 5 \\ 6 \end{bmatrix}.$$

We obtain the solution x as

```
>> A=[1 2;3 4]; B=[5; 6]; x=inv(A)*B
x =
    -4.0000
     4.5000
```

Thus,

$$y = -4 \text{ and } z = 4.5.$$

The system of equations $\begin{matrix} y + 2z = 5 \\ 3y + 4z = 6 \end{matrix}$ can be solved graphically. In particular, we have the following MATLAB statement:

```
>> y=-10:0.1:0; z=(-y+5)/2; plot(y,z); hold on; z=(-3*y+6)/4; plot(y,z)
```

Figure 3.10 illustrates that the solutions are $y = -4$ and $z = 4.5$. Chapter 4 covers two- and three-dimensional plotting and graphics. The graphical solution is given just to illustrate and verify the results.

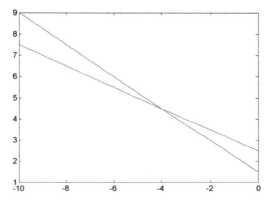

Figure 3.10. Graphical solution of the system of linear equations $\begin{matrix} y + 2z = 5 \\ 3y + 4z = 6 \end{matrix}$

As another example, using MATLAB, let us solve the system of the third-order linear algebraic equations given by

$$Ax = B, \text{ where } A = \begin{bmatrix} 1 & 2 & 3 \\ 4 & 5 & 0 \\ 6 & 7 & 8 \end{bmatrix} \text{ and } B = \begin{bmatrix} 10 \\ 20 \\ 30 \end{bmatrix}.$$

Our goal is to find $x(x_1, x_2, \text{ and } x_3)$. We have

```
>> A=[1 2 3;4 5 0;6 7 8]; B=[10; 20; 30]; x=inv(A)*B
x =
  -1.6667e+000
   5.3333e+000
   3.3333e-001
```

That is, the following solution is obtained $x = \begin{bmatrix} -1.67 \\ 5.33 \\ 0.33 \end{bmatrix}.$

The multiplications of A and x should give the matrix B. We have

```
>> B=A*x
B =
   1.0000e+001
   2.0000e+001
   3.0000e+001
```

Thus, the solution is correct.

In addition to solving linear algebraic equations, MATLAB performs a great number of other matrix computations. Among the most useful is the computation of eigenvalues and eigenvectors using the `eig` function. If A is a square matrix, then `eig(A)` returns the eigenvalues of A in a vector, while `[V,D]=eig(A)` returns the spectral decomposition of A (here, V is a matrix whose columns are eigenvectors of A, while D is a diagonal matrix whose diagonal entries are eigenvalues: thus the equation $AV=VD$ holds). If A is diagonalizable, then V is invertible, while if A is symmetric, then V is orthogonal $V^T V = I$.

Let us study the following example. For the matrix $A = \begin{bmatrix} 1 & 2 & 3 \\ 7 & 8 & 9 \\ 4 & 5 & 6 \end{bmatrix}$ find the eigenvalues and eigenvectors. We start with the MATLAB help. In particular,

```
>> help eig
 EIG    Eigenvalues and eigenvectors.
    E = EIG(X) is a vector containing the eigenvalues of a square
    matrix X.

    [V,D] = EIG(X) produces a diagonal matrix D of eigenvalues and a
    full matrix V whose columns are the corresponding eigenvectors so
    that X*V = V*D.

    [V,D] = EIG(X,'nobalance') performs the computation with balancing
    disabled, which sometimes gives more accurate results for certain
    problems with unusual scaling.

    E = EIG(A,B) is a vector containing the generalized eigenvalues
    of square matrices A and B.

    [V,D] = EIG(A,B) produces a diagonal matrix D of generalized
    eigenvalues and a full matrix V whose columns are the
    corresponding eigenvectors so that A*V = B*V*D.
```

```
    EIG(A,B,'chol') is the same as EIG(A,B) for symmetric A and symmetric
    positive definite B.  It computes the generalized eigenvalues of A and B
    using the Cholesky factorization of B.
    EIG(A,B,'qz') ignores the symmetry of A and B and uses the QZ algorithm.
    In general, the two algorithms return the same result, however using the
    QZ algorithm may be more stable for certain problems.
    The flag is ignored when A and B are not symmetric.

    See also CONDEIG, EIGS.
 Overloaded methods
    help lti/eig.m
    help sym/eig.m
```

Thus, the eigenvalues and eigenvectors are found using the `[V,D]=eig(A)` statement. We have

```
>> A = [1 3 2;7 8 9;4 5 6]; [V,D]=eig(A); A, V, D
A =

     1      3      2
     7      8      9
     4      5      6


V =

   -0.2377    -0.8259    -0.5241
   -0.8206     0.5595    -0.4071
   -0.5196     0.0702     0.7480


D =

   15.7266         0         0
         0   -1.2025         0
         0         0    0.4759
```

It is easy to verify that $AV - VD = 0$. In particular,

```
>> A = [1 3 2;7 8 9;4 5 6]; [V,D]=eig(A); O=A*V-V*D
O =
  1.0e-014 *
    0.3109    -0.0555    -0.0111
    0.3553    -0.2665    -0.1332
    0.1776    -0.1138    -0.1776
```

Many numerical problems involve the application of inverse matrices. Finding inverse matrices in MATLAB is straightforward using the `inv` function.

For matrix $A = \begin{bmatrix} 1 & 2 & 3 \\ 0 & 4 & 0 \\ 5 & 6 & 7 \end{bmatrix}$, find the inverse matrix, calculate the eigenvalues, derive

$B = 10A^3 A^{-1}$, and find the determinant of B. Using the inv, eig, and det functions, we have

```
>> A=[1 2 3;0 4 0;5 6 7]; B=10*(A^3)*(A)^(-1); inv(A), B, eig(B), det(B)
ans =
 -8.7500e-001 -1.2500e-001   3.7500e-001
            0  2.5000e-001             0
  6.2500e-001 -1.2500e-001  -1.2500e-001
B =
  1.6000e+002   2.8000e+002   2.4000e+002
            0   1.6000e+002             0
  4.0000e+002   7.6000e+002   6.4000e+002
ans =
  8.0816e+000
  7.9192e+002
  1.6000e+002
ans =
  1.0240e+006
```

That is, $A^{-1} = \begin{bmatrix} -0.875 & -0.125 & 0.375 \\ 0 & 0.25 & 0 \\ 0.625 & -0.125 & -0.125 \end{bmatrix}$, $B = \begin{bmatrix} 160 & 280 & 240 \\ 0 & 160 & 0 \\ 400 & 760 & 640 \end{bmatrix}$, the eigenvalues of the matrix B are

8.1, 791.9, 160, and the determinant is 1024000.

We performed the matrix multiplications. The entry-by-entry multiplication, instead of the usual matrix multiplication, can be performed using a dot before the multiplication operator; for example, a.*b. As an illustration, let us perform the entry-by-entry multiplication of two three-by-three matrices

$A = \begin{bmatrix} 1 & 2 & 3 \\ 4 & 5 & 6 \\ 7 & 8 & 9 \end{bmatrix}$ and $B = \begin{bmatrix} 10 & 10 & 10 \\ 100 & 1 & 100 \\ 1 & 1 & 1 \end{bmatrix}$. We have

```
>> A=[1 2 3;4 5 6;7 8 9]; B=[10 10 10;100 1 100;1 1 1]; C=A.*B
C =
    10    20    30
   400     5   600
     7     8     9
```

MATLAB allows us to generate the random matrices. For example, a five-by-five matrix can be randomly generated using the rand function. We have

```
>> R=rand(5)
R =
   9.5013e-001   7.6210e-001   6.1543e-001   4.0571e-001   5.7891e-002
   2.3114e-001   4.5647e-001   7.9194e-001   9.3547e-001   3.5287e-001
   6.0684e-001   1.8504e-002   9.2181e-001   9.1690e-001   8.1317e-001
   4.8598e-001   8.2141e-001   7.3821e-001   4.1027e-001   9.8613e-003
   8.9130e-001   4.4470e-001   1.7627e-001   8.9365e-001   1.3889e-001
```

The random matrices, arrays, and number generation are accomplished using rand. Different sequences of random matrices, arrays, and numbers are produced for each execution. The complete description of the rand function is available as follows:

```
>> help rand
 RAND   Uniformly distributed random numbers.
    RAND(N) is an N-by-N matrix with random entries, chosen from
    a uniform distribution on the interval (0.0,1.0).
    RAND(M,N) and RAND([M,N]) are M-by-N matrices with random entries.
    RAND(M,N,P,...) or RAND([M,N,P,...]) generate random arrays.
    RAND with no arguments is a scalar whose value changes each time it
    is referenced.  RAND(SIZE(A)) is the same size as A.

    RAND produces pseudo-random numbers.  The sequence of numbers
    generated is determined by the state of the generator.  Since MATLAB
    resets the state at start-up, the sequence of numbers generated will
    be the same unless the state is changed.

    S = RAND('state') is a 35-element vector containing the current state
    of the uniform generator.  RAND('state',S) resets the state to S.
    RAND('state',0) resets the generator to its initial state.
    RAND('state',J), for integer J, resets the generator to its J-th state.
    RAND('state',sum(100*clock)) resets it to a different state each time.

    This generator can generate all the floating point numbers in the
    closed interval [2^(-53), 1-2^(-53)].  Theoretically, it can generate
    over 2^1492 values before repeating itself.

    MATLAB Version 4.x used random number generators with a single seed.
```

```
RAND('seed',0) and RAND('seed',J) cause the MATLAB 4 generator to be
used.
RAND('seed') returns the current seed of the MATLAB 4 uniform generator.
RAND('state',J) and RAND('state',S) cause the MATLAB 5 generator to be
used.
  See also RANDN, SPRAND, SPRANDN, RANDPERM.
```

The range of values generated by the `rand` function can be different from what is needed. Therefore, scaling is necessary. The general expression for scaling and shifting is

$R = Shifting + Scaling*$`rand()`,

and the following example illustrates the application of the above formula:

```
>> R=ones(5)+0.1*rand('5)
R =
    1.0583    1.0226    1.0209    1.0568    1.0415
    1.0423    1.0580    1.0380    1.0794    1.0305
    1.0516    1.0760    1.0783    1.0059    1.0874
    1.0334    1.0530    1.0681    1.0603    1.0015
    1.0433    1.0641    1.0461    1.0050    1.0768
```

The average (mean) value can be found using the `mean` function. For vectors, mean(x) is the mean value of the elements in x. For matrices, mean(X) is a row vector containing the mean value of each column. In contrast, for arrays, mean(x) is the mean value of the elements along the first non-singleton dimension of x.

The median value is found by making use of the `median` function. For vectors, median(x) is the median value of the elements in x. For matrices, median(X) is a row vector containing the median value of each column. For arrays, median(x) is the median value of the elements along the first nonsingleton dimension of x.

To illustrate the `mean` and `median` functions, the following example is introduced:

```
>> R=rand(5), Rmean=mean(R), Rmedian=median(R),
R =
    0.6756    0.1210    0.2548    0.2319    0.1909
    0.6992    0.4508    0.8656    0.2393    0.8439
    0.7275    0.7159    0.2324    0.0498    0.1739
    0.4784    0.8928    0.8049    0.0784    0.1708
    0.5548    0.2731    0.9084    0.6408    0.9943
Rmean =
    0.6271    0.4907    0.6132    0.2480    0.4747
Rmedian =
    0.6756    0.4508    0.8049    0.2319    0.1909
```

Thus, using `rand`, we generated the random 5 × 5 matrix R. Then, applying the `mean` and `median` functions, we found the mean and median values of each column of R.

MATLAB has functions to round floating point numbers to integers. These functions are `round`, `fix`, `ceil`, and `floor`. The following illustrates the application of these functions:

```
>> f=[-0.1 -0.5 0.1 .5 1 1.9],R=round(f),F=fix(f),C=ceil(f),FL=floor(f),S=sum(f)
f =
 -1.0000e-001 -5.0000e-001  1.0000e-001  5.0000e-001  1.0000e+000  1.9000e+000
R =
     0    -1     0     1     1     2
F =
     0     0     0     0     1     1
C =
     0     0     1     1     1     2
FL =
    -1    -1     0     0     1     1
S =
   2.9000e+000
```

Symbols and Punctuation. The standard notations are used in MATLAB. To practice, type the examples given. The answers and comments are given in Table 3.1.

Table 3.1. MATLAB Problems

Problems with MATLAB syntaxes	Answers						Comments
>> a=2+3	a = 5						MATLAB arithmetic
>> 2+3	ans = 5						
>> a=2*3	a = 6						
>> 2*3	ans = 6						
>> a=sqrt(5*5)	a = 5						
>> sqrt(5*5)	ans = 5						
>> a=1+2j; b=3+4j; c=a*b	c = -5.0000 +10.0000i						Complex variables
>> a=[0 2 4 6 8 10]	a = 0	2	4	6	8	10	Vectors
>> a=[0:2:10]	a = 0	2	4	6	8	10	
>> a=0:2:10	a = 0	2	4	6	8	10	
>> a(:)'	a = 0	2	4	6	8	10	
>> a=[0:2:10];	c =						
>> b=a(:)*a(:)'	0	0	0	0	0	0	Forming matrix b
	0	4	8	12	16	20	
	0	8	16	24	32	40	
	0	12	24	36	48	60	
	0	16	32	48	64	80	
	0	20	40	60	80	100	
>> b(3,4)	ans = 24						Element (3,4)
>> b(3,:)	ans = 0	8	16	24	32	40	Third row
>> c=b(:,4:5)	c =						Forming a new matrix
	0	0					
	12	16					
	24	32					
	36	48					
	48	64					
	60	80					
>> a(:)'*a(:)	ans = 220						

MATLAB Operators, Characters, Relations, and Logics. It was demonstrated how to use summation, subtractions, multiplications, etc. We can use the relational and logical operators. In particular, we can apply 1 to symbolize "true" and 0 to symbolize "false." The MATLAB operators and special characters are listed below.

```
Arithmetic operators
        plus      - Plus                                  +
        uplus     - Unary plus                            +
        minus     - Minus                                 -
        uminus    - Unary minus                           -
        mtimes    - Matrix multiply                       *
        times     - Array multiply                        .*
        mpower    - Matrix power                          ^
        power     - Array power                           .^
        mldivide  - Backslash or left matrix divide       \
        mrdivide  - Slash or right matrix divide          /
        ldivide   - Left array divide                     .\
        rdivide   - Right array divide                    ./
        kron      - Kronecker tensor product              kron
Relational operators
```

```
          eq        - Equal                                    ==
          ne        - Not equal                                ~=
          lt        - Less than                                <
          gt        - Greater than                             >
          le        - Less than or equal                       <=
          ge        - Greater than or equal                    >=

Logical operators
          and       - Logical AND                              &
          or        - Logical OR                               |
          not       - Logical NOT                              ~
          xor       - Logical EXCLUSIVE OR
          any       - True if any element of vector is nonzero
          all       - True if all elements of vector are nonzero
Special characters
          colon     - Colon                                    :
          paren     - Parentheses and subscripting             ( )
          paren     - Brackets                                 [ ]
          paren     - Braces and subscripting                  { }
          punct     - Function handle creation                 @
          punct     - Decimal point                            .
          punct     - Structure field access                  .
          punct     - Parent directory                         ..
          punct     - Continuation                             ...
          punct     - Separator                                ,
          punct     - Semicolon                                ;
          punct     - Comment                                  %
          punct     - Invoke operating system command          !
          punct     - Assignment                               =
          punct     - Quote                                    '
          transpose - Transpose                                .'
          ctranspose- Complex conjugate transpose              '
          horzcat   - Horizontal concatenation                 [,]
          vertcat   - Vertical concatenation                   [;]
          subsasgn  - Subscripted assignment                   ( ),{ },.
          subsref   - Subscripted reference                    ( ),{ },.
          subsindex - Subscript index
Bitwise operators
          bitand    - Bit-wise AND
          bitcmp    - Complement bits
          bitor     - Bit-wise OR
          bitmax    - Maximum floating point integer
          bitxor    - Bit-wise XOR
          bitset    - Set bit
          bitget    - Get bit
          bitshift  - Bit-wise shift
Set operators
          union     - Set union
          unique    - Set unique
          intersect - Set intersection
          setdiff   - Set difference
          setxor    - Set exclusive-or
          ismember  - True for set member
```

For example, the MATLAB operators &, |, ~ stand for "logical AND", "logical OR", and "logical NOT".

The operators == and ~= check for equality. Let us illustrate the application of == using two matrices $A = \begin{bmatrix} 1 & 1 & 1 \\ 0 & 0 & 0 \\ 1 & 1 & 1 \end{bmatrix}$ and $B = \begin{bmatrix} 1 & 1 & 1 \\ 10 & 10 & 10 \\ 0 & 0 & 0 \end{bmatrix}$. We have

```
>> A=[1 1 1; 0 0 0; 1 1 1]; B=[1 1 1; 10 10 10; 0 0 0]; C=A==B, D=A|B
C =
       1       1       1
       0       0       0
       0       0       0

D =
       0       0       0
       1       1       1
       1       1       1
```

One concludes that MATLAB performs Boolean operations on vectors element-wise. For this purpose, based on Boolean algebra, MATLAB regards any nonzero real element as true, and zero as false. MATLAB uses & for the Boolean AND operator, | for OR, and ~ for NOT. In addition, the user can run a cumulative Boolean OR or Boolean AND across all the elements of a matrix or vector. If A is a vector or matrix, any(A) returns true if any element of A is non-zero; all(A) returns true if all the elements of A are nonzero.

Other MATLAB operators can be straightforwardly applied in a similar manner.

There are many other matrix functions in MATLAB related to matrix factorizations. For example, the following functions are commonly used (see the help options for a complete description):

- lu computes the LU factorization of a matrix,
- chol computes the Cholesky factorization of a symmetric positive definite matrix,
- qr computes the QR factorization of a matrix,
- svd computes the singular values or singular value decomposition of a matrix,
- cond, condest, rcond compute or estimate various condition numbers,
- norm computes various matrix or vector norms.

Different norms may be found. In particular, using the help command, we have

```
>> help norm

 NORM   Matrix or vector norm.
    For matrices...
      NORM(X) is the largest singular value of X, max(svd(X)).
      NORM(X,2) is the same as NORM(X).
      NORM(X,1) is the 1-norm of X, the largest column sum,
                  = max(sum(abs((X)))).
      NORM(X,inf) is the infinity norm of X, the largest row sum,
                  = max(sum(abs((X')))).
      NORM(X,'fro') is the Frobenius norm, sqrt(sum(diag(X'*X))).
      NORM(X,P) is available for matrix X only if P is 1, 2, inf or 'fro'.

    For vectors...
      NORM(V,P) = sum(abs(V).^P)^(1/P).
      NORM(V) = norm(V,2).
      NORM(V,inf) = max(abs(V)).
      NORM(V,-inf) = min(abs(V)).

    See also COND, RCOND, CONDEST, NORMEST.
```

```
Overloaded methods
   help ss/norm.m
   help lti/norm.m
   help frd/norm.m
   help idmodel/norm.m
```

Strings and Basic Operations with Strings. Arrays can be used to hold data of any type. To illustrate this, we consider storing strings in character arrays. Strings variables are mainly used for labeling output and passing the names of m-files as arguments to other functions. Therefore, they are not usually important in numerical analysis, but strings guarantee flexibility in programming. Strings are matrices with character elements. The normal rules of assignment and variable creation are applied. String constants (letters) are enclosed in single quotes, and the following example shows how to create (declare) string variables:

```
>> First='John'; Last='Johnson'; Name=[First,'    ',Last]
Name =
John    Johnson
```

Thus, two string variables were defined (declared), and a new string variable was created.

The size of string variables is determined by the length of the strings. In particular,

```
>> whos
  Name        Size          Bytes  Class
  First       1x4           8   char array
  Last        1x7           14  char array
  Name        1x15          30  char array
Grand total is 26 elements using 52 bytes
```

The commonly used string operations are comparison, concatenation, reading strings from files, element-wise string operations, passing strings, etc.

Display Formats. In the MATLAB environment, five digits are displayed by default. However, MATLAB maintains and computes in a double precision 16 decimal places, and it just rounds the numbers. For example, `format long` will display all 16 digits, `format short` will return to the shorter display. It is possible to use the commands `format short e` and `format long e`. Using the help option, we have

```
>> help format
 FORMAT Set output format.
    All computations in MATLAB are done in double precision.
    FORMAT may be used to switch between different output
    display formats as follows:
       FORMAT          Default. Same as SHORT.
       FORMAT SHORT    Scaled fixed point format with 5 digits.
       FORMAT LONG     Scaled fixed point format with 15 digits.
       FORMAT SHORT E  Floating point format with 5 digits.
       FORMAT LONG E   Floating point format with 15 digits.
       FORMAT SHORT G  Best of fixed or floating point format with 5 digits.
       FORMAT LONG G   Best of fixed or floating point format with 15 digits.
       FORMAT HEX      Hexadecimal format.
       FORMAT +        The symbols +, - and blank are printed
                       for positive, negative and zero elements.
                       Imaginary parts are ignored.
       FORMAT BANK     Fixed format for dollars and cents.
       FORMAT RAT      Approximation by ratio of small integers.
    Spacing:
       FORMAT COMPACT  Suppress extra line-feeds.
       FORMAT LOOSE    Puts the extra line-feeds back in.
```

Polynomial Analysis. Polynomial analysis, curve fitting, and interpolation are easily performed. We consider a polynomial

$$p(x) = 10x^{10} + 9x^9 + 8x^8 + 7x^7 + 6x^4 + 5x^5 + 4x^4 + 3x^3 + 2x^2 + 1x + 0.5.$$

To find the roots, we use the `roots` function:

```
>> p=[10 9 8 7 6 5 4 3 2 1 0.5]; roots(p)
ans =
    0.6192 + 0.5138i
    0.6192 - 0.5138i
   -0.7159 + 0.2166i
   -0.7159 - 0.2166i
   -0.4689 + 0.5597i
   -0.4689 - 0.5597i
    0.2298 + 0.6890i
    0.2298 - 0.6890i
   -0.1142 + 0.6913i
   -0.1142 - 0.6913i
```

As illustrated, different formats are supported by MATLAB. The numerical values are displayed in 15-digit fixed and 15-digit floating-point formats if `format long` and `format long e` are used, respectively. Five digits are displayed if `format short` and `format short e` are assigned to be used. For example, in `format short e`, we have

```
>> format short e; p=[10 9 8 7 6 5 4 3 2 1 0.5]; roots(p)
ans =
   6.1922e-001 +5.1377e-001i
   6.1922e-001 -5.1377e-001i
  -7.1587e-001 +2.1656e-001i
  -7.1587e-001 -2.1656e-001i
  -4.6895e-001 +5.5966e-001i
  -4.6895e-001 -5.5966e-001i
   2.2983e-001 +6.8904e-001i
   2.2983e-001 -6.8904e-001i
  -1.1423e-001 +6.9125e-001i
  -1.1423e-001 -6.9125e-001i
```

In general, the polynomial is expressed as

$$p(x) = a_n x^n + a_{n-1} x^{n-1} + \ldots + a_2 x^2 + a_1 x + a_0.$$

The functions `conv` and `deconv` perform convolution and deconvolution (polynomial multiplication and division). Consider two polynomials

$$p_1(x) = x^4 + 2x^3 + 3x^2 + 4x + 5 \text{ and } p_2(x) = 6x^2 + 7x + 8$$

To find $p_3(x) = p_1(x) p_2(x)$ we use the `conv` function. In particular,

```
>> p1=[1 2 3 4 5]; p2=[6 7 8]; p3=conv(p1,p2)
p3 =
     6    19    40    61    82    67    40
```

Thus, we find

$$p_3(x) = 6x^6 + 19x^5 + 40x^4 + 61x^3 + 82x^2 + 67x + 40.$$

It is easy to see that $p_4(x) = \dfrac{p_3(x)}{p_1(x)} = \dfrac{6x^6 + 19x^5 + 40x^4 + 61x^3 + 82x^2 + 67x + 40}{x^4 + 2x^3 + 3x^2 + 4x + 5} = 6x^2 + 7x + 8 = p_2(x)$

This can be verified using the `deconv` function. In particular, we have

```
>> p4=deconv(p3,p1)
p4 =
     6     7     8
```

Comprehensive analysis can be performed using the MATLAB polynomial algebra and numerics. For example, let us evaluate the polynomial

$$p_3(x) = 6x^6 + 19x^5 + 40x^4 + 61x^3 + 82x^2 + 67x + 40$$

at the points 0, 3, 6, 9, and 12. This problem has a straightforward solution using the `polyval` function. We have
```
>> x=[0:3:12]; y=polyval(p3,x)
y =
         40        14857       496090      4624771     23591212
```
Thus, the values of $p_3(x)$ at $x = 0, 3, 9$, and 12 are 40, 14857, 496090, 4624771, and 23591212.

As illustrated, MATLAB enables different operations with polynomials (e.g., calculations of roots, convolution, etc.). In addition, advanced commands and functions are available, such as curve fitting, differentiation, interpolation, etc. We download polynomials as row vectors containing coefficients ordered by descending powers. For example, we download the polynomial $p(x) = x^3 + 2x + 3$ as
```
>> p=[1 0 2 3]
```
The following functions are commonly used: `conv` (multiply polynomials), `deconv` (divide polynomials), `poly` (polynomial with specified roots), `polyder` (polynomial derivative), `polyfit` (polynomial curve fitting), `polyval` (polynomial evaluation), `polyvalm` (matrix polynomial evaluation), `residue` (partial-fraction expansion), `roots` (find polynomial roots), etc.

The `roots` function calculates the roots of a polynomial.
```
>> p=[1 0 2 3]; r=roots(p)
r =
   0.5000 + 1.6583i
   0.5000 - 1.6583i
  -1.0000
```
The function `poly` returns to the polynomial coefficients, and
```
>> p=poly(r)
p =
   1.0000   -0.0000    2.0000    3.0000
```
The `poly` function computes the coefficients of the characteristic polynomial of a matrix. For example,
```
>> A=[1 2 3; 0 4 5; 0 6 7]; c=poly(A)
c =
   1.0000  -12.0000    9.0000    2.0000
```
The roots of this polynomial, computed using the `roots` function, are the characteristic roots (eigenvalues) of the matrix A. In particular,
```
>> r=roots(c)
r =
   11.1789
    1.0000
   -0.1789
```
The `polyval` function evaluates a polynomial at a specified value. For example, to evaluate $p(x) = x^3 + 2x + 3$ at $s=10$, we have
```
>> p=[1 0 2 3]; p10=polyval(p,10)
p10 =
        1023
```
The `polyder` function computes the derivative of any polynomial. To obtain the derivative of the polynomial $p(x) = x^3 + 2x + 3$, the MATLAB statement is
```
>> p=[1 0 2 3]; der=polyder(p)
der =
     3     0     2
```
The `polyder` function can be straightforwardly applied to compute the derivative of the product or quotient of polynomials. For example, for two polynomials $p_1(x) = x^3 + 2x + 3$ and $p_2(x) = x^4 + 4x + 5$, we have
```
>> p1=[1 0 2 3]; p2=[1 0 0 4 5]; p=conv(p1,p2), der=polyder(p1,p2)
p =
     1     0     2     7     5     8    22    15
der =
     7     0    10    28    15    16    22
```

The data fitting can be easily performed. The `polyfit` function finds the coefficients of a polynomial that fits a set of data in a least-squares sense. Assume we have the data (x and y) as given by
$x = [0\ 1\ 2\ 3\ 4\ 5\ 6\ 7\ 8\ 9]$ and $y = [1\ 2.5\ 2\ 3\ 3\ 3\ 2.5\ 2.5\ 2\ 1]$.
Then, to fit the data by the polynomial of the order three, we have
```
>> x=[0 1 2 3 4 5 6 7 8 9]; y=[1 2.5 2 3 3 3 2.5 2.5 2 1]; p=polyfit(x,y,3)
p =
    0.0010    -0.1040    0.8478    1.2028
```
Thus, one obtains $p(x) = 0.001x^3 - 0.104x^2 + 0.8478x + 1.2028$.

The resulting plots, plotted using the following MATLAB statement,
```
>> plot(x,y,'-',x,polyval(p,x),':')
```
of the data and its approximation by the polynomial are illustrated in Figure 3.11.

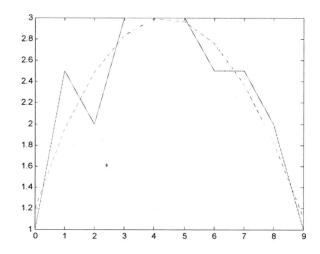

Figure 3.11. Plots of the xy data ($x = [0\ 1\ 2\ 3\ 4\ 5\ 6\ 7\ 8\ 9]$ and $y = [1\ 2.5\ 2\ 3\ 3\ 3\ 2.5\ 2.5\ 2\ 1]$) and its approximation by $p(x) = 0.001x^3 - 0.104x^2 + 0.8478x + 1.2028$

Interpolation (estimation of values that lie between known data points) is important in signal and image processing. MATLAB implements a number of interpolation methods that balance the smoothness of the data fit with the execution speed and memory usage. The one-, two- and three-dimensional interpolations are performed by using the `interp1`, `interp2`, and `interp3` functions. The interpolation methods should be specified, and we have `interp1(x,y,xi,method)`.

The nearest neighbor interpolation method is designated by `nearest`, while the linear, cubic spline, and cubic interpolation methods are specified by the `linear`, `spline` and `cubic` functions. Choosing an interpolation method, one must analyze the smoothness, memory, and computation time requirements.

Example 3.4.1.

Consider the nonlinear magnetic circuit. Ampere's law states that the line integral of $\vec{B}$ around the closed path is proportional to the *net current* through the enclosed area. However, the value of permeability of the ferromagnetic material depends on the external field, and μ is not constant. This effect is observed due to the *saturation magnetization* phenomena. In general, one should use the nonlinear magnetization curves.

That is, the equation $L = \dfrac{N\Phi}{i} = \dfrac{\psi}{i} = const$ is valid *only* if the magnetic system is linear.

Consider a set of data for the flux linkage – current relation for an electromagnetic motion device. We use $i = [0\ 0.2\ 0.4\ 0.6\ 0.8\ 1\ 1.2\ 1.4\ 1.6\ 1.8\ 2]$
and $\Phi = [0\ 0.022\ 0.044\ 0.065\ 0.084\ 0.1\ 0.113\ 0.123\ 0.131\ 0.136\ 0.138]$.

Using MATLAB, curve fitting, interpolation, and approximation can be performed (see the script and the results).

MATLAB Script

```
% NUMERICAL ANALYSIS OF THE CURRENT - FLUX DATA
        % The current-flux data points
I=linspace(0,2,11);
F=[0 0.022 0.044 0.065 0.084 0.1 0.113 0.123 0.131 0.136 0.138];
subplot(3,2,1)
plot(I,F,'o'); axis([0 2 0 0.14]);
xlabel('Current'),ylabel('Flux')
title('The plot of the Current - Flux data')
pause;
        % Differentiation of the current-flux data
dI=I(1:length(I)-1);
dF=diff(F)./diff(I);
subplot(3,2,2)
plot(dI,dF); axis([0 2 0 0.14]);
xlabel('Current'),ylabel('dFlux / dCurrent')
title('Derivative dFlux /dCurrent as a function of Current')
pause;
        % Interpolation of the current-flux curve
I_interval=linspace(0,2,1001);
F_interpol=interp1(I,F,I_interval,'spline');
subplot(3,2,3)
plot(I,F,'o',I_interval,F_interpol,'-'); axis([0 2 0 0.14]);
xlabel('Current'),ylabel('Flux')
title('Smoothing of the Current - Flux curve using cubic spline
interpolation')
pause;
        % Differentiation of the interpolated current-flux curve
dI_interval=I_interval(1:length(I_interval)-1);
dF_interpol=diff(F_interpol)'./diff(I_interval);
subplot(3,2,4)
plot(dI_interval,dF_interpol); axis([0 2 0 0.14]);
xlabel('Current'),ylabel('dFlux / dCurrent')
title('Derivative dFlux /dCurent as a function of Current')
pause;
    % Interpolation of the current-flux curve by N-order polynomials
N=3
polynomial=polyfit(I,F,N)
F_interpolated=polyval(polynomial,I_interval);
subplot(3,2,5)
plot(I,F,'o',I_interval,F_interpolated,'-'); axis([0 2 0 0.14]);
xlabel('Current'),ylabel('Flux')
title('Interpolation of the Current - Flux curve by N-order polynomials')
pause;
        % Differentiation of the interpolated current-flux curve
polynomial_derivatives=polyder(polynomial)
dF_inter=polyval(polynomial_derivatives,I_interval);
subplot(3,2,6)
plot(I_interval,dF_inter); axis([0 2 0 0.14]);
xlabel('Current'),ylabel('dFlux / dCurrent')
title('Derivative dFlux /dCurrent as a function of Current')
clear; disp('End');
```

Figure 3.12 plots the data, and the variations of the inductance are evident. Approximating $\Phi = f(i)$ by the third-order polynomial is found to be

$$\Phi = -0.0048i^3 - 0.016i^2 + 0.12i - 0.00075 .$$

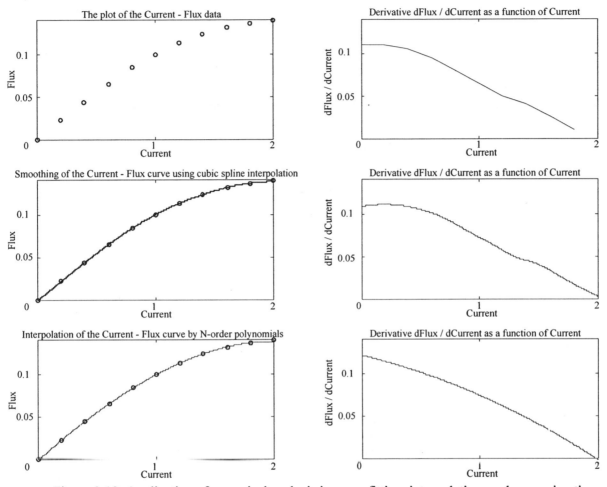

Figure 3.12. Application of numerical analysis in curve fitting, interpolation, and approximation

3.5. Conditions and Loops

The logical operators in MATLAB are $<$, $>$, $<=$, $>=$, $==$ (logical equals), and $\sim=$ (not equal). These are binary operators which return the values 0 and 1 (for scalar arguments). To illustrate them, we have

```
>> a=20>5
a =
         1
>> a=20<5
a =
         0
>> a=20==5
a =
         0
```

These logical operators have limited features, and therefore, loops, conditions, control statements, and control structures (sequence, selection, and repetition structures) are embedded in all programming languages. In particular, MATLAB has standard `if-elseif-else`, `switch`, and `while` structures. The general form of the pseodocode for the `if` conditional statement is

```
if [expression 1]
   statements
elseif [expression 2]
   statements
else
   statements
end
```

As an example, running the following MATLAB statements for two different grades C – and C + (with 1.7 and 2.3 GPA),

```
John_grade=1.7;
if John_grade>=2.0
display('Passed')
else
display('Failed')
end
```

and

```
John_grade=2.3;
if John_grade>=2.0
display('Passed')
else
display('Failed')
end
```

the following two results are displayed in the Command Window:

```
ans =
Failed
```

and

```
ans =
Passed
```

Here, the passing and failing conditions were used. When the condition is satisfied (true), the student passes the course, while if the condition is not guaranteed (false), the student fails the course.

As another example, running the following MATLAB statement

```
x=rand(1);
if x<=0.33 y=0;
elseif x>=0.33 y=1;
else y=x.^2;
end; x, y
```

the answers are found and displayed in the Command Window. In particular, we have

```
x =
    0.9501
y =
    1
```

Control Structures. The `if` selection structure (conditional statement) allows us to design programs that make decisions about what commands to execute. This decision-making is performed choosing among alternative actions based upon the particular (specific) conditions. The basic statement, to illustrate the basic features, is

```
if a>0
x=a^3;
end
```

Thus, we assign x be the equal to a^3 if a is positive. We have an `end` statement to terminate the program. We define an `else` clause which is executed if the condition given (`if` statement) is not true. For example,

```
if a>0
x=a^3;
  else
  x=-a^4;
end
```

Hence, if $a = 5$, $x = 125$, and if $a = -5$, $x = -625$. Here, we need one `end`.

Using the MATLAB help, we have:

1.   `if` structure:

```
>> help if
 IF  IF statement condition.
    The general form of the IF statement is

        IF expression
          statements
        ELSEIF expression
          statements
        ELSE
          statements
        END
    The statements are executed if the real part of the expression
    has all non-zero elements. The ELSE and ELSEIF parts are optional.
    Zero or more ELSEIF parts can be used as well as nested IF's.
    The expression is usually of the form expr rop expr where
    rop is ==, <, >, <=, >=, or ~=.

    Example
        if I == J
          A(I,J) = 2;
        elseif abs(I-J) == 1
          A(I,J) = -1;
        else
          A(I,J) = 0;
        end
    See also RELOP, ELSE, ELSEIF, END, FOR, WHILE, SWITCH.
```

2.   `else` structure:

```
>> help else
 ELSE   Used with IF.
    ELSE is used with IF.  The statements after the ELSE are executed
    if all the preceding IF and ELSEIF expressions are false.

    The general form of the IF statement is
        IF expression
          statements
        ELSEIF expression
          statements
        ELSE
          statements
        END
    See also IF, ELSEIF, END.
```

3.   `elseif` structure:
```
>> help elseif

 ELSEIF IF statement condition.
     ELSEIF is used with IF. The statements after the ELSEIF are
     executed if the expression is true and all the preceding IF and
     ELSEIF expressions are false. An expression is considered true if
     the real part has all non-zero elements.

     ELSEIF does not need a matching END, while ELSE IF does.

     The general form of the IF statement is
         IF expression
            statements
         ELSEIF expression
            statements
         ELSE
            statements
         END
     See also IF, ELSE, END.
```

4.   `switch` structure:
```
>> help switch
 SWITCH Switch among several cases based on expression.
     The general form of the SWITCH statement is:

         SWITCH switch_expr
           CASE case_expr,
              statement, ..., statement
           CASE {case_expr1, case_expr2, case_expr3,...}
              statement, ..., statement
           ...
           OTHERWISE,
              statement, ..., statement
         END
     The statements following the first CASE where the switch_expr matches
     the case_expr are executed.  When the case expression is a cell array
     (as in the second case above), the case_expr matches if any of the
     elements of the cell array match the switch expression.  If none of
     the case expressions match the switch expression then the OTHERWISE
     case is executed (if it exists).  Only one CASE is executed and
     execution resumes with the statement after the END.

     The switch_expr can be a scalar or a string.  A scalar switch_expr
     matches a case_expr if switch_expr==case_expr.  A string
     switch_expr matches a case_expr if strcmp(switch_expr,case_expr)
     returns 1 (true).

     Only the statements between the matching CASE and the next CASE,
     OTHERWISE, or END are executed.  Unlike C, the SWITCH statement
     does not fall through (so BREAKs are unnecessary).

     Example:
     To execute a certain block of code based on what the string, METHOD,
     is set to,
```

```
     method = 'Bilinear';
     switch lower (METHOD)
        case {'linear','bilinear'}
          disp('Method is linear')
        case 'cubic'
          disp('Method is cubic')
        case 'nearest'
          disp('Method is nearest')
        otherwise
          disp('Unknown method.')
     end
   Method is linear
   See also CASE, OTHERWISE, IF, WHILE, FOR, END.
```

The following conclusions can be made.

1. The `if` selection structure performs an action if a condition is true or skips the action if the condition is false.
2. The `if - else` selection structure performs an action if a condition is true and performs a different action if the condition is false.
3. The `switch` selection structure performs one of many different actions depending on the value of an expression.

Therefore, the `if` structure is called a single-selection structure because it performs (selects) or skips (ignores) a single action. The `if - else` structure is called a double-selection structure because it performs (selects) between two different actions. The `switch` structure is called a multiple-selection structure because it selects among many different actions.

Using the results given it is obvious that we can expand the `if` conditional statement (single-selection structure) using other possible conditional structures. If the first condition is not satisfied, it looks for the next condition, and so on, until it either finds an `else`, or finds the `end`. For example,

```
if a>0
x=a^3;
  elseif a==0,
        x-j;
  else
        x=-a^4;
end
```

This script verifies whether a is positive (and, if $a>0$, $x=a^3$), and if a is not positive, it checks whether a is zero (if this is true, $x = j = \sqrt{-1}$). Then, if a is not zero, it does the else clause, and if $a<0$, $x = -a^4$. In particular,

```
a=2;
if a>0
x=a^3;
  elseif a==0,
        x=j;
  else
        x=-a^4;
end; x
```

gives

```
x =
    8
```

```
while
a=0;
if a>0
x=a^3;
  elseif a==0,
        x=j;
  else
        x=-a^4;
end; x
```
results in
```
x =
        0 + 1.0000i
```
In addition to the selection structures (conditional statements), the repetition structures `while` and `for` are used to optimize and control the program. The `while` structure is described below:
```
>> help while
 WHILE  Repeat statements an indefinite number of times.
    The general form of a WHILE statement is:

        WHILE expression
          statements
        END

    The statements are executed while the real part of the expression
    has all non-zero elements. The expression is usually the result of
    expr rop expr where rop is ==, <, >, <=, >=, or ~=.
    The BREAK statement can be used to terminate the loop prematurely.
    For example (assuming A already defined):
            E = 0*A; F = E + eye(size(E)); N = 1;
            while norm(E+F-E,1) > 0,
                E = E + F;
                F = A*F/N;
                N = N + 1;
            end
    See also FOR, IF, SWITCH, BREAK, END.
```
Thus, the `while` structure repeats as long as the given expression is true (nonzero):
```
>> x=0.1;
  while 1+x>1
     x=x/10;
  end; x
```
and the answer is
```
x =
  1.0000e-016
```
The MATLAB `for` structure is comparable to a FORTRAN do loop and the C `for` structure. The `for` structure repeats the statements in the loop as the loop index takes on the values in a given row vector. For example,
```
>> for n=[1 2 3 4 5 6 7 8 9 10]'
   disp(n.*n)
   end
```
The resulting answer is
```
     1
     4
     9
    16
    25
```

```
 36
 49
 64
 81
100
```

The built-in function `disp` displays the argument. The loop is terminated by the `end`.

The `for` structure allows you to make a loop or series of loops to be executed several times. It is functionally very similar to the `for` structure in C. We may choose not to use the variable i as an index, because you may redefine the complex variable $i = \sqrt{-1}$. Typing

```
for z = 1:4
k
end
```

causes the program to make the variable z count from 1 to 4, and print its value for each step. For the above statement, we have

```
z =

    1
z =

    2
z =

    3
z =

    4
```

In general, the loop can be constructed in the form

```
for i=1:n, <program>, end
```

Here we will repeat program for each index value i.

The complete description of the `for` repetition structure is given below:

```
>> help for
 FOR    Repeat statements a specific number of times.
    The general form of a FOR statement is:
        FOR variable = expr, statement, ..., statement END
      The columns of the expression are stored one at a time in
    the variable and then the following statements, up to the
    END, are executed. The expression is often of the form X:Y,
    in which case its columns are simply scalars. Some examples
    (assume N has already been assigned a value).
        FOR I = 1:N,
            FOR J = 1:N,
                A(I,J) = 1/(I+J-1);
            END
        END
    FOR S = 1.0: -0.1: 0.0, END steps S with increments of -0.1
    FOR E = EYE(N), ... END  sets E to the unit N-vectors.
    Long loops are more memory efficient when the colon expression appears
    in the FOR statement since the index vector is never created.
    The BREAK statement can be used to terminate the loop prematurely.
    See also IF, WHILE, SWITCH, BREAK, END.
```

The loop must have a matching `end` statement to indicate which commands should be executed several times. You can have nested `for` structures. For example,

```
for m=1:3
    for n=1:3
    x(m,n)=m+n*i;
    end
end; x
```

generates (creates) the x matrix as

```
x =
    9     17     25
   10     18     26
   11     19     27
```

To terminate `for` and `while`, the `break` statement is used.

3.6. Illustrative Examples

Example 3.6.1.
Find the values of a, b, and c as given by the following expressions

$$a = 5x^2 - 6y + 7z, \quad b = \frac{3y^2}{4x - 5z^3} \quad \text{and} \quad c = \left(1 + \frac{1}{x^2}\right)^{-1}$$

if $x = 10$, $y = -20$ and $z = 30$.
Solution.
In the MATLAB Command Window, to find a, we type the statements

```
>> x=10; y=-20; z=30; a=5*x^2-6*y+7*z
```

Pressing the Enter key, we have the result. In particular,

```
a =
   830
```

That is, $a = 830$.

To find b, we type

```
>> x=10; y=-20; z=30; b=3*y^2/(4*x-5*z^3)
```

and the value for b is found. In particular,

```
b =
   -0.0089
```

Thus, $b = -0.0089$
Finally, to find the value of c, we have

```
>> x=10; y=-20; z=30; c=(1+1/x^2)^-1
```

and pressing the Enter key, the c value is displayed. That is, making use of

```
c =
   0.9901
```

we conclude that $c = 0.9901$. □

Example 3.6.2.
Use MATLAB to calculate the value of $e^{17.11}$.
Solution.
This problem is solved as follows:

```
» e=exp(17.11)
e =
   2.6964e+007
```

□

Example 3.6.3.
Given the complex number $N = 13 - 7i$. Using MATLAB, perform the following numerical calculations:
a.   Find the magnitude of N.
b.   Find the phase angle of N.
c.   Determine the complex conjugate of N.

Solution.
The complex number is downloaded as
```
>> N=13-7i
```
We can use either i or j for the imaginary number. The three problems can be straightforwardly solved. In particular,

a.
```
>> abs(N)
ans =
   14.7648
```
b.
```
>> angle(N)
ans =
   -0.4939
```
c.
```
>> conj(N)
ans =
   13.0000 + 7.0000i
```

□

Example 3.6.4.
For a shell with an external diameter $r_1 = 10$ and internal diameter $r_2 = 2$, find the volume which is given by the following formula:
$$V = \frac{4}{3}\pi\left(r_1^3 - r_2^3\right).$$
Solution.
To solve this problem, the MATLAB statement (typed in the Command Window) is
```
>> r1=10; r2=2; V=(4*pi/3)*(r1^3-r2^3)
```
Here, we use the pi which is the constant π. Then, using the numerical result displayed,
```
V =
   4.1553e+003
```
we conclude that $V = 4155$. □

Example 3.6.5.
For a shell with an external diameter $r_1 = 3, 4, 5, 6, 7, 8, 9$, and 10 and internal diameter $r_2 = 2$, find the values for volume $V = \frac{4}{3}\pi\left(r_1^3 - r_2^3\right)$. Calculate and plot a nonlinear function $V = f(r_1)$ for the r_1 given.

Solution.
In the MATLAB Command Window we type
```
>> r1=3:1:10; r2=2; V=(4*pi/3)*(r1.^3-r2^3); plot(V,r1)
```
Then, values for V are found to be
```
V =
   1.0e+003 *
      0.0796    0.2346    0.4901    0.8713    1.4032    2.1112    3.0201
   4.1553
```
To plot the nonlinear function $V = f(r_1)$, we have
```
>> r1=3:1:10; r2=2; V=(4*pi/3)*(r1.^3-r2^3);  plot(V,r1)
```
and the plot is illustrated in Figure 3.13.

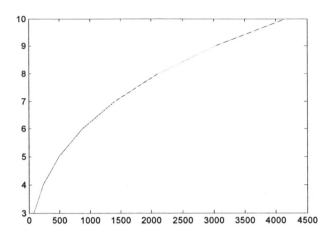

Figure 3.13. Nonlinear function: volume versus the external radius $V=f(r_1)$ □

Example 3.6.6.

Use the `linspace` function and increment method to create a vector A with 15 equally spaced values, beginning with 7.0 and ending with 47.5.

Solution.

Using `linspace`, in the Command Window, we type

```
>> A=linspace(7.0, 47.5, 15)
```

where 7.0 is the first (initial) value, 47.5 is the final value, and 15 is the number of values to be displayed. Pressing the Enter key, the following is displayed in the Command Window:

```
A =
  Columns 1 through 9
   7.0000    9.8929   12.7857   15.6786   18.5714   21.4643   24.3571   27.2500   30.1429
  Columns 10 through 15
  33.0357   35.9286   38.8214   41.7143   44.6071   47.5000
```

The first value is 7.0, the final value is 47.5, and 15 numbers are displayed.

The increment method can be used. The increment value is found using the equation

$$\text{Increment} = \frac{\text{Final Value} - \text{Initial Value}}{\text{Number of Increments} - 1}.$$

Thus, we enter the following statement,

```
>> Increment=(47.5-7.0)/(15-1)
```

and press the Enter key. We have

```
Increment =
    2.8929
```

Because a value of 2.8929 is now assigned to be the increment, we can enter

```
>> A=[7.0:Increment:47.5]
```

The result is

```
A =
Columns 1 through 9
7.0000    9.8929   12.7857   15.6786   18.5714   21.4643   24.3571   27.2500   30.1429
Columns 10 through 15
33.0357   35.9286   38.8214   41.7143   44.6071   47.5000
```

□

Example 3.6.7.

Use `linspace` and apply the increment method to create vector B with starting (initial) value of 7 and final (ending) value of 23 with increment of 0.16 between values. Display only the 18th value in each case.

Solution.

Increment method. We enter

```
>> B=[7:0.16:23];
>> Display=B(18)
```

Here, the first line is the vector, and the second line indicates the value we wish to display. Pressing the Enter key, we have

```
Display =
    9.7200
```

Using the `linspace` function, we must first find the number of values that will be found using the following equation:

$$\text{Number of Values} = \frac{\text{Final Value} - \text{Initial Value}}{\text{Increment}} + 1.$$

Thus, in the command line, enter the equation and press Enter key:

```
>> Number=((23-7)/(.16))+1
Number =
   101
```

This means that the 101 values would have been displayed under the given conditions. Now, using `linspace` and `display`, we type

```
>> B=linspace(7,23,Number);
>> Display=B(18)
Display =
    9.7200
```

□

Example 3.6.8.

For the given the matrices $C = \begin{bmatrix} 6 & 9 & 5 & 1 \\ 8 & 7 & 2 & 3 \\ 1 & 3 & 4 & 4 \\ 5 & 2 & 8 & 2 \end{bmatrix}$ and $D = \begin{bmatrix} 4 & 8 \\ 3 & 7 \\ 2 & 3 \\ 5 & 1 \end{bmatrix}$, in MATLAB perform the following:

a.   Create matrix E1 with the two middle columns of C using the colon operator.
b.   Create matrix E2 with rows 1 and 2 and columns 2 and 3 of C using the colon operator.
c.   Create matrix E3 by placing E1 and D side by side.
d.   Find the product of C_{24} and D_{12}.

Solution.

First, we download the matrices C and D as

```
>> C=[6 9 5 1;8 7 2 3;1 3 4 4;5 2 8 2];
>> D=[4 8;3 7;2 3;5 1];
```

a.   The matrix E1 is created as

```
>> E1=C(:,2:3)
E1 =
     9     5
     7     2
     3     4
     2     8
```

b.	The matrix E2 is generated as
```
>> E2=C(1:2,2:3)
E2 =
        9        5
        7        2
```
c.	The matrix E3 is created as
```
>> E3=[E1,D]
E3 =
        9        5        4        8
        7        2        3        7
        3        4        2        3
        2        8        5        1
```
d.	The product of the value in row 2 and column 4 of matrix C and the value in row 1 and column 2 in matrix D is found as
```
>> C(2,4)*D(1,2)
```
We use the numbers for row and column location in matrices C and D. Pressing the Enter key, we have
```
ans =
       24
```
In fact, the product of 8 and 3 is 24.	□

Example 3.6.9.
We have the following arrays F = [3 21 6 17], G = [4 27 9 3], and H = [1 2 9 15].

a.	Combine F, G and H into a matrix K1 such that F is in the first row of K1, G is in the second row of K1, and H is the third row of K1.
b.	Combine F, G and H into a matrix K2 such that F is in the first column of K2, G is in the second column of K2, and H is the third column of K2.

Solution.
First, we download the arrays assigned as
```
>> F=[3 21 6 17]; G=[4 27 9 3]; H=[1 2 9 15];
```
a.	The matrix K1 is created and displayed using the following statement
```
>> K1=[F;G;H]
K1 =
        3       21        6       17
        4       27        9        3
        1        2        9       15
```
b.	The matrix K2 is generated as
```
>> K2=[F',G',H']
K2 =
        3        4        1
       21       27        2
        6        9        9
       17        3       15
```
Here, the transpose symbol ' transforms a horizontal array into a vertical one.	□

Example 3.6.10.

Given matrices A and B as $A = \begin{bmatrix} 7 & 2 \\ 3 & 1 \end{bmatrix}$ and $B = \begin{bmatrix} 2 & 3 \\ -4 & -5 \end{bmatrix}$, calculate the following:

a.   A + B
b.   A − B
c.   2*B
d.   A/4
e.   A.*B
f.   B.*A
g.   A*B
h.   B*A
k.   A.^2
l.   A^2
m.   A.^B
n.   A./B

using pencil and paper. Verify the results using MATLAB.

Solution.

First, we download matrices A and B as
```
>> A=[7 2;3 1]; B=[2 3;-4 -5];
```
If one wants to display these matrices, the first semicolon outside the brackets must be replaced by a comma, and remove the second semicolon. In particular, typing
```
>> A=[7 2;3 1], B=[2 3;-4 -5]
```
and pressing the Enter key, the following is displayed
```
A =
     7     2
     3     1
B =
     2     3
    -4    -5
```
a.   A + B

Typing
```
>> A+B
```
and pressing the Enter key, we have
```
ans =
   9   5
  -1  -4
```
b.   A − B

Making use of
```
>> A-B
```
and pressing the Enter key, one has
```
ans =
     5    -1
     7     6
```
c.   2*B

It is obvious that the following must be typed:
```
>> 2*B
```
The answer is
```
ans =
     4     6
    -8   -10
```

d.   A/4

To find the resulting matrix, we have

```
>> A/4
```

Then, pressing the Enter key, we find

```
ans =
     1.7500    0.5000
     0.7500    0.2500
```

e.   A.*B

To multiply the matrices' elements (entries), we type

```
>> A.*B
```

The answer is displayed pressing the Enter key. In particular,

```
ans =
     14       6
    -12      -5
```

f.   B.*A

We type

```
>> B.*A
```

and have the resulting answer:

```
ans =
     14       6
    -12      -5
```

g.   A*B

To multiply the matrices, we type

```
>> A*B
```

By pressing the Enter key, the resulting matrix is found to be

```
ans =
      6      11
      2       4
```

h.   B*A

The matrices are multiplied using the following statement:

```
>> B*A
```

We have the following answer pressing the Enter key:

```
ans =
  23   7
 -43 -13
```

k.   A.^2

In order to squire the elements (entries) of matrix A, we type in the Command Window

```
>> A.^2
```

Pressing the Enter key, we have

```
ans =
     49       4
      9       1
```

l.   A^2

Here we need to multiply matrix A by A. We have

```
>> A^2
```

The result is

```
ans =
     55      16
     24       7
```

m.   A.^B

We type

```
>> A.^B
```
and the following answer is displayed:
```
ans =
    49.0000    8.0000
     0.0123    1.0000
```
n. A./B

By typing in the Command Window
```
>> A./B
```
we obtain
```
ans =
     3.5000    0.6667
    -0.7500   -0.2000
```

□

Example 3.6.11.

Given the matrix $A = \begin{bmatrix} 12.11 & -7.9 & 9.23 \\ 5.06 & 6.35 & 21.7 \\ -3.34 & 2.67 & 14.38 \end{bmatrix}$, using MATLAB do the following:

a.   Find the natural logarithm of the absolute value of each element of A.
b.   Find the base 10 logarithm of the absolute value of each element of A.
c.   Find the square root of each element in A.
d.   Calculate the hyperbolic cosine of each entry of A.
e.   Round each element in A to the nearest integer.
f.   Round each element in A to the next higher integer.
g.   Truncate each element of A to the next lower integer toward zero.
h.   Find the sum of the elements in each column of A.
k.   Find the product of the elements in each row of A.
l.   Find the maximum value in each row of A.
m.   Find the minimum value in each row of A.
n.   Sort the elements in each column of A in ascending order.
o.   Sort the elements in each row of A in ascending order.
p.   Find the mean of the values in each column of A.
q.   Find the size of A.

Solution.

First, we download matrix A as
```
>> A=[12 -7 9;5 6 21;-3 2 14];
```
To solve the problems and find the numerical values, we type in the Command Window using the corresponding statements listed below. To find the answers, the Enter key must be pressed. We have

Part a
```
>> log(abs(A))
ans =
    2.4940    2.0669    2.2225
    1.6214    1.8485    3.0773
    1.2060    0.9821    2.6658
```
Part b
```
>> log10(abs(A))
ans =
    1.0831    0.8976    0.9652
    0.7042    0.8028    1.3365
    0.5237    0.4265    1.1578
```

Part c
```
>> sqrt(A)
ans =
    3.4799        0 + 2.8107i   3.0381
    2.2494        2.5199        4.6583
    0 + 1.8276i   1.6340        3.7921
```
Part d
```
>> cosh(A)
ans =
  1.0e+009 *
    0.0001    0.0000    0.0000
    0.0000    0.0000    1.3279
    0.0000    0.0000    0.0009
```
It is evident that another format should be used. For example, using the `format short e` we find
```
>> cosh(A)
ans =
  8.1377e+004   5.4832e+002   4.0515e+003
  7.4210e+001   2.0172e+002   6.5941e+008
  1.0068e+001   3.7622e+000   6.0130e+005
```
Part e
```
>> round(A)
ans =
    12    -8     9
     5     6    22
    -3     3    14
```
Part f
```
>> ceil(A)
ans =
    13    -7    10
     6     7    22
    -3     3    15
```
Part g
```
>> fix(A)
ans =
    12    -7     9
     5     6    21
    -3     2    14
```
Part h
```
>> sum(A)
ans =
   13.8300    1.1200   45.3100
```
Part k
```
>> prod(A')'
ans =
 -883.0249
  697.2427
 -128.2380
```
Part l
```
>> max(A)
ans =
   12.1100    6.3500   21.7000
```

Part m
```
>> max(A')
ans =
   -7.9000
    5.0600
   -3.3400
```
Part n
```
>> sort(A)
ans =
   -3.3400   -7.9000    9.2300
    5.0600    2.6700   14.3800
   12.1100    6.3500   21.7000
```
Part o
```
>> sort(A')'
ans =
   -7.9000    9.2300   12.1100
    5.0600    6.3500   21.7000
   -3.3400    2.6700   14.3800
```
Part p
```
>> mean(A)
ans =
    4.6100    0.3733   15.1033
```
Part q
```
>> size(A)
ans =
     3     3
```

□

Example 3.6.12.
Given polynomials $f = 15x^3 - 7x^2 + 2x + 4$ and $g = 9x^2 - 17x + 3$, do the following problems:

a.   find the product of f and g,
b.   find the quotient and remainder of f divided by g,
c.   find the roots of g.

Solution.
We download two polynomials as
```
>> f=[15 -7 2 4]; g=[9 -17 3];
```
a.   The product of f and g is found using the conv function. In particular,
```
>> fg=conv(f,g)
fg =
   135  -318   182   -19   -62    12
```
b.   Quotient and remainder of f divided by g is found using deconv. Specifically,
```
>> [Quotient, Remainder]=deconv(f,g)
Quotient =
    1.6667    2.3704
Remainder =
    0.0000         0   37.2963   -3.1111
```
c.   The roots function is applied to find the roots of f.
```
>> roots(f)
ans =
    0.4672 + 0.5933i
    0.4672 - 0.5933i
   -0.4676
```

□

Example 3.6.13.

Write an m-file which will generate a table of conversions from inches to centimeters using the conversion factor 1 inch = 2.54 cm. Prompt the user to enter the starting number of inches. Increment the inch value by 3 on each line. Display a total of 10 lines. Include a title and column heading in the table.

Solution.

The m-file should be written. Fiurthermore, to execute an m-file, MATLAB must be able to find it. This means that a directory in MATLAB's path must be found. The current working directory is always on the path. To display or change the path, we use the `path` function. To display or change the working directory, the user must use `cd`. As usual, `help` will provide more information.

To solve the problem, the following m-file is written. Comments are identified by the `%` symbol.

```
%This program will generate a table of conversions from inches to centimeters.
%The user will be allowed to enter the initial inch value.
%The values will be incremented by 3 inches, with a %total of 10 lines printed.
%User input is equal to the variable inch_initial
inch_initial=input('Enter the initial length in inches:  ')
%Calculate largest inch value to be printed (limit table to 10 lines of text)
inch_final=inch_initial+5*9;
%Increment value by 3
inches=[inch_initial:3:inch_final];
%Convert inches to centimeters
centimeters=inches.*2.54;
%Table of values
table=[inches; centimeters];
%Format the table
fprintf('Conversion from Inches to Centimeters\n')
fprintf('Inches      Centimeters\n\n')
fprintf('%6.3f       %6.3f\n', table)
```

Assigning the initial length to be 10, the following results are displayed:

```
Enter the initial length in inches:  10

inch_initial =
    10

Conversion from Inches to Centimeters
Inches Centimeters

10.000 25.400
13.000 33.020
16.000 40.640
19.000 48.260
22.000 55.880
25.000 63.500
28.000 71.120
31.000 78.740
34.000 86.360
37.000 93.980
40.000 101.600
43.000 109.220
46.000 116.840
49.000 124.460
52.000 132.080
55.000 139.700
```

□

Example 3.6.14.

Write an m-file that will calculate the area of circles ($A = \pi r^2$) with radii ranging from 3 to 8 meters at an increment between values entered by the user in the Command Window. Generate the results in a table using disp and fprintf, with radii in the first column and areas in the second column. When fprintf is used, print the radii with two digits after the decimal point and the areas with four digits after the decimal point.

Solution.

To solve the problem, the MATLAB script is developed and listed below.

```
%This program calculates area of circles with radii ranging from 3 to 8
%An increment is specified by the user
%One table is displayed using disp and the other using fprintf
%Radii have two digits and areas have four digits after the decimal point
%User input is equal to the variable increment
increment=input('Enter the increment value for the radii:  ')
%Increment radii
r=[3:increment:8];
%Equation for area
A=pi*r.^2;
table1=[r; A];
%Transpose table1
table2=table1';
%Disp is used to generate the table
disp('Areas of Circles with Different Radii')
disp(' Radius      Area')
disp(' Meters     Square Meters')
%Transposed table printed
disp(table2)
%fpintf is used to generate the table
fprintf('\n')
fprintf('Areas of Circles with Different Radii\n')
fprintf('Radius       Area\n')
fprintf('Meters       Square Meters\n')
fprintf('%5.2f       %10.4f\n', table1)
%Table automatically transposed
```

Assigning the increment to be 1, we have

```
Enter the increment value for the radii:  1

increment =
    1

Areas of Circles with Different Radii
  Radius      Area
  Meters     Square Meters
    3.0000   28.2743
    4.0000   50.2655
    5.0000   78.5398
    6.0000  113.0973
    7.0000  153.9380
    8.0000  201.0619

Areas of Circles with Different Radii
Radius    Area
Meters    Square Meters
  3.00     28.2743
  4.00     50.2655
  5.00     78.5398
  6.00    113.0973
  7.00    153.9380
  8.00    201.0619
```

□

Example 3.6.15.

Write an m-file which allows the user to enter (download) the temperatures in degrees Fahrenheit and return the temperature in degrees Kelvin. Use the formulas $C° = 5(F° - 32)/9$ and $K = C° + 273.15$. The output should include both the Fahrenheit and Kelvin temperatures. Make three variations of the output as:

a.   Output temperatures as decimals with 5 digits following the decimal point,

b.   Output temperatures in exponential format with 7 significant digits,

c.   Output temperatures with 4 significant digits.

Solution

The following MATLAB script allows us to solve the problem:

```
%This program allows the user to enter a temperature in degrees Fahrenheit and will
%return the temperature in degrees Kelvin in three different formats.
%User input is equal to the variable "Fahrenheit"
Fahrenheit=input('Enter a temperature in degrees Fahrenheit:  ')
%Convert from Fahrenheit to Kelvin
Kelvin=5*(Fahrenheit-32)/9+273.15;
fprintf('Kelvin:\n')
%Part a: output temperature as decimals with 5 digits following the decimal point
fprintf('%.5f \n', Kelvin)
%Part b:  output temperature in exponential format with 7 significant digits
fprintf('%.6e \n', Kelvin)
%Part c:  output temperature in general format with 4 significant digits
fprintf('%.4g \n\n', Kelvin)
```

For 100°F, the results displayed are given below:

```
Enter a temperature in degrees Fahrenheit:  100

Fahrenheit =
   100

Kelvin:
310.92778
3.109278e+002
310.9
```

□

Example 3.6.16.

A spring's potential energy is found as $E = kx^2/2$, where k is the spring constant; x is the spring displacement. The spring force is $F = kx$.

Using the data for five different springs as given in Table 3.2, write an m-file to find the displacement and potential energy stored in each spring. Output the results in a table that displays the spring number, displacement in meters, and potential energy in joules. The calculated values should have three digits following the decimal point.

Table 3.2. Spring Data

Spring	1	2	3	4	5
Force (N)	23	123	5	79	8
Spring constant, k	145	33	12	17	34

Solution.

The problem is solved by making use of the following MATLAB script:

```
%This program calculates the displacement and potential energy of springs.
%The force and spring constant will be entered by the user for each of five springs
%The program will print the output in three columns
%Input the vector values for force and constant "k"
force=[23 123 5 79 8];
k=[145 33 12 17 34];
%Increment spring number
spring_number=[1:1:5];
```

```
%Calculate displacement
displacement=force./k,
potential=(k.*(displacement.^2))/2;
%Calculate potential energy stored in the spring
%Table of values
table=[spring_number;displacement;potential];
fprintf('Spring Number    Displacement Potential Energy\n')
fprintf('                 (meters)                (Joules)\n')
%print output
fprintf('%1.0f                    %7.3f                    %7.3f\n', table)
```

The results displayed in the Command Window are documented below:

Spring Number	Displacement (meters)	Potential Energy (Joules)
1	0.159	1.824
2	3.727	229.227
3	0.417	1.042
4	4.647	183.559
5	0.235	0.941

□

Example 3.6.17.

The formula for the volume of a truncated cone is $V = \dfrac{\pi R^3}{3\tan\theta} - \dfrac{\pi}{3}(R - y\tan\theta)^2\left(\dfrac{R}{\tan\theta} - y\right)$.

Here, y is the height; R is the radius of the base; θ is the angle in radians formed by the centerline and the side of the cone at the ape.

Find the volume for radii $R = 1$, 2 and 3 meters if $y = 5$ meters and $\theta = 20°$. Calculate three volumes.

Solution.

The m-file is written. In particular,

```
%This program calculates volume of a truncated cone after the user inputs cone height,
%radius of the base, and the angle in radians formed by the centerline and the side of
%the cone at the apex
%Prompt user to input data, input assigned to the specified variable names
y=input('Enter the height of the cone in meters:  \n')
R=input('Enter the three radii in meters:  \n')
t=input('Enter the angle in degrees:  \n')
%Convert angle from degrees to radians
t=t*pi/100;
%Calculate volumes for the tree radii
V=((pi*R.^3)/(3*tan(t)))-(pi/3)*((R-y*tan(t)).^2).*((R./(tan(t)))-y);
%Display calculated output for three radii
disp(V)
```

The results displayed in the Command Window are documented below:

```
Enter the height of the cone in meters:
3

y =

    3

Enter the three radii in meters:
[1 2 3]

R =

    1     2     3

Enter the angle in degrees:
20

t =

    20

    2.8794    20.8627    57.6956
```

The three volumes are found to be 2.8794, 20.8627, and 57.6956.   □

Example 3.6.18.

Write a MATLAB script which accepts the radius and height as inputs and returns the volume of the cone with those dimensions.

Solution.

The script (ch3618.m) is given below.

```
function V=ch3618(r,h)
%This program accepts the radius and height of a cone and calculates the cone volume
%User types in the function's name the variables separated by a comma
V=(1/3)*(pi*r.^2)*h;
```

The numerical results for $r = 5$ and $h = 10$ are

```
>> ch3618(5,10)

ans =
  261.7994
```

Thus, $V = 261.7994$. □

Example 3.6.19.

Write an m-file that computes the time t at which an object thrown vertically upward with the initial velocity v will reach a height h. There are two solutions for t in the height equation $h(t) = vt - \frac{1}{2}gt^2$ because the equation is quadratic. Test the file if $h = 100$ m, $v = 50$ m/sec, and $g = 9.81$ m/sec^2.

Solution.

The MATLAB script ch3619.m is

```
function t=ch3619(g,v,h)
%This program computes the time at which an object will reach a certain height.
%The user must input the gravity constant, the initial velocity and the height
%Two outputs will be displayed for t
%The first t is the time the object reaches the specific height on the way up
%The second t is the time when the object reaches/passes the height on the way down
%Terms of the equation are separated in ascending order of the exponents
C=[-.5*g;v;-h]
%Function roots is used to compute the two values of time
T=roots(C)
```

Numerical results are

```
>> ch3619(9.81,50,100)

C =
   -4.9050
   50.0000
 -100.0000


T =
    7.4612
    2.7324
```

□

Example 3.6.20.

Write the MATLAB file to solve linear algebraic equations. Develop an m file in order to solve the following sets of linear algebraic equations:

a. $6x - 3y + 4z = 41$
   $12x + 5y - 7z = -26$
   $-5x + 2y + 6z = 14$
b. $12x - 5y = 11$
   $-3x + 4y + 7z = -3$
   $6x + 2y + 3z = 22$
c. $2.5x_4 + 5x_3 + x_1 - 2x_2 = -4$
   $25x_2 - 6.2x_3 + 18x_4 + 10x_1 = 2.9$
   $28x_4 + 25x_1 - 30x_2 - 15x_3 = -5.2$
   $-3.2x_1 + 12x_3 - 8x_4 = -4.$

Solution.

The following m-file is written:

```
%This program solves linear equations using the downloaded matrices
%Three sets of matrices are
Aa=[6 -3 4;12 5 -7;-5 2 6]; Ba=[41;-26;14];
Ab=[12 -5 0;-3 4 7;6 2 3]; Bb=[11;-3;22];
Ac=[1 -2 5 2.5;10 25 -6.2 18;25 -30 -15 28;-3.2 0 12 -8]; Bc=[-4;2.9;-5.2;-4];
%Solve the equations
part_a=inv(Aa)*Ba;
part_b=(Ab^(-1))*Bb;
part_c=Ac\Bc;
%Print the results
fprintf('Part a: \n')
fprintf(' x        y         z \n')
fprintf('%3.2f       %3.2f %3.2f \n\n', part_a)
fprintf('Part b: \n')
fprintf(' x        y          z \n')
fprintf('%3.2f       %3.2f %3.2f \n\n', part_b)
fprintf('Part c: \n')
fprintf(' x1       x2      x3       x4 \n')
fprintf('%3.2f       %3.2f %3.2f  %3.2f \n\n', part_c)
```

The displayed results are

```
Part a:
x       y       z
2.00    -3.00   5.00

Part b:
x       y       z
3.00    5.00    -2.00

Part c:
x1      x2      x3      x4
0.13    0.20    -0.55   -0.38
```

Thus, the solutions of the algebraic equations are found.

□

Example 3.6.21.

Electric circuits are described (modeled) using Kirchhoff's voltage and current laws. The electric circuit under consideration is described by the following set of five algebraic equations:

$$R_1 i_1 + R_2 i_2 - v_1 = 0$$
$$- R_2 i_2 + R_3 i_3 + R_5 i_5 = 0$$
$$v_2 + R_4 i_4 - R_3 i_3 = 0$$
$$- i_1 + i_2 + i_3 + i_4 = 0$$
$$- i_4 - i_3 + i_5 = 0$$

a.   Calculate the five unknown currents (i_1, i_2, i_3, i_4, and i_5) using the following resistances and voltages as: $R_1 = 470$ ohm, $R_2 = 300$ ohm, $R_3 = 560$ ohm, $R_4 = 100$ ohm, $R_5 = 1000$ ohm, $v_1 = 5$V, and $v_2 = 10$V. Label the answers with current number and units. .

b.   Using the resistances given above and $v_1 = 5$V, find the range of positive voltages v_2 for which none of the currents exceeds 50 mA. The currents may be positive or negative. None of the currents may be less than -50 mA or greater than 50 mA.

Solution.

The MATLAB script is documented below.

```
%This program calculates the value of five currents using Kirchhoff's voltage law
%Part A. Variable values
R1=470; R2=330; R3=560; R4=100; R5=1000; v1=5; v2=10;
%Matrices used to solve the equation
A=[R1 R2 0 0 0;0 -R2 R3 0 R5;0 0 -R3 R4 0; -1 1 1 1 0;0 0 -1 -1 1];
B=[v1;0;-v2;0;0];
%Vector for current number
I=[1:5];
%Solve the linear algebraic equation
C=(A\B)';
%Create a table to output current number and current value
table=[I;C];
%Print a table that outputs the current values
fprintf('Part A: \n')
fprintf('Current Number        Current Value \n')
fprintf('                      (Amperes)     \n')
fprintf('--------------        ------------- \n')
fprintf('   %4.0f                 %8.6f\n', table)
%Part B:
%Form a loop to find the range of positive voltages v2 (currents cannot exceed 0.05A)
%value of subscript n
n=1;
%Use a range of v2 between 0V and 30V, incrementing by 0.1
%The absolute value of current (vector C) is used to avoid 2 loops
%Subscript n is incriminated by 1
for v2=0:0.1:30
    B=[v1;0;-v2;0;0];
    C=A\B;
    if abs(C)<0.05
        v(n)=v2;
        n=n+1;
    end
end
%Find minimum and maximum values of v2 and assign to two variables
v_max=max(v);
v_min=min(v);
%Print the output
fprintf('\n\nPart B: \n')
fprintf('The range of voltages v2 for which no currents are bellow\n')
fprintf('     -50mA or above 50mA is %4.1f V to %4.1f V. \n\n', v_min, v_max)
```

The results are

```
Part A:
Current Number          Current Value
                        (Amperes)

---------------         --------------
      1                    0.004178
      2                    0.009201
      3                    0.014391
      4                   -0.019413
      5                   -0.005022

Part B:
The range of voltages v2 for which no currents are bellow
      -50mA or above 50mA is   0.0 V to 24.7 V.
```

□

Example 3.6.22.

The height, horizontal distance, and speed of a projectile launched with a speed v at an angle A to the horizontal line are given by the following formulas:

$$h(t) = vt \sin A - \tfrac{1}{2} g t^2 , \quad x(t) = vt \cos A \text{ and } v(t) = \sqrt{v^2 - 2vgt \sin A + g^2 t^2} .$$

The projectile will strike the ground when $h(t) = 0$, and the time of the hit is $t_{hit} = 2 \dfrac{v}{g} \sin A$.

Suppose that $A = 30°$, $v = 40$ m/s, and $g = 9.81$ m/s^2. Use logical operators to find the times (with the accuracy to the nearest hundredth of a second) when

a.   The height is no less than 15 meters,

b.   The height is no less than 15 meters and the speed is no greater than 36 m/sec.

Solution.

The following MATLAB script is developed to solve the problem.

```
%This program finds the times at which the conditions specified bellow are satisfied
%Parameters
A=30; vo=40; g=9.81;
%Part a:  Determine the times at which the height is no less than 15 meters.
%Increment time by 0.01
time=[0:0.01:5];
%Find height (h) for different values of time
h=vo*time.*sin(A*pi/180)-0.5*g*time.^2;
%Determine times when height is greater than 15 meters
times=find(h>=15);
%Find the maximum and minimum value for times
max_time=max(times)/100;
min_time=min(times)/100;
%Print the results
fprintf('\nThe height is at least 15 m when the time is between\n')
fprintf('     %.2f seconds and %.2f seconds.\n\n', min_time, max_time)
%Part b: determine t at which h is no less than 15 m and v is no more than 36 m/sec
%Increment time by 0.01
time=[0:0.01:5];
%Find height (h) and velocity (v) for different values of time
h=vo*time.*sin(A*pi/180)-0.5*g*time.^2;
v=sqrt((vo^2)-(2*vo*g*time.*sin(A*pi/180))+(g^2*time.^2));
%Determine times when heigh is greater than 15 m and velocity is no more than 36 m/sec
vector=find(h>=15 & v<=36);
%Find the maximum and minimum value for times
max_time=max(times);
min_time=min(times);
%Print the results
fprintf('\n\nThe height is at least 15 m and the velocity is no less than 36 m/s\n')
fprintf('when the time is between %f seconds and %f seconds.\n\n', min_time, max_time)
```

In the Comand Window, we have the results

```
The height is at least 15 m when the time is between 1.01 seconds and 3.09 seconds.
The height is at least 15 m and the velocity is no less than 36 m/s
when the time is between 101.000000 seconds and 309.000000 seconds.
```

☐

REFERENCES

1. *MATLAB 6.5 Release 13,* CD-ROM, MathWorks, Inc., 2002.
2. Hanselman, D. and Littlefield, B., *Mastering MATLAB 5*, Prentice Hall, Upper Saddle River, NJ, 1998.
3. Palm, W. J., *Introduction to MATLAB for Engineers*, McGraw-Hill, Boston, MA, 2001.
4. Recktenwald G., *Numerical Methods with MATLAB: Implementations and Applications.* Prentice Hall, Upper Saddle River, NJ, 2000.
5. *User's Guide. The Student Edition of MATLAB: The Ultimate Computing Environment for Technical Education*, MathWorks, Inc., Prentice Hall, Upper Saddle River, NJ, 1995.

Chapter 4

MATLAB GRAPHICS

MATLAB has outstanding graphical, visualization and illustrative capabilities [1 - 4]. A graph is a collection of points, in two, three, or more dimensions, that may or may not be connected by lines or polygons. It was emphasized that MATLAB is designed to work with vectors and matrices rather than functions. Matrices are a convenient way to store numerical numbers.

4.1. Plotting

In MATLAB, the user can plot numerical data stored as vectors and matrices. This data can be obtained performing numerical calculations, evaluating functions, or reading the stored data from files. Single and multiple curves can be created.

The dependent variable can be easily evaluated as a function of the independent variable. For example, consider

$$y(x) = f(x), \text{ e.g., } y(x) = x^{1/3}, y(x) = x^2, y(x) = e^{-x}, y(x) = \sin(x), \text{ etc.}$$

To create a line plot of y versus x, the MATLAB statement is

```
>> x=[. . . .]  % cretae x data
>> y=[. . . .]  % cretae y data
>> plot(x,y)    % plotting statement
```

Illustrative Example 4.1.1.

Plot the following data in MATLAB:

```
>> x=[0 1 2 3 4 5 6 7 8 9 10 20 30 40 50 60 70 80 90 100];   % cretae x data
>> y=[2 3 4 5 6 7 7 7 7 7 10 11 12 10 10 10 14 15 15 14];     % cretae y data
>> plot(x,y)                                                  % plot
```

Solution.

The resulting plot is illustrated in Figure 4.1.a. By using the following statement

```
>> x=[0 1 2 3 4 5 6 7 8 9 10 20 30 40 50 60 70 80 90 100];   % cretae x data
>> y=[2 3 4 5 6 7 7 7 7 7 10 11 12 10 10 10 14 15 15 14];     % cretae y data
>> plot(x,y,'o')                                             % plot
```

we obtain the plot as documented in Figure 4.1.b.

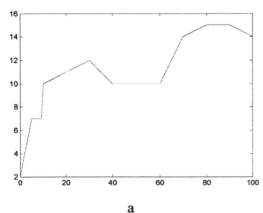 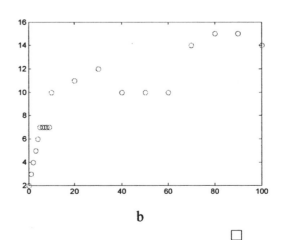

a   b

Figure 4.1. Data plots   □

By default, the `plot` function connects the data with a solid line. Using `plot(x,y,'o')`, the data is connected by symbol o.

As has been shown, `plot` is the simplest way of graphing and visualizing the data. If x is a vector, `plot(x)` will plot the elements of x against their indices. For example, let us plot the vector. We type

```
>> x=[1 2 3 4 5 6 7 8 9 10]; plot(x)
```

and the resulting plots are given in Figure 4.2.

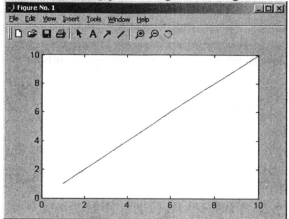 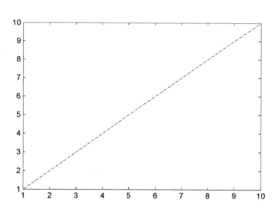

Figure 4.2. Plots of the vector x

Illustrative Example 4.1.2.
Plot sin(x) if x varies from 1 to 10 letting the increment to be 0,1.
Solution.
We can use the following statement

```
>> x=1:0.1:10; plot(x,sin(x))
```

and the resulting plot is given in Figure 4.3.a. In contrast, making use of the following statement,

```
>> x=1:0.25:10; plot(x,sin(x),'o')
```

we have the plot illustrated in Figure 4.3.b.

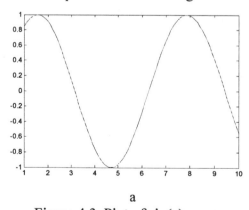 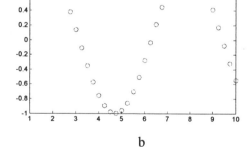

a   b

Figure 4.3. Plot of sin(x)   □

Thus, we can plot two vectors as arguments, and the `plot` function creates a graph with the first argument as the abscissa values, and the second vector as ordinate values. The simple graph was created in the *xy* cartesian plane: see sin (x). Another example is given here:

```
>> x=[1 2 3 4 5 6 7 8 9 10]; y=[0 2 4 6 8 10 8 6 4 2]; plot(x,y)
```

The resulting graph is displayed in Figure 4.4.

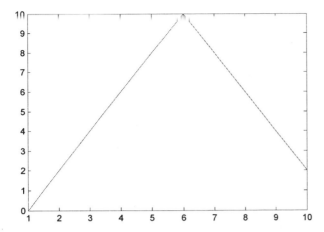

Figure 4.4. Plot of two vectors *x* and *y*

Let us illustrate how to calculate the function $x(t) = e^{-t}\sin(2t)$ if *t* varies from 0 to 8 sec, and then plot the resulting function. We will use the colon notation (: is the special character) to create the time array. For example, typing `t=0:1:8`, we have

```
>> t=0:1:12
t =
   0    1    2    3    4    5    6    7    8    9   10   11   12
```

Thus, we assign the time interval `t=0:0.1:8`, then calculates $x(t) = e^{-t}\sin(2t)$, and plot the function. In particular,

```
>> t=0:0.1:8; x=exp(-t).*sin(2*t), plot(t,x)
```

Eighty-one values of the entries of the vector (array) *x* are

```
x =
Columns 1 through 8
      0      0.1798    0.3188    0.4183    0.4809    0.5104    0.5115    0.4894
Columns 9 through 16
   0.4491    0.3959    0.3345    0.2691    0.2034    0.1405    0.0826    0.0315
Columns 17 through 24
  -0.0118   -0.0467   -0.0731   -0.0915   -0.1024   -0.1067   -0.1054   -0.0996
Columns 25 through 32
  -0.0904   -0.0787   -0.0656   -0.0519   -0.0384   -0.0256   -0.0139   -0.0037
Columns 33 through 40
   0.0048    0.0115    0.0165    0.0198    0.0217    0.0222    0.0217    0.0202
Columns 41 through 48
   0.0181    0.0156    0.0128    0.0100    0.0072    0.0046    0.0022    0.0002
Columns 49 through 56
  -0.0014   -0.0027   -0.0037   -0.0043   -0.0046   -0.0046   -0.0044   -0.0041
Columns 57 through 64
  -0.0036   -0.0031   -0.0025   -0.0019   -0.0013   -0.0008   -0.0003    0.0001
Columns 65 through 72
   0.0004    0.0006    0.0008    0.0009    0.0010    0.0010    0.0009    0.0008
Columns 73 through 80
   0.0007    0.0006    0.0005    0.0004    0.0002    0.0001    0.0000   -0.0000
Column 81
  -0.0001
```

The resulting plot is illustrated in the Figure 4.5.

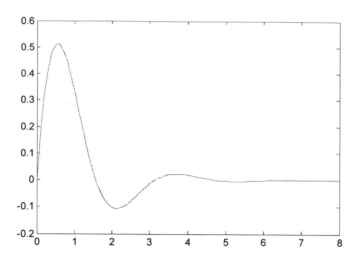

Figure 4.5. Plot of the function $x(t) = e^{-t}\sin(2t)$

The function `plot(t,x)` uses the built-in `plot` function and gives a very basic plot. The first variable is on the horizontal axis and the second variable is on the vertical axis. There are many ways to use `plot`. For example, you can change the style and color of the line. Using `plot(t,y,':')` gives the dotted line. To have the green dashdot line, type `plot(t,x,'g-.')`.

The following options are available:

```
solid    -        red      r
dashed   --       green    g
dotted   :        blue     b
dashdot  -.       white    w
```

We can use the `help plot` for detail information. That is, using

```
>> help plot
```

the user has

```
PLOT    Linear plot.
   PLOT(X,Y) plots vector Y versus vector X. If X or Y is a matrix,
   then the vector is plotted versus the rows or columns of the matrix,
   whichever line up.  If X is a scalar and Y is a vector, length(Y)
   disconnected points are plotted.

   PLOT(Y) plots the columns of Y versus their index.
   If Y is complex, PLOT(Y) is equivalent to PLOT(real(Y),imag(Y)).
   In all other uses of PLOT, the imaginary part is ignored.

   Various line types, plot symbols and colors may be obtained with
   PLOT(X,Y,S) where S is a character string made from one element
   from any or all the following 3 columns:

            y      yellow      .     point          -      solid
            m      magenta     o     circle         :      dotted
            c      cyan        x     x-mark         -.     dashdot
            r      red         +     plus           --     dashed
            g      green       *     star
```

```
        b      blue       s      square
        w      white      d      diamond
        k      black      v      triangle (down)
                          ^      triangle (up)
                          <      triangle (left)
                          >      triangle (right)
                          p      pentagram
                          h      hexagram
For example, PLOT(X,Y,'c+:') plots a cyan dotted line with a plus
at each data point; PLOT(X,Y,'bd') plots blue diamond at each data
point but does not draw any line.

PLOT(X1,Y1,S1,X2,Y2,S2,X3,Y3,S3,...) combines the plots defined by
the (X,Y,S) triples, where the X's and Y's are vectors or matrices
and the S's are strings.

For example, PLOT(X,Y,'y-',X,Y,'go') plots the data twice, with a
solid yellow line interpolating green circles at the data points.

The PLOT command, if no color is specified, makes automatic use of
the colors specified by the axes ColorOrder property.  The default
ColorOrder is listed in the table above for color systems where the
default is yellow for one line, and for multiple lines, to cycle
through the first six colors in the table.  For monochrome systems,
PLOT cycles over the axes LineStyleOrder property.
PLOT returns a column vector of handles to LINE objects, one
handle per line.
The X,Y pairs, or X,Y,S triples, can be followed by
parameter/value pairs to specify additional properties
of the lines.
See also SEMILOGX, SEMILOGY, LOGLOG, GRID, CLF, CLC, TITLE, XLABEL,
YLABEL, AXIS, AXES, HOLD, COLORDEF, LEGEND, SUBPLOT, and STEM.
Overloaded methods
    help idmodel/plot.m
    help iddata/plot.m
```

The results are integrated in Table 4.1.

Table 4.1. Colors, Symbols, and Line Types Used in `Plot`

Line	Color	Symbol
- solid	y yellow	. point
: dotted	m magenta	o circle
-. dash dotted	c cyan	x x-mark
-- dashed	r red	+ plus
	g green	* star
	b blue	s square
	w white	d diamond
	k black	v triangle (down)
		^ triangle (up)
		< triangle (left)
		> triangle (right)
		p pentagram
		h hexagram

To illustrate the `plot` function and options we have, using the MATLAB statements

```
>> t=0:0.25:10; y=sin(t); plot(t,y,'rd:')
```

and

```
>> t=0:0.25:10; y=sin(t); plot(t,y,'k<-')
```

you calculate the function $x = \sin t$ and plot the results, as documented in Figures 4.6.a and b.

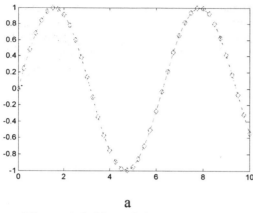
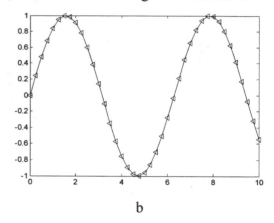

a   b

Figure 4.6. Plot of sin(*t*)

The discrete values of *t* are connected by lines to have continuous function. The discrete and piecewise continuous functions can be plotted. For example, the `stem` function can be used. Figure 4.7 illustrates the plot for sin(*t*) at instances 1, 2, 3, 4, 5, 6, 7, 8, 9, and 10. In particular, we use

```
>> n=1:10; stem(n,sin(n))
```

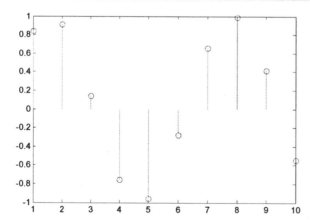

Figure 4.7. Plot of sin(*n*)

Thus, two- and three-dimensional (as will be illustrated latter) plots and coordinate transformations are supported by MATLAB. The basic commands and functions are reported in Tables 4.2 to 4.5.

Table 4.2. Basic Plots and Graphs Functions and Commands

Bar	Vertical bar chart
Barh	Horizontal bar chart
Hist	Plot histograms
Histc	Histogram count
Hold	Hold current graph
loglog	Plot using log-log scales
Pie	Pie plot
Plot	Plot vectors or matrices.
Polar	Polar coordinate plot
semilogx	Semi-log scale plot
semilogy	Semi-log scale plot
subplot	Create axes in tiled positions

Table 4.3. Three-Dimensional Plotting

Bar3	Vertical 3D bar chart
Bar3h	Horizontal 3D bar chart
Comet3	3D comet plot
cylinder	Generate cylinder
fill3	Draw filled 3D polygons in three-dimensional space
plot3	Plot lines and 3D points (in three-dimensional space)
quiver3	3D quiver (or velocity) plot
Slice	Volumetric slice plot
sphere	Generate sphere
stem3	Plot discrete surface data
waterfall	Waterfall plot

Table 4.4. Plot Annotation and Grids

clabel	Add contour labels to a contour plot
datetick	Date formatted tick labels
grid	Grid lines for 2D and 3D plots
gtext	Place text on a 2D graph using a mouse
legend	Graph legend for lines and patches
plotyy	Plot graphs with Y tick labels on the left and right
title	Titles for 2D and 3D plots
xlabel	X-axis labels for 2D and 3D plots
ylabel	Y-axis labels for 2D and 3D plots
zlabel	Z-axis labels for 3D plots

Table 4.5. Surface, Mesh, and Contour Plots

contour	Contour (level curves) plot
contourc	Contour computation
contourf	Filled contour plot
hidden	Mesh hidden line removal mode
meshc	Combination mesh/contourplot
mesh	3D mesh with reference plane
peaks	A sample function of two variables
surf	3D shaded surface graph
surface	Create surface low-level objects
surfc	Combination surf/contourplot
surfl	3D shaded surface with lighting
trimesh	Triangular mesh plot
trisurf	Triangular surface plot

Let us illustrate the MATLAB application within an example.

Illustrative Example 4.1.3.

Calculate and plot the function $f(t) = \sin(100t)e^{-2t} + \sin(100t)\cos(100t + 1)e^{-5t}$, $0 \le t \le 0.1$ sec.

Solution.

To calculate and plot the function $f(t) = \sin(100t)e^{-2t} + \sin(100t)\cos(100t+1)e^{-5t}$ for $0 \le t \le 0.1$ sec, we assign the time interval of interest ($0 \le t \le 0.1$ sec), calculate $f(t)$ with the desired smoothness assigning increment (for example, 101 values), and plot this function. We have the following statement:

```
» t=linspace(0,.1,100);f=sin(100*t).*exp(-2*t)+sin(100*t).*cos(100*t+1).*exp(-5*t);
» plot(t,f)
```

The resulting plot for $f(t)$ is given in Figure 4.8.

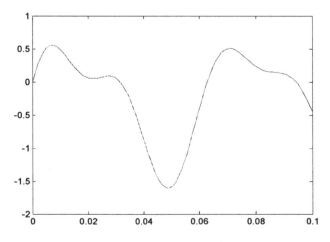

Figure 4.8. Plot of the function $f(t) = \sin(100t)e^{-2t} + \sin(100t)\cos(100t+1)e^{-5t}$ □

One can change the type of line used to connect the points by including a third argument specifying line type. The syntax is `plot(x,y,'-')`. The line types available are: `'-'` solid line (default), `'--'` dashed line, `':'` dotted line, and `'-.'` dashdot line. The default line type is solid. However, a graph is a discrete-time array. One can use a mark to indicate each discrete value. This can be done by using a different set of characters to specify the line-type argument. If we use a ' . ', each sample is marked by a point. Using a + marks each sample with a + sign, * uses stars, o uses circles, and x uses x's. For example, assigning the time interval t=0:1:12, let us calculate $x = \sin t$, and plot the function. We have

```
>> t=0:.25:12; x=sin(t); plot(t,x,'+')
```

The resulting plot is illustrated in the Figure 4.9.

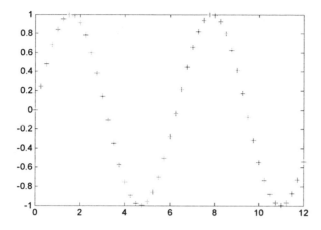

Figure 4.9. The plot of $x = \sin t$

We can also plot several graphs on the same axis. For example, let us calculate and plot two functions $x = \sin t$ and $x = \sin(0.5t)$. We type

```
>> t=0:.25:12; x1=sin(t); x2=sin(0.5*t); plot(t,x1,t,x1,'+',t,x2,t,x2,'o')
```

and the resulting plots are illustrated in Figure 4.10.

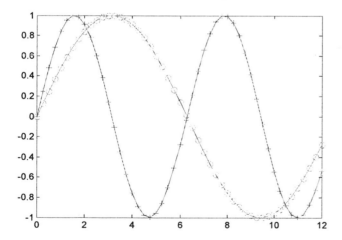

Figure 4.10. Plots of $x = \sin t$ and $x = \sin(0.5t)$

The user can change the axes scale, and the logarithmic scale functions are the following:

- `loglog`   (logarithmic x- and y-axis scale),
- `semilogy`   (linear x-axis and logarithmic y-axis scale),
- `semilogx`   (linear y-axis and logarithmic x-axis scale).

We can have the text labels on the graphs and axes. The following labeling statements are used for title, *x*- and *y*-axis:

```
>>  title('Graphic')
>>  xlabel('X-axis label')
>>  ylabel('Y-axis label')
```

It was explicitly illustrated that two-dimensional plots are created using the `plot` function, and in the simplest form, `plot` takes two arguments,

```
>> plot(xdata,ydata)
```

where `xdata` and `ydata` are vectors containing the data.

It is important to emphasize that `xdata` and `ydata` vectors must be the same length and both must be the same type (both must be either row or column vectors). Additional arguments to `plot` provide other options, including the ability to plot multiple data sets, and use different colors, symbols, and line types.

Illustrative Example 4.1.4.

Plot the function $x(t) = \dfrac{2+\sin t}{2-\cos\frac{1}{4}t}e^{-0.05t}, 0 \le t \le 30$.

Solution.

To calculate *x*(*t*) and plot the function, the following MATALB script is developed:

```
t=0:0.05*pi:30;              %   t vector, 0<=t<=30 with increment 0.05*pi
x=exp(-0.05*t).*(2.+sin(t))./(2.-cos(0.25*t)); % calculate x vector values
plot(t,x,':')               %   create the plot
xlabel('t (time)');         %   label the x-axis
ylabel('function x(t)');    %   label the y-axis
title('Function x(t)');     %   plot title
```

The plot is illustrated in Figure 4.11.

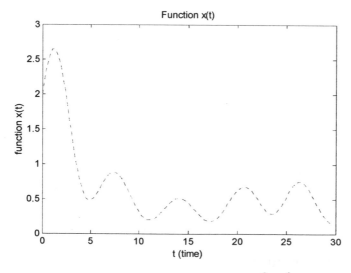

Figure 4.11. Plot of the function $x(t) = \dfrac{2+\sin t}{2-\cos\frac{1}{4}t}e^{-0.05t}, 0 \le t \le 30$ □

The commonly used annotation functions are listed in Table 4.6.

Table 4.6. MATLAB Annotation Functions

Function	Description	Help
Axis	Set the minimum and maximum values of axis	help axis
Grid	Draw grid line corresponding to the thickness of *x* and *y* axes	help grid
Gtext	Add text to a location indicated iteratively with mouth input	help gtext
Legend	Set symbols and line types for multiple curves on the same plot	help legend
Text	Add text at the specified location on the plot	help text
Title	Add a title string (text) above the plot	help title
Xlabel, ylabel	Label the *x* and *y* axes with a text string (text)	help xlabel help ylabel

The `plot` function allows us to generate multiple curves on the same figure using the following syntax

```
plot(x1,y1,s1,x2,y2,...)
```

where the first data set represented by the vector pair `(x1,y1)` is plotted with the symbol definition `s1`, the second data set `(x2,y2)` is plotted with symbol definition `s2`, etc. It should be emphasized that the vectors must have the same length (size). Thus, the length of `x1` and `y1` must be the same. The length (size) of `x2` and `y2` must be the same, but in general, can be different from the length of `x1` and `y1`. The separate curves can be labeled using `legend`.

Illustrative Example 4.1.5.
Calculate and plot two functions

$$x_1(t) = \frac{2 + \sin t}{2 - \cos \frac{1}{4}t} e^{-0.05t}, 0 \le t \le 30 \text{ and } x_2(t) = \frac{2 + \sin t}{2 - \cos \frac{1}{4}t} e^{-0.2t}, 0 \le t \le 30.$$

Solution.
The following MATLAB script is developed:

```
t=0:0.05*pi:30;       % t vector, t varies from 0 to 30, increment is 0.05*pi
x1=exp(-0.05*t).*(2.+sin(t))./(2.-cos(0.25*t)); %calculate x1 vector values
x2=exp(-0.2*t).*(2.+sin(t))./(2.-cos(0.25*t)); %calculate x2 vector values
plot(t,x1,':',t,x2,'--')                % create the plots for x1 and x2
xlabel('t (time)');                     % label the x-axis
ylabel('functions x1(t) and x2(t)');    % label the y-axis
title('Functions x1(t) and x2(t)');     % plot title
```

The resulting plots are shown in Figure 4.12.

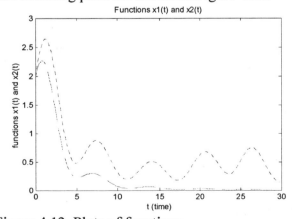

Figure 4.12. Plots of functions

The `axis` command is used to control the limits and scaling of the current graph. Typing

```
axis([minx  maxx  miny  maxy]
```

we assign a four-element vector to set the minimum and maximum ranges for the axes. The first element is the minimum x-value, while the second is the maximum x-value. The third and fourth elements are the minimum and maximum y-values, respectively.

Let us calculate (for $0 \leq t \leq 30$ sec) and plot (in $0 \leq t \leq 20$ sec) functions $x_1(t) = \dfrac{2+\sin t}{2-\cos\frac{1}{4}t}e^{-0.05t}$ and $x_2(t) = \dfrac{2+\sin t}{2-\cos\frac{1}{4}t}e^{-0.2t}$. The plots should be plotted using the x-axis from -1 to 3. The following MATLAB script is used:

```
t=0:0.05*pi:30;      % t vector, t varies from 0 to 30, increment is 0.05*pi
x1=exp(-0.05*t).*(2.+sin(t))./(2.-cos(0.25*t)); %calculate x1 vector values
x2=exp(-0.2*t).*(2.+sin(t))./(2.-cos(0.25*t));  %calculate x2 vector values
plot(t,x1,':',t,x2,'--')          %  create the plots for x1 and x2
axis([0  20  -1  3])              %  axis assignment
xlabel('t (time)');               %  label the x-axis
ylabel('functions x1(t) and x2(t)');  %  label the y-axis
title('Functions x1(t) and x2(t)');   %  plot title
```

The plots are documented in Figure 4.13.

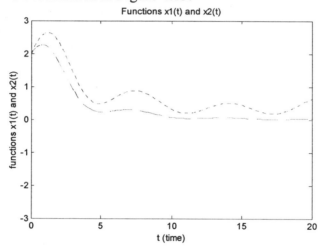

Figure 4.13. Plots of $x_1(t) = \dfrac{2+\sin t}{2-\cos\frac{1}{4}t}e^{-0.05t}$ and $x_2(t) = \dfrac{2+\sin t}{2-\cos\frac{1}{4}t}e^{-0.2t}$

It was illustrated that MATLAB provides the vectorized arithmetic capabilities.

Illustrative Example 4.1.6.

Calculate functions $f_1(x) = \dfrac{x}{1+x^4}$ and $f_2(x) = \dfrac{x}{1+\sin x+x^4}$ if $-5 \leq x \leq 5$.

Solution.

We have the folowing statement:

```
>> x=-5:0.25:5; f1=x./(1+x.^4); f2=x./(1+sin(x)+x.^4);plot(x,f1,'+',x,f2,'o')
```

The graphs of these two functions are illustrated in Figure 4.14.

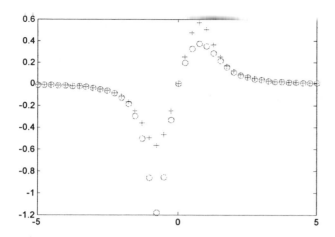

Figure 4.14. Plots of the functions $f_1(x) = \dfrac{x}{1+x^4}$ and $f_2(x) = \dfrac{x}{1+\sin x + x^4}$, $-5 \le x \le 5$ □

The `hold` command will keep the current plot and axes even if you plot another graph. The new graph will just be put on the current axes.

Let us calculate the nonlinear functions $x(t) = \left|\dfrac{\sin 50t}{t}\right|\cos(t+\pi)$, $y(t) = \left|\dfrac{\sin 50t}{t}\right|\sin(t+\pi)$ and plot them if $-10\pi \le t \le 10\pi$. Then, holding the plot, calculate the function $10e^z$, for $z = -0.01 + 0.5i$ to $z = -1 + 50i$ (z is the complex variable, and let the size of the z array be 991). Plot the function $10e^z$.

The MATLAB script is given below, and the resulting plots are given in Figure 4.15.

```
t=[-10*pi:.0001:10*pi];
xy=abs(sin(50*t)./t);
x=xy.*cos(t+pi);
y=xy.*sin(t+pi);
plot(x,y,'b'); hold on;
z=(-0.01+j*0.5)*[1:.1:100];
y=10*exp(z);
plot(real(y),imag(y),'g');
```

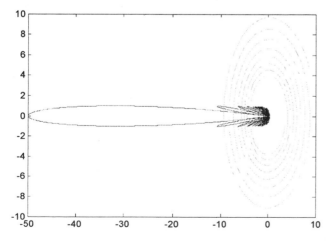

Figure 4.15. Functions plots

Plotting Multiple Graphs. The `subplot` command allows the user to display multiple plots in the same window and print them together. In particular, `subplot(m,n,p)` partitions the figure window into an m-by-n matrix of subplots and selects the pth subplot for the current plot. The plots are numbered along first the top row of the figure window, then the second row,

and so on. The order for p is as follows: $\begin{bmatrix} 1 & 2 \\ \hline 3 & 4 \end{bmatrix}$. Thus, `subplot` partitions the window into

multiple windows, and one or many of the subwindows can be selected for the specified graphs. In general, `subplot` divides the graphics window into the specified number of quadrants. As mentioned, m is the number of vertical divisions, n is the number of horizontal divisions, and p is the selected window for the current plot (p must be less than or equal to m times n). For example, `subplot(1,2,1)` will create two full-height, half-width windows for graphs, and select the first (left window) as active for the first graph.

To plot the data, the basic steps must be followed. To illustrate the MATLAB capabilities, we study the modified previous example with the sequential steps as documented in Table 4.7.

Table 4.7. Sequential Steps to Calculate, Plot, and Visualize the Data

Step	MATLAB Statements and Results

1. Perform calculations and prepare the data.	`t=[-10*pi:.0001:10*pi];`
	`xy=abs(sin(50*t)./t);`
	`x=xy.*cos(t+pi);`
	`y=xy.*sin(t+pi);`
	and
	`z=(-0.01+j*0.5)*[1:.1:100];`
	`y=10*exp(z);`

2. Select a window and position a plot region within the specified window.	`subplot(2,2,1);`
	and
	`subplot(2,2,2);`

3. Use plotting function assigning the line styles, marker characteristics, axis limits, marks, text, grid, hold, etc.	`plot(x,y,'b');`
	and
	`plot(real(y),imag(y),'g');`

4. Annotate the plots with axis labels, legend, and text.	`xlabel('x');ylabel('y');title('x-y');`
	and
	`xlabel('Re(y)');ylabel('Im(y)');`
	`title('Re(y)-Im(y)');`

5. Save, export, print, and use data and plots in data-intensive analysis.
 	
MATLAB script
`t=[-10*pi:.0001:10*pi];`
`xy=abs(sin(50*t)./t);`
`x=xy.*cos(t+pi); y=xy.*sin(t+pi);`
`subplot(2,2,1); plot(x,y,'b');`
`xlabel('x');ylabel('y');title('x-y');`
`z=(-0.01+j*0.5)*[1:.1:100];`
`y=10*exp(z);`
`subplot(2,2,2);`
`plot(real(y),imag(y),'g');`
`xlabel('Re(y)');ylabel('Im(y)');`
`title('Re(y)-Im(y)');`	

To plot the functions, the `ezplot` plotter is also frequently used. Let us plot the function $y = \sin^4 x \cos x + e^{-|x|} \cos^4 x$ using `ezplot`. To plot this function, we type

```
>> ezplot('sin(x)^4*cos(x)+exp(-abs(x))*cos(x)^4')
```

The resulting plot is documented in Figure 4.16.

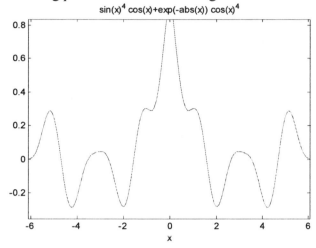

Figure 4.16. Plot of a nonlinear function $y = \sin^4 x \cos x + e^{-|x|} \cos^4 x$ □

4.2. Two- and Three-Dimensional Graphics

Two- and three-dimensional graphics is supported by MATLAB. If x, y and z are vectors with the same size (length), they can be plotted using `plot3`. In particular, `plot3(x,y,z)` generates a line in three dimensions through the points whose coordinates are the elements of x, y, and z and then produces a 2-dimensional projection of that line on the screen. In particular, we have the following MATLAB help:

```
>> help plot3
 PLOT3  Plot lines and points in 3-D space.
    PLOT3() is a three-dimensional analogue of PLOT().
    PLOT3(x,y,z), where x, y and z are three vectors of the same length,
    plots a line in 3-space through the points whose coordinates are the
    elements of x, y and z.
    PLOT3(X,Y,Z), where X, Y and Z are three matrices of the same size,
    plots several lines obtained from the columns of X, Y and Z.
    Various line types, plot symbols and colors may be obtained with
    PLOT3(X,Y,Z,s) where s is a 1, 2 or 3 character string made from
    the characters listed under the PLOT command.
    PLOT3(x1,y1,z1,s1,x2,y2,z2,s2,x3,y3,z3,s3,...) combines the plots
    defined by the (x,y,z,s) fourtuples, where the x's, y's and z's are
    vectors or matrices and the s's are strings.
    Example: A helix:
        t = 0:pi/50:10*pi;
        plot3(sin(t),cos(t),t);
    PLOT3 returns a column vector of handles to LINE objects, one
    handle per line. The X,Y,Z triples, or X,Y,Z,S quads, can be
    followed by parameter/value pairs to specify additional
    properties of the lines.
    See also PLOT, LINE, AXIS, VIEW, MESH, SURF.
```

As given in the MATLAB help, to create a helix, we type in the Command Window
```
>> t=0:0.02*pi:25*pi;x=sin(t);y=cos(t);z=t;plot3(x,y,z);
```
and the three-dimensional plot is illustrated in Figure 4.17.

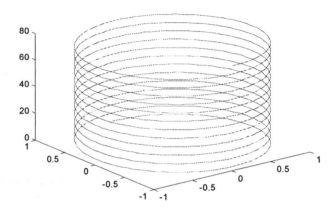

Figure 4.17. Three-dimensional plot

Consider a scalar function of two variables $z = f(x,y)$. This function defines a surface in the three-dimensional space. In MATLAB, the surface can be graphically represented using `mesh`, `meshc`, `surf`, `surfc`, `surfl`, and other commands and functions. In general, the function $z = f(x,y)$ is calculated and stored as the Z matrix, and a grid is defined, e.g., $Z(i,j) = f(x(i),y(j))$. To evaluate the functions, `meshgrid` is used. In particular, the (x,y) data is generated to evaluate $z = f(x,y)$. The statement
```
>> [X,Y]=meshgrid(xg,yg)
```
creates matrices X and Y as given by

$$X = \begin{bmatrix} xg_1 & xg_2 & \cdots & xg_n \\ xg_1 & xg_2 & \cdots & xg_n \\ \vdots & \vdots & \ddots & \vdots \\ xg_1 & xg_2 & \cdots & xg_n \end{bmatrix} \text{ and } Y = \begin{bmatrix} yg_1 & yg_1 & \cdots & yg_1 \\ yg_2 & yg_2 & \cdots & yg_2 \\ \vdots & \vdots & \ddots & \vdots \\ yg_m & yg_m & \cdots & yg_m \end{bmatrix}$$

where xg_i and yg_i are the vectors defining the grid lines perpendicular to the x- and y-axis.

Thus, the matrix data can be plotted and visualized. The arguments to `plot3` are matrices of the same size, and the plot lines are obtained from the columns of X, Y, and Z. To display a function of two variables $z = f(x,y)$, one forms matrices X and Y consisting of repeated rows and columns over the domain of the function. These matrices are used to evaluate and graph the function of two variables. The `meshgrid` function transforms the domain specified by vectors x and y into matrices X and Y (rows of X map vector x and columns of Y map vector y). In particular,
```
>> help meshgrid
 MESHGRID   X and Y arrays for 3-D plots.
   [X,Y] = MESHGRID(x,y) transforms the domain specified by vectors
   x and y into arrays X and Y that can be used for the evaluation
   of functions of two variables and 3-D surface plots.
   The rows of the output array X are copies of the vector x and
   the columns of the output array Y are copies of the vector y.
   [X,Y] = MESHGRID(x) is an abbreviation for [X,Y] = MESHGRID(x,x).
```

```
[X,Y,Z] = MESHGRID(x,y,z) produces 3-D arrays that can be used to
evaluate functions of three variables and 3-D volumetric plots.
For example, to evaluate the function  x*exp(-x^2-y^2) over the
range  -2 < x < 2,   -2 < y < 2,
    [X,Y] = meshgrid(-2:.2:2, -2:.2:2);
    Z = X .* exp(-X.^2 - Y.^2);
    mesh(Z)
MESHGRID is like NDGRID except that the order of the first two input
and output arguments are switched (i.e., [X,Y,Z] = MESHGRID(x,y,z)
produces the same result as [Y,X,Z] = NDGRID(y,x,z)).  Because of
this, MESHGRID is better suited to problems in cartesian space,
while NDGRID is better suited to N-D problems that aren't spatially
based.   MESHGRID is also limited to 2-D or 3-D.
See also SURF, SLICE, NDGRID.
```

We can calculate the nonlinear functions $z(x,y) = x^2 y e^{-x^2-y^2}$ if $-4 \le x \le 4$ and $-4 \le y \le 4$. The x, y, and z can be plotted using a three-dimensional plot applying meshgrid. In particular, the statement is

```
>> [x,y]=meshgrid([-4:0.1:4]);z=x.*x.*y.*exp(-x.^2-y.^4); plot3(x,y,z)
```

The three-dimensional plot is documented in Figure 4.18.

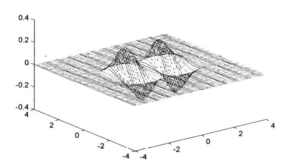

Figure 4.18. Three-dimensional plot, $z(x,y) = x^2 y e^{-x^2-y^2}$ if $-4 \le x \le 4$ and $-4 \le y \le 4$.

Illustrative Example 4.2.1.

Calculate and plot the sinc-like function $z(x,y) = \dfrac{\sin\sqrt{x^2+y^2+\varepsilon}}{\sqrt{x^2+y^2+\varepsilon}}$, $\varepsilon = 1 \times 10^{-10}$ if $-10 \le x \le 10$ and $-10 \le y \le 10$.

Solution.

We apply meshgrid, plot3 and mesh. In particular, making use of

```
>> [x,y]=meshgrid([-10:0.2:10]);xy=sqrt(x.^2+y.^2)+1e-10;z=sin(xy)./xy;plot3(x,y,z)
```

and

```
>> [x,y]=meshgrid([-10:0.2:10]);xy=sqrt(x.^2+y.^2)+1e-10;z=sin(xy)./xy;mesh(z)
```

the three-dimensional plots are illustrated in Figure 4.19.

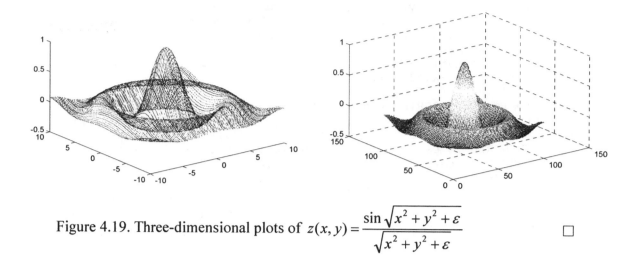

Figure 4.19. Three-dimensional plots of $z(x,y) = \dfrac{\sin \sqrt{x^2 + y^2 + \varepsilon}}{\sqrt{x^2 + y^2 + \varepsilon}}$ □

Using the subplot commands, let us plot four mesh-plots. We have the following MATLAB statements

```
>>[x,y]=meshgrid([-10:0.5:10]);xy=sqrt(x.^2+y.^2)+1e-10;z=sin(xy)./xy;
>>subplot(2,2,1);mesh(x);subplot(2,2,2);mesh(y);subplot(2,2,3);mesh(z);subplot(2,2,4);mesh(x,y,z)
```

and the resulting plots are illustrated in Figure 4.20.

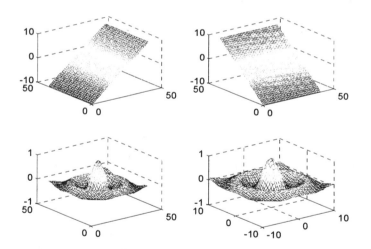

Figure 4.20. Mesh-plots of *x*, *y*, *z*, and *xyz*

Illustrative Example 4.2.2.

Study and plot the quadratic function $z(x,y) = 1 - \frac{1}{4}x^2 - \frac{1}{4}y^2$ in the region $-10 \le x \le 10$ and $-10 \le y \le 10$.

Solution.

The following MATLAB statements are used to attain our objective

```
>> x=linspace(-10,10,25); y=linspace(-10,10,25); [X,Y]=meshgrid(x,y); Z=1-(X.^2+Y.^2)/4;
>> subplot(2,2,1);mesh(x,y,Z);title('mesh plot'); subplot(2,2,2);surf(x,y,Z);title('surf plot');
>> subplot(2,2,3);surfc(x,y,Z);title('surfc plot');subplot(2,2,4);surfl(x,y,Z);title('surfl plot');
```

and the corresponding three-dimensional plots are documented in Figure 4.21.

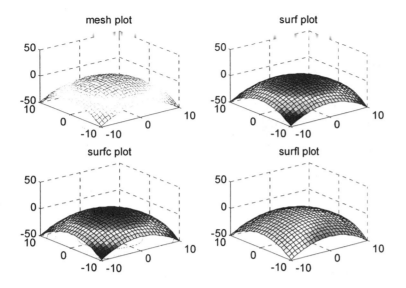

Figure 4.21. Plot of $z(x,y) = 1 - \frac{1}{4}x^2 - \frac{1}{4}y^2$ if $-10 \le x \le 10$ and $-10 \le y \le 10$ □

MATLAB creates a surface by calculating the *z*-points (data) above a rectangular grid in the *xy* plane. Plots are formed by joining adjacent points with straight lines. MATLAB generates different forms of surface plots. In particular, mesh-plots are wire-frame surfaces that color only the lines connecting the defining points, while surface plots display both the connecting lines and the faces of the surface in color. Functions `mesh` and `surf` create surface plots, `meshc` and `surfc` generate surface plots with contour under-plot, `meshz` creates surface plots with curtain plot (as the reference plane), `pcolor` makes flat surface plots (value is proportional only to color), `surfl` creates surface plots illuminated from a specified direction, and `surface` generates low-level functions (on which high-level functions are based) for creating surface graphics objects.

The `mesh` and `surf` functions create three-dimensional surface plots of matrix data. Specifically, if *Z* is a matrix for which the elements $Z(i,j)$ define the height of a surface over an underlying (i,j) grid, then `mesh(Z)` generates and displaces a colored, wire-frame three-dimensional view of the surface. Similarly, `surf(Z)` generates and displaces a colored, faceted three-dimensional view of the surface.

The functions that generate surfaces can use two additional vector or matrix arguments to describe surfaces. Let *Z* be an *m*-by-*n* matrix, *x* be an n-vector, and *y* be an m-vector. Then, `mesh(x,y,Z,C)` gives a mesh surface with vertices having color $C(i,j)$ and located at the points $(x(j), y(i), Z(i,j))$, where *x* and *y* are the columns rows of *Z*.

If *X, Y, Z,* and *C* are matrices of the same dimensions, then `mesh(X,Y,Z,C)` is a mesh surface with vertices having color $C(i,j)$ located at the points $(X(i,j), Y(i,j), Z(i,j))$.

Using the spherical coordinates, a sphere can be generated and plotted applying the Hadamard matrix (orthogonal matrix commonly used in signal processing coding theory). We have the MATLAB statement as given below,

```
k=6; n=2^k; theta=pi*(-n:2:n)/n; phi=(pi/2)*(-n:2:n)'/n;
X=cos(phi)*cos(theta); Y=cos(phi)*sin(theta); Z=sin(phi)*ones(size(theta));
colormap([1 1 1;1 1 1]); C=hadamard(2^k); surf(X,Y,Z,C);
```

and Figure 4.22 illustrates the resulting sphere.

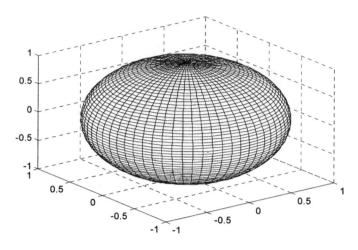

Figure 4.22. Three-dimensional sphere

Finally we illustrate two- and three-dimensional graphics through examples as given in Table 4.8.

Table 4.8. MATLAB Two- and Three-Dimensional Graphics

Problems with MATLAB Syntax	Plot
`>> x=-10:0.1:10; y=x.^3; plot(x,y)`	
`>> t=-10:0.1:10;` `>> x=t.^2;y=t.^3;z=t.^4; plot3(x,y,z);`	

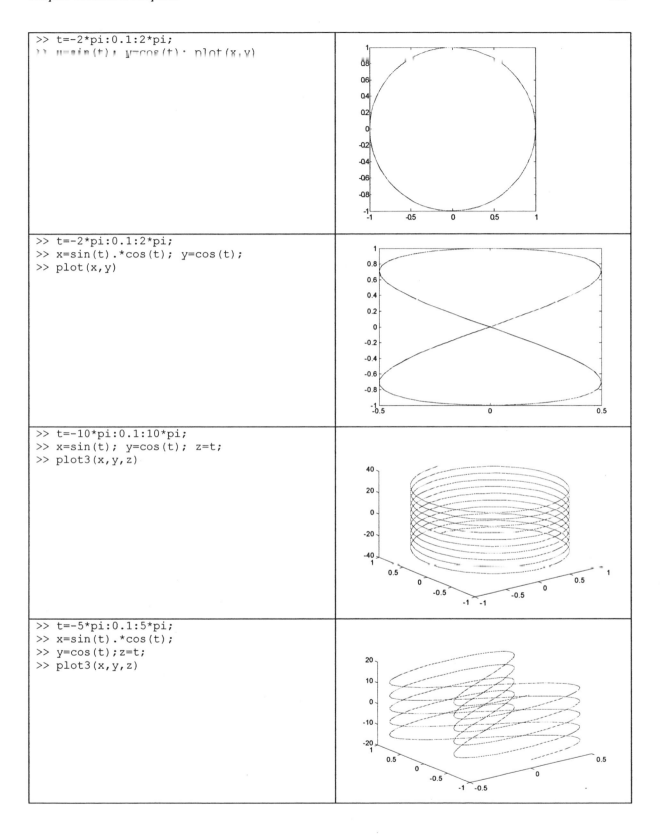

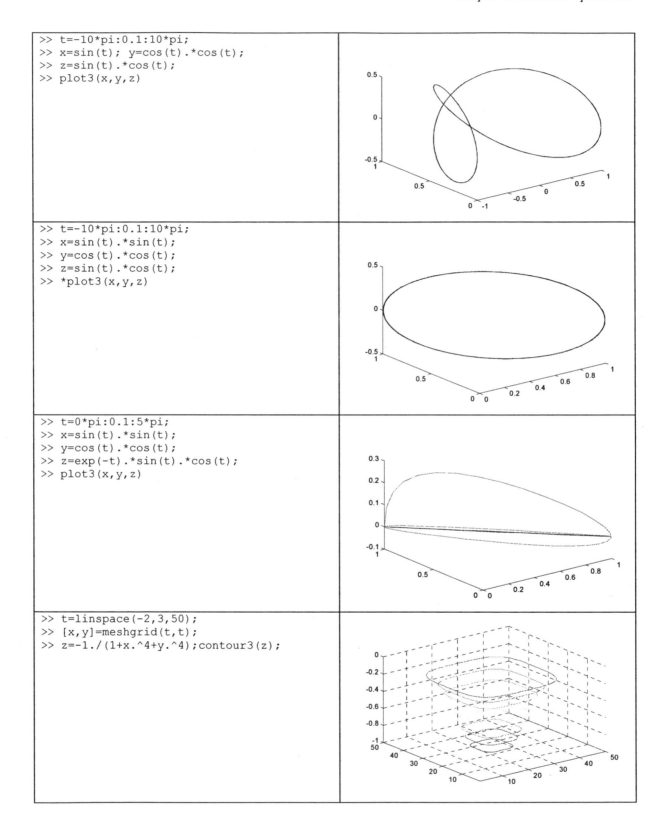

```
>> t=-10*pi:0.1:10*pi;
>> x=sin(t); y=cos(t).*cos(t);
>> z=sin(t).*cos(t);
>> plot3(x,y,z)
```

```
>> t=-10*pi:0.1:10*pi;
>> x=sin(t).*sin(t);
>> y=cos(t).*cos(t);
>> z=sin(t).*cos(t);
>> *plot3(x,y,z)
```

```
>> t=0*pi:0.1:5*pi;
>> x=sin(t).*sin(t);
>> y=cos(t).*cos(t);
>> z=exp(-t).*sin(t).*cos(t);
>> plot3(x,y,z)
```

```
>> t=linspace(-2,3,50);
>> [x,y]=meshgrid(t,t);
>> z=-1./(1+x.^4+y.^4);contour3(z);
```

MATLAB has animation capabilities. Advanced animation functions, commands and examples are reported in the specialized books and user manuals. Let us illustrate the simple examples.

As illustrated in Table 4.8, the circle was calculated and plotted using the MATLAB statement

```
>> t=-2*pi:0.1:2*pi; x=sin(t); y=cos(t); plot(x,y)
```

Let us animate the bead going around a circular path. We will calculate the bead positions and draw (plot) the bead path using the comet comand. In particular, the statement is

```
>> t=-4*pi:0.01:4*pi; x=sin(t); y=cos(t); comet(x,y)
```

The bead and the circular path at $t = 4\pi$ and $t = -\pi$ are illustrated in Figure 4.23.

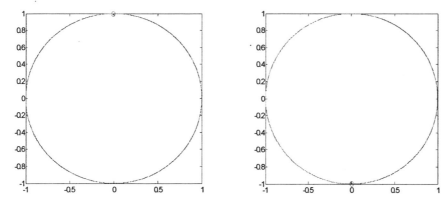

Figure 4.23. Bead location and circular path

Using movie, moviein, and getframe, the movies can be made. In particular, the animated sequence of plots are used to create movies. Each figure is stored as the movie frame, and frames (stored as column vectors using getframe) can be played on the screen. The generalized and specific MATLAB scripts are given below

```
Nframes=3;                % assign the number of frames
Mframe=moviein(Nframes);  % frame matrix
for i=1:Nframes
x=[   ]; y=[   ]; z=[   ]; % create the data
plot3(x,y,z) or plot(x,y); % other 3D and 2D plotting can be used
Mframes(:,i)=getframe;
end
N=2;
movie(Mframe,N)           % play the movie frames N times
```

and

```
t=-2*pi:0.1:2*pi;
Nframes=3;                % number of frames
Mframe=moviein(Nframes);  % frame matrix
for i=1:Nframes
x=sin(t); y=cos(t);       % data
plot(x,y);
Mframes(:,i)=getframe;
end
for j=1:Nframes
x=sin(t); y=sin(t).*cos(t); % data
plot(x,y);
Mframes(:,j)=getframe;
end
N=2;
movie(Mframe,N)           % play the movie frames N times
```

The resulting frames are documented in Figure 4.24.

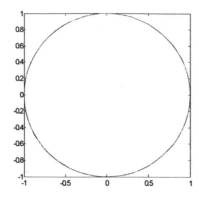 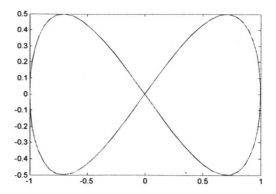

Figure 4.24. Movie frames

It is obvious that `for` loops can be used. A simple example is given below to clculate the quadratic function x^2 in the region from -8 to 8 and increment 2. We have the following MATLAB statement,

```
for i=-8:2:8
    x=i^2; i, x
end
```

and the numerical values are given below:

```
i =
    -8
x =
    64

i =
    -6
x =
    36
i =
    -4
x =
    16

i =
    -2
x =
    4

i =
    0
x =
    0

i =
    2
x =
    4

i =
    4
x =
```

```
        16
i =
        6
x =
        36

i =
        8
x =
        64
```

As an illustrative example, the reader is advised to use the following MATLAB script to create a "movie".

```
t=-2*pi:0.1:2*pi;
Nframes=50;                % number of frames
Mframe=moviein(Nframes);   % matrix frame
i=0; j=0;
for i=1:Nframes
    i=i+1;
x=sin(10*i*t); y=cos(10*i*t);              % data
plot(x,y);
Mframes(:,i)=getframe;
end
for j=1:Nframes
    j=j+1;
x=sin(2*j*t); y=sin(4*j*t).*cos(6*j*t); % data
plot(x,y);
Mframes(:,j)=getframe;
end
N=2;
movie(Mframe,N)                % play the movie frames N times
```
Four of the resulting frames are given in Figure 4.25.

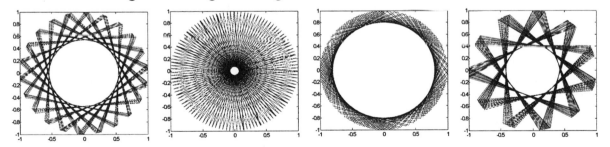

Figure 4.25. Four movie frames

Another example which can be used is based on the MATLAB script given below

```
t=-2*pi:0.1:2*pi;
Nframes=5;                 % number of frames
Mframe=moviein(Nframes);   % matrix frame
i=0; j=0;
for i=1:Nframes
i=i+1;
    for j=1:Nframes
    j=j+1;
x=sin(i*j*t); y=cos(i*j*t);    % data
```

```
plot(x,y);
Mframes(:,i)=getframe;
    end
end
N=2;
movie(Mframe,N)               % play the movie frames N times
```
The MATLAB script which makes the three-dimensional "movie" is documented below:
```
t=-3:0.05:3;
Nframes=6;                    % number of frames
Mframe=moviein(Nframes);     % matrix frame
i=0; j=0;
for i=0:2:Nframes
    i=i+2;
[x,y]=meshgrid([t]);
xy=sqrt(x.^(i^2)+y.^(i^2))+1e-5; z=sin(xy)./xy;
plot3(x,y,z);
Mframes(:,i)=getframe;
end
for j=0:2:Nframes
    j=j+2;
[x,y]=meshgrid([t]);
xy=sqrt(x.^(2*j)+y.^(4*j))+1e-5; z=cos(xy).*sin(xy)./xy;
plot3(x,y,z);
Mframes(:,j)=getframe;
end
N=2;
movie(Mframe,N)               % play the movie frames N times
```
To create a graph of a surface in three-dimensional space (or a contour plot of a surface), it was shown that MATLAB evaluates the function on a regular rectangular grid. This was done by using meshgrid. For example, one creates one-dimensional vectors describing the grids in the x- and y-directions. Then, these grids are spead into two dimensions using meshgrid. In particular,

```
>> x=0:0.2*pi:10*pi; y=0:0.2*pi:10*pi; [X,Y]=meshgrid(x,y); whos
  Name      Size            Bytes  Class
  X         51x51           20808  double array
  Y         51x51           20808  double array
  x         1x51              408  double array
  y         1x51              408  double array
Grand total is 5304 elements using 42432 bytes
```

Using the meshgrid comand, we created a vector X with the x-grid along each row, and a vector Y with the y-grid along each column. Then, using vectorized functions and/or operators, it is easy to evaluate a function $z = f(x,y)$ of two variables (x and y) on the rectangular grid. As an example,
```
>> z=sin(X).*cos(Y).*exp(-0.001*X.^2);
```
Having created the matrix containing the samples of the function, the surface can be graphed using either mesh or the surf,
```
>> mesh(x,y,z)
>> surf(x,y,z)
```
and the resulting plots are given in Figures 4.26.a and b, respectively. The difference is that surf shades the surface, while mesh does not.

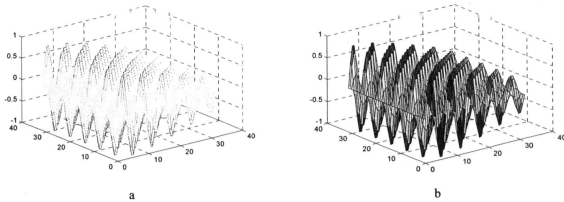

Figures 4.26. Three-dimensional plots

In addition, a contour plot can be created using the contour function, as in Figure 4.27.

```
>> contour(x,y,z)
```

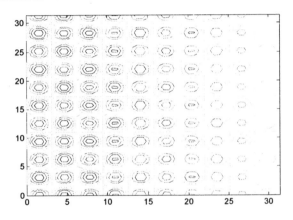

Figure 4.27. Three-dimensional plot

We can use the help command to learn the additional options to effectively use mesh, surf, and contour.

4.3. Illustrative Examples

Example 4.3.1.

Calculate (for $-5 \le t \le 5$ sec) and plot the function $x(t) = 2 + 3\sin(\pi t + 10)e^{-0.35t}$. The plot should be made using the *x*- and *y*-axis from -20 to 20 and -6 to 6, respectively.

Solution.

The following MATLAB script is developed:

```
%Sinusoidal function
t=-5:.01:5;
x=2*ones(size(t))+3*sin(pi*t+10).*exp(-0.35*t);
plot(t,x),title('Sinusoidal function');
axis([-6,6,-20,20]);
xlabel('time, t [second]'); ylabel('x(t)'); grid;
text(0,5.5,'x(t)=2+3*sin(pi*t+10)*exp(-0.35t)');
```

The resulting plot is shown in Figure 4.28.

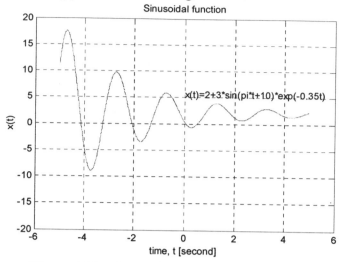

Figure 4.28. Plots of functions $x(t) = 2 + 3\sin(\pi t + 10)e^{-0.35t}$ □

Example 4.3.2.

Calculate and plot the discrete function $x(n) = 25\cos(\pi n + 5)e^{-0.1n}$ if $0 \le n \le 40$.

Solution.

The following MATLAB script is developed using the `stem` function:

```
%Discrete sinusoidal sequence
n=0:1:40;
x=25*cos(pi*n+5).*exp(-0.1*n);
stem(n,x);
axis([0 40 -10 10]); grid;
text(10,5,'x(n)=25cos(pi*n+5)exp(-0.1n)');
```

The resulting plot is documented in Figure 4.29.

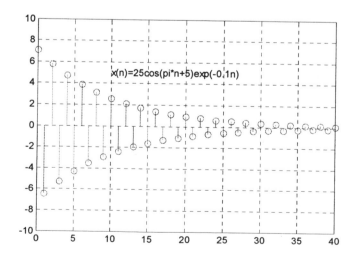

Figure 4.29. Plots of functions $x(n) = 25\cos(\pi n + 5)e^{-0.1n}$ □

Example 4.3.3.

The experimental data of tension in a steel bar is given by Table 4.9. Plot the two sets of experimental data with elongation as the independent variable and the tension as the independent variable. Connect the data points point-to-point with line segments. Label the curves with either `text` or `gtext`.

Table 4.9. Experimental Data to be Plotted

Elongation (inches $\times 10^{-3}$)	Increasing Tension Force (lbs)	Decreasing Tension Force (lbs)
0	0	0
1	1,000	0
2	1,700	1,500
3	3,300	2,200
4	4,500	3,600
5	7,000	5,900
6	10,400	8,700
7	12,100	11,400
8	13,300	12,900
9	14,100	13,300
10	14,700	14,700

Solution.

The MATLAB file written to solve the problem is documented below,

```
%This program creates the graph based upon the tension test for a steel bar
%The plot includes two lines: for increasing and decreasing tension forces
%Vectors for elongation (E), tension force increasing (Ti), tension
E=[0:10];
Ti=[0 1000 1700 3300 4500 7000 10400 12100 13300 14100 14700];
Td=[0 0 1500 2200 3600 5900 8700 11400 12900 13300 14700];
%Plot E versus Ti with a line -*-*- and plot E versus Ti with a line -o-o-
plot(E,Ti,'-*',E,Td,'-o')
%Label the plot line
gtext('Increasing tension force')
gtext('Decreasing tension force')
%Increment x- and y-axis
x=[0:10];
y=[0:1000:15000];
%Label x- and y-axis
xlabel('Tension Force  (lbs)')
ylabel('Elongation  (inches*10^3)')
%Title the graph
title('Tension of Steel Bars')
%Add a grid to the graph
grid on
```

The resulting plot is illustrated in Figure 4.30.

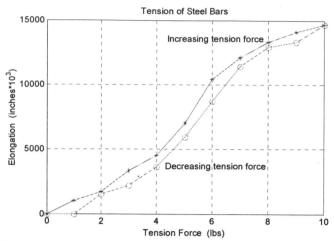

Figure 4.30. Tension in the steel bar

Example 4.3.4.

The height $h(t)$ and horizontal distance $x(t)$ traveled by a ball thrown at an angle A with a speed v are given by the following equations: $h(t) = vt \sin A - \frac{1}{2}gt^2$ and $x(t) = vt \cos A$. The acceleration due to gravity is $g = 9.81$ m/sec^2. Solve the following problems.

a. Suppose the ball is thrown with the velocity $v = 10$ m/sec at an angle 35°. Compute how height of the ball will change and how long it will take the ball to hit the ground. This problem can be solved using graphical and analytical methods.

b. Use the values for v and A to numerically calculate and plot the ball's trajectory (plot h versus x for positive values h). Use `axis` to restrict the height to positive values.

c. Plot the trajectories for $v=10$ m/sec corresponding to any three values of the angle A. Use `axis` to restrict the height to positive values. Use different line types for the three curves.

Solution.

Here is the MATLAB script to be used:

```
%This program uses two equations to find the value of height and distance
%Part a: calculate ball height, horizontal distance and time
g=9.81; v=10; A=35; T=[0:.1:2];
%Find maximum height (h) and horizontal distance (x)
h=v*T.*sin(A*pi/180)-0.5*g*T.^2;
x=v*T.*cos(A*pi/180);
%Use the MATALB max function
maxh=max(h);
%At maximum height, v=0, manipulating the equation time=1/2 of the trip is found
%Total time is the value*2
t=2*(maxh/(.5*g))^.5;
%Find the distance
maxx=v*t*cos(A*pi/180);
%Display the results to the user
fprintf('maximum height: %f meters\n', maxh)
fprintf('maximum horizantal distace: %f meters\n', maxx)
fprintf('time: %f seconds\n',t)
%Part b
```

```
%Plot ball's trajectory (height as a function of horizontal distance)
t=[0:0.1:t];
subplot(2,1,1)
plot(x,h,'--')
x=[0:.5:maxx]; y=[0:.5:maxh];
xlabel('Horizontal Distance Traveled  x(t)   (meters)')
ylabel('Height  h(t)   (meters)')
title('Ball Trajectory (Horizontal and Vertical Distances) as a Function of Time')
grid on
axis ([0 maxx 0 3])
%Part c
%Plot trajectories for 3 (given) values of A
%Assign three different angles: 20, 30 and 45 degrees
A1=20; A2=30; A3=45;
%Find h and x for each angle
h1=v*T.*sin(A1*pi/180)-0.5*g*T.^2;
x1-v*T.*cos(A1*pi/180);
h2=v*T.*sin(A2*pi/180)-0.5*g*T.^2;
x2=v*T.*cos(A2*pi/180);
h3=v*T.*sin(A3*pi/180)-0.5*g*T.^2;
x3=v*T.*cos(A3*pi/180);
%Format the graph
x=[0:.5:maxx]; y=[0:.5:maxh]; t=[0:0.1:2];
subplot(2,1,2)
plot(x1,h1,':',x2,h2,'-. ',x3,h3,'-')
xlabel('Horizontal Distance Traveled  x(t)   (meters)')
ylabel('Height  h(t)   (meters)')
title('Ball Trajectory as a Function of Time for Different Angle Values')
grid on
legend('20 degrees','30 degrees','45 degrees')
axis ([0 12 0 4])
```

The resulting plots are documented in Figure 4.31.

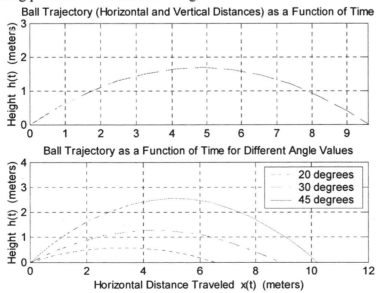

Figure 4.31. Ball trajectory

The results displayed in the Command Window are
```
maximum height: 1.675659 meters
maximum horizantal distace: 9.575639 meters
time: 1.168970 seconds
```

□

Example 4.3.5.

Create four subplots for vectors *x* and *y*. Use the subplots to plot the data as linear, semilogx, semilogy, and loglog plots. Use data markers, titles to identify the plots, and the grid. Connect points with line segments. Recall the following equations:

1.	Straight line on linear plot:	$y = mx + b$
2.	Straight line on loglog plot:	$y = bx^m$
3.	Straight line on semilogx plot:	$y = be^{mx}$
4.	Straight line on semilogy plot:	$y = be^{my}$

Solution.

The following m-file is written:
```
%Creates four plots for a given set of vectors using
%linear, loglog, semilogy and semilogx plots
%Given vectors
x=[2.5 3 3.5 4 4.5 5 5.5 6 7 8 9 10];
y=[1500 1220 1050 915 810 745 690 620 520 480 410 390];
%Linear plot - plots x as a function of y, a straight line segment should form
subplot(2,2,1)
plot(x,y,'o',x,y,'--')
xlabel('x')
ylabel('y')
title('Linear Plot of x versus y')
grid on
%loglog plot - plot both x and y on a log scale
%forms a straight line, a y=b*x^m equation
subplot(2,2,2)
loglog(x,y,'o',x,y,'--')
xlabel('x')
ylabel('y')
title('Loglog Plot of x versus y')
grid on
%semilogy plot - plot x on log scale and y on linear scale
subplot(2,2,3)
semilogy(x,y,'o',x,y,'--')
xlabel('x')
ylabel('y')
title('Semilogy Plot of x versus y')
grid on
%semilogx plot - plot y on log scale and x on linear scale
subplot(2,2,4)
semilogx(x,y,'o',x,y,'--')
xlabel('x')
ylabel('y')
title('Semilogx Plot of x versus y')
grid on
```
Four plots are documented in Figure 4.32.

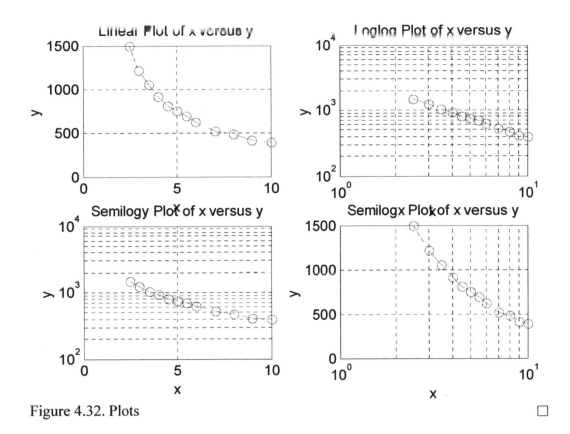

Figure 4.32. Plots ☐

Example 4.3.6.

The bulk modulus of SiC versus temperature is given as [5]:

$$B = [203_{T=20}, 200_{T=250}, 197_{T=500}, 194_{T=750}, 191_{T=1000}, 188_{T=1200}, 186_{T=1400}, 184_{T=1500}].$$

The temperature is given in $^\circ$C. Perform the data fitting.

Solution.

The interpolation is performed using the `spline` solver (spline fit). The MATLAB file is:

```
T=[20 250 500 750 1000 1200 1400 1500]; % Temperature Data Array
B=[203 200 197 194 191 188 186 184];    % Bulk Modulus Data Array
Tinterpol=20:10:1500;
Binterpol=spline(T,B,Tinterpol);        % Spline Interpolation
plot(T,B,'o',Tinterpol,Binterpol,'-');  % Plotting Statement
xlabel('Temperature, deg C');
ylabel('Bulk Modulus, GPa');
title('Temperature-Bulk Modulus Data and Spline Interpolation');
```

The resulting temperature – bulk modulus plot of the interpolated spline data (solid line) and the data values used are given in Figure 4.33.

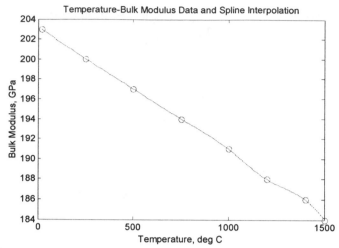

Figure 4.33. Temperature – bulk modulus data and its spline interpolation.   ☐

REFERENCES

1. *MATLAB 6.5 Release 13,* CD-ROM, MathWorks, Inc., 2002.
2. Hanselman, D. and Littlefield, B., *Mastering MATLAB 5*, Prentice Hall, Upper Saddle River, NJ, 1998.
3. Palm, W. J., *Introduction to MATLAB for Engineers*, McGraw-Hill, Boston, MA, 2001.
4. *User's Guide. The Student Edition of MATLAB: The Ultimate Computing Environment for Technical Education*, MathWorks, Inc., Prentice Hall, Upper Saddle River, NJ, 1995.
5. Lyshevski, S. E., *MEMS and NEMS: Systems, Devices, and Structures,* CRC Press, Boca Raton, FL, 2002.

Chapter 5

MATLAB APPLICATIONS: NUMERICAL SIMULATIONS OF DIFFERENTIAL EQUATIONS AND INTRODUCTION TO DYNAMIC SYSTEMS

5.1. Solution of Differential Equations and Dynamic Systems Fundamentals

To study real-world systems, one can use the MATLAB environment [1]. In particular, the dynamic systems are modeled using lumped-parameters and high-fidelity mathematical models given in the form of nonlinear differential (ordinary and partial) and difference equations [2 - 5]. These equations must be numerically or analytically solved, and the MATLAB environment offers the needed features. Then, the data-intensive analysis can be accomplished in MATLAB. The commonly used solvers to numerically solve ordinary nonlinear and linear differential equations are the ode23, ode113, ode15S, ode23S, ode23T, ode23TB, and ode45 solvers. Below is the description of the ode45 solver.

```
>> help ode45
 ODE45  Solve non-stiff differential equations, medium order method.
    [T,Y] = ODE45(ODEFUN,TSPAN,Y0) with TSPAN = [T0 TFINAL] integrates the
    system of differential equations y' = f(t,y) from time T0 to TFINAL with
    initial conditions Y0. Function ODEFUN(T,Y) must return a column vector
    corresponding to f(t,y). Each row in the solution array Y corresponds to
    a time returned in the column vector T. To obtain solutions at specific
    times T0,T1,...,TFINAL (all increasing or all decreasing), use
    TSPAN = [T0 T1 ... TFINAL].

    [T,Y] = ODE45(ODEFUN,TSPAN,Y0,OPTIONS) solves as above with default
    integration properties replaced by values in OPTIONS, an argument created
    with the ODESET function. See ODESET for details. Commonly used options
    are scalar relative error tolerance 'RelTol' (1e-3 by default) and vector
    of absolute error tolerances 'AbsTol' (all components 1e-6 by default).

    [T,Y] = ODE45(ODEFUN,TSPAN,Y0,OPTIONS,P1,P2...) passes the additional
    parameters P1,P2,... to the ODE function as ODEFUN(T,Y,P1,P2...), and to
    all functions specified in OPTIONS. Use OPTIONS = [] as a place holder if
    no options are set.

    ODE45 can solve problems M(t,y)*y' = f(t,y) with mass matrix M that is
    nonsingular. Use ODESET to set the 'Mass' property to a function MASS if
    MASS(T,Y) returns the value of the mass matrix. If the mass matrix is
    constant, the matrix can be used as the value of the 'Mass' option. If
    the mass matrix does not depend on the state variable Y and the function
    MASS is to be called with one input argument T, set 'MStateDependence' to
    'none'. ODE15S and ODE23T can solve problems with singular mass matrices.

    [T,Y,TE,YE,IE] = ODE45(ODEFUN,TSPAN,Y0,OPTIONS...) with the 'Events'
    property in OPTIONS set to a function EVENTS, solves as above while also
    finding where functions of (T,Y), called event functions, are zero. For
    each function you specify whether the integration is to terminate at a
    zero and whether the direction of the zero crossing matters. These are
    the three vectors returned by EVENTS: [VALUE,ISTERMINAL,DIRECTION] =
    EVENTS(T,Y). For the I-th event function: VALUE(I) is the value of the
    function, ISTERMINAL(I)=1 if the integration is to terminate at a zero of
    this event function and 0 otherwise. DIRECTION(I)=0 if all zeros are to
    be computed (the default), +1 if only zeros where the event function is
    increasing, and -1 if only zeros where the event function is
    decreasing. Output TE is a column vector of times at which events
```

occur. Rows of YE are the corresponding solutions, and indices in vector
IE specify which event occurred.

SOL = ODE45(ODEFUN,[T0 TFINAL],Y0...) returns a structure that can be
used with DEVAL to evaluate the solution at any point between T0 and
TFINAL. The steps chosen by ODE45 are returned in a row vector SOL.x.
For each I, the column SOL.y(:,I) contains the solution at SOL.x(I).
If events were detected, SOL.xe is a row vector of points at which events
occurred. Columns of SOL.ye are the corresponding solutions, and indices
in vector SOL.ie specify which event occurred. If a terminal event has
been detected, SOL.x(end) contains the end of the step at which the event
occurred. The exact point of the event is reported in SOL.xe(end).

Example
        [t,y]=ode45(@vdp1,[0 20],[2 0]);
        plot(t,y(:,1));
    solves the system y' = vdp1(t,y), using the default relative error
    tolerance 1e-3 and the default absolute tolerance of 1e-6 for each
    component, and plots the first component of the solution.

See also
    other ODE solvers: ODE23, ODE113, ODE15S, ODE23S, ODE23T, ODE23TB
    options handling: ODESET, ODEGET
    output functions: ODEPLOT, ODEPHAS2, ODEPHAS3, ODEPRINT
    evaluating solution: DEVAL
    ODE examples: RIGIDODE, BALLODE, ORBITODE

NOTE:
    The interpretation of the first input argument of the ODE solvers and
    some properties available through ODESET have changed in this version
    of MATLAB. Although we still support the v5 syntax, any new
    functionality is available only with the new syntax. To see the v5
    help, type in the command line
    more on, type ode45, more off

The following examples illustrate the application of the MATLAB ode45 solver.

MATLAB Illustrative Example.
The following set of two nonlinear differential equations, called the van der Pol
equations,

$$\frac{dx_1(t)}{dt} = x_2, \, x_1(t_0) = x_{10},$$

$$\frac{dx_2(t)}{dt} = \mu\left[(1 - x_1^2)x_2 - x_1\right], \, x_2(t_0) = x_{20},$$

has been used as an illustrative example to solve ordinary differential equations using different
solvers over the last 18 years (the author integrated this MATLAB example into the engineering
curriculum in 1985). Two m-files [1] to solve these differential equations are given below:

• MATLAB script with ode15s solver and plotting statements (file name: vdpode.m):
```
function   vdpode(MU)
%VDPODE  Parameterizable van der Pol equation (stiff for large MU).
%   For the default value of MU = 1000 the equation is in relaxation
%   oscillation, and the problem becomes very stiff. The limit cycle has
%   portions where the solution components change slowly and the problem is
%   quite stiff, alternating with regions of very sharp change where it is
%   not stiff (quasi-discontinuities). The initial conditions are close to an
%   area of slow change so as to test schemes for the selection of the
%   initial step size.
%
%   The subfunction J(T,Y,MU) returns the Jacobian matrix dF/dY evaluated
```

```
%    analytically at (T,Y). By default, the stiff solvers of the ODE Suite
%    approximate Jacobian matrices numerically. However, if the ODE Solver
%    property Jacobian is set to @J with ODESET, a solver calls the function
%    to obtain dF/dY. Providing the solvers with an analytic Jacobian is not
%    necessary, but it can improve the reliability and efficiency of
%    integration.
%
%    L. F. Shampine, Evaluation of a test set for stiff ODE solvers, ACM
%    Trans. Math. Soft., 7 (1981) pp. 409-420.
%
%    See also ODE15S, ODE23S, ODE23T, ODE23TB, ODESET, @.

%    Mark W. Reichelt and Lawrence F. Shampine, 3-23-94, 4-19-94
%    Copyright 1984-2002 The MathWorks, Inc.
%    $Revision: 1.18 $  $Date: 2002/04/08 20:04:56 $

if nargin < 1
  MU = 1000;      % default
end

tspan = [0; max(20,3*MU)];                % several periods
y0 = [2; 0];
options = odeset('Jacobian',@J);

[t,y] = ode15s(@f,tspan,y0,options,MU);

figure;
plot(t,y(:,1));
title(['Solution of van der Pol Equation, \mu = ' num2str(MU)]);
xlabel('time t');
ylabel('solution y_1');

axis([tspan(1) tspan(end) -2.5 2.5]);

% -----------------------------------------------------------------
function dydt = f(t,y,mu)
dydt = [           y(2)
        mu*(1-y(1)^2)*y(2)-y(1) ];
% -----------------------------------------------------------------

function dfdy = J(t,y,mu)
dfdy = [           0                    1
        -2*mu*y(1)*y(2)-1      mu*(1-y(1)^2) ];
```

- MATLAB script with a set of differential equations to be solved (file name: vdp1000.m):

```
function dydt = vdp1000(t,y)
%VDP1000  Evaluate the van der Pol ODEs for mu = 1000.
%
%    See also ODE15S, ODE23S, ODE23T, ODE23TB.

%    Jacek Kierzenka and Lawrence F. Shampine
%    Copyright 1984-2002 The MathWorks, Inc.
%    $Revision: 1.5 $  $Date: 2002/04/08 20:04:56 $

dydt = [y(2); 1000*(1-y(1)^2)*y(2)-y(1)];
```

Both files vdpode.m and vdp1000.m are in the particular MATLAB directory. Let these files be in the directory cd c:\MATLAB6p5\toolbox\matlab\demos. Then, to run these programs, we type in the Command Window

```
>> cd c:\MATLAB6p5\toolbox\matlab\demos
```

To perform numerical simulations, run the file vdpode.m by typing in the Command Window

```
>> vdpode
```

and pressing the Enter key. The resulting plot for the evolution of the state variable $x_1(t)$ is documented in Figure 5.1 (note that the initial conditions were assigned to be $x_0 = \begin{bmatrix} x_{10} \\ x_{20} \end{bmatrix} = \begin{bmatrix} 2 \\ 0 \end{bmatrix}$ and $\mu = 1000$). Please note that in the MathWorks vdpode.m file to solve ordinary differential equations, the solver ode15s is used, and the plotting statement is plot(t,y(:,1)).

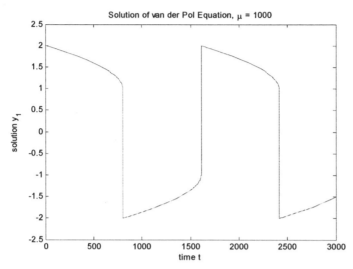

Figure 5.1. Dynamics of the state $x_1(t)$

The user can modify the file vdpode.m. For example, if we need to plot $x_1(t)$ and $x_2(t)$, as well as visualize the results plotting $x_1(t)$, $x_2(t)$ and t in three-dimensional plot (x_1, x_2, t), the following lines can be added to vdpode.m (the variable x_2 was divided by 100):

```
% Two-dimensional plot
plot(t,y(:,1),'-',t,y(:,2)/100,':');
xlabel('Time (seconds)');
title('Solution of van der Pol equation: x1 and x2/100');
pause
% 3-D plot w(y1,y2,t)
plot3(y(:,1),y(:,2)/100,t)
xlabel('x1'), ylabel('x2/100'), zlabel('time')
text(0,0,0,'0 Origin')
```
The resulting plots are illustrated in Figure 5.2.

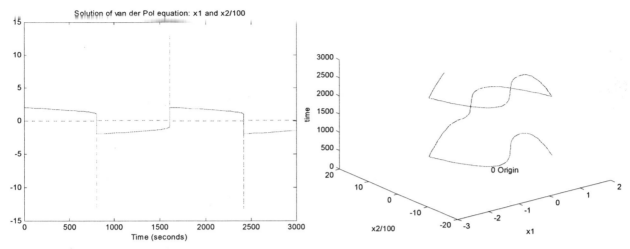

Figure 5.2. Evolution of the state variables using two- and tree-dimensional plots □

Example 5.1.1.
Numerically solve a system of highly nonlinear differential equations using the MATLAB ode45 solver

$$\frac{dx_1(t)}{dt} = -15x_1 + 10|x_2| + 10x_1x_2x_3, \; x_1(t_0) = x_{10},$$

$$\frac{dx_2(t)}{dt} = -5x_1x_2 - \sin x_1 + x_2 - x_3, \; x_2(t_0) = x_{20},$$

$$\frac{dx_3(t)}{dt} = -5x_1x_2 + 10x_2 \cos x_1 - 15x_3, \; x_3(t_0) = x_{30}.$$

Two m-files (c5_1_1a.m and c5_1_1b.m) are developed in order to numerically simulate this set of nonlinear differential equations. The initial conditions must be assigned, and let

$$x_0 = \begin{bmatrix} x_{10} \\ x_{20} \\ x_{30} \end{bmatrix} = \begin{bmatrix} 15 \\ -15 \\ 10 \end{bmatrix}.$$ The evolution of the state variables $x_1(t)$, $x_2(t)$, and $x_3(t)$ must be plotted. To

illustrate the transient responses of $x_1(t)$, $x_2(t)$, and $x_3(t)$, the plot command is used. Three-dimensional graphics is also available and integrated in the first m-file. A three-dimensional plot is obtained using x_1, x_2, and x_3 as the variables by making use of plot3. Comments, which are not executed, appear after the % symbol. These comments explain particular steps in MATLAB scripts.

MATLAB script with ode45 solver and plotting (two- and three-dimensional) statements using plot and plot3 (c5_1_1a.m):

```
echo on; clear all
tspan=[0 3];        % initial and final time
y0=[15 -15 10]';     % initial conditions
[t,y]=ode45('c5_1_1b',tspan,y0);    %ode45 MATLAB solver
% Plot of the time history found by solving
% three differential equations assigned in the file c5_1_1b.m
plot(t,y(:,1),'--',t,y(:,2),'-',t,y(:,3),':');
xlabel('Time (seconds)');
title('Solution of Differential Equations: x1, x2 and x3');
pause
% 3-D plot w(y1,y2,y3)
```

```
plot3(y(:,1),y(:,2),y(:,3))
xlabel('x1'), ylabel('x2'), zlabel('x3')
text(15,-15,10,'x0 Initial')
text(0,0,0,'0 Origin')
v=axis
pause; disp('END')
```

MATLAB script with a set of differential equations to be solved (c5_1_1b.m):

```
function yprime = difer(t,y);
a11=-15; a12=10; a13=10; a21=-5; a22=-2; a31=-5; a32=10; a33=-15;
yprime=[a11*y(1,:)+a12*abs(y(2,:))+a13*y(1,:)*y(2,:)*y(3,:);...
a21*y(1,:)*y(2,:)+a22*sin(y(1,:))-y(2,:)+y(3,:);...
a31*y(1,:)*y(2,:)+a32*cos(y(1,:))*y(2,:)+a33*y(3,:)];
```

To calculate the transient dynamics and plot the transient dynamics, type in the Command window » c5_1_1a and press the Enter key. The resulting transient behavior and three-dimensional plot are documented in Figures 5.3 and 5.4.

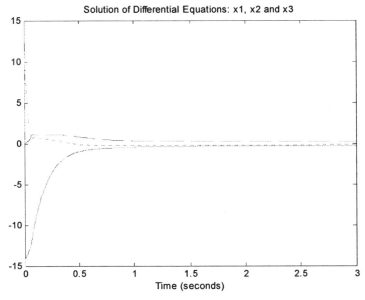

Figure 5.3. Evolution of the state variables, $x_0 = \begin{bmatrix} x_{10} \\ x_{20} \\ x_{30} \end{bmatrix} = \begin{bmatrix} 15 \\ -15 \\ 10 \end{bmatrix}$

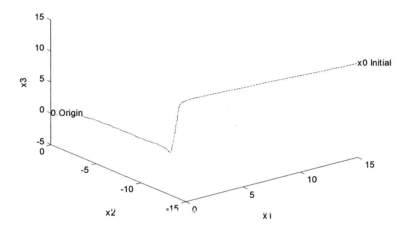

Figure 5.4. Three-dimensional plot ☐

A set of differential equations was assigned. However, to apply MATLAB, first mathematical models for real-word systems must be developed. Thus, numerical and analytical simulation and analysis of systems is a two-step process. Mathematical models depict the time-dependent mathematical relationships among the system's inputs, states, events, and outputs.

The Lagrange equations of motion, as well as Kirchhoff's and Newton's laws, can be used to develop mathematical models described by differential or difference equations. The real-world systems integrate many components, subsystems, and devices. Multivariable dynamic systems are studied with different levels of comprehensiveness. Consider the aircraft in Figure 5.5. In aircraft as well as in other flight vehicles (missiles, projectiles, rockets, spacecraft, etc.) and surface/undersea vehicles (ships, submarines, torpedoes, etc.), control surfaces are actuated by electromechanical actuators. Therefore, the actuator must be studied. These actuators are controlled by power amplifiers, and therefore the circuitry must be examined as well. Mechanical systems (rigid-body aircraft and actuators' torsional-mechanical dynamics) are modeled using Newtonian mechanics, the electromagnetics of electromechanical actuators are studied using Maxwell's equations, and the circuitry dynamics is usually modeled using Kirchhoff's laws [3, 4].

Figure 5.5. Aircraft

The aircraft outputs are the Euler angles θ, φ, and ψ. The reference inputs are the desired (assigned by the pilot or flight computer) Euler angles, which are denoted as r_θ, r_ϕ and r_ψ. For rigid-body aircraft, the longitudinal and lateral dynamics are modeled using the following state variables: the forward velocity v; the angle of attack α; the pitch rate q; the pitch angle θ; the sideslip angle β; the roll rate p; the yaw rate r; the roll angle ϕ; the yaw angle ψ. As was emphasized, the aircraft is controlled by displacing the control surfaces (right and left horizontal stabilizers, right and left leading- and trailing-edge flaps, right and left rudders). That is, a multi-input/multi-output dynamic system (e.g., aircraft, submarines, cars, etc.) must be simulated and analyzed in the MATLAB environment.

Having introduced the basics in flight control, the MATLAB demo offers a great number of illustrative examples which should be used. For example, the numerical simulations for the F-14 fighter are performed as illustrated in Figure 5.6.

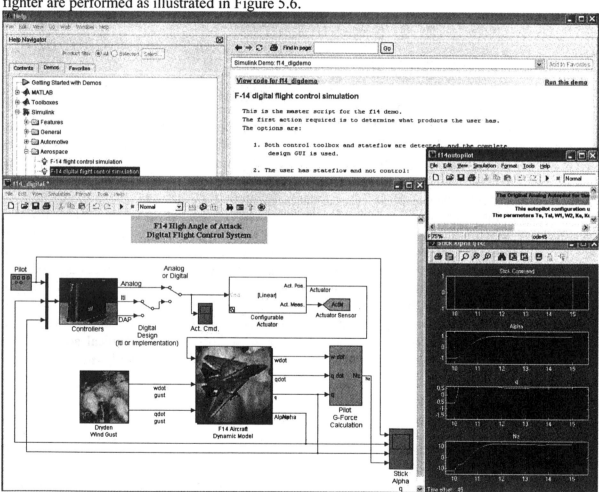

Figure 5.6. Simulations of the F-14 fighter using MATLAB demo

It was emphasized that the aircraft is controlled by changing the angular displacement of the flight control surfaces, and servo-systems are used to actuate ailerons, elevators, canards, flaps, rudders, stabilizers, tips, and other control surfaces. To deflect ailerons, canards, fins, flaps, rudders, and stabilizers, hydraulic and electric motors have been applied. A direct-drive control surface *servo* driven by an electric motor is shown in Figure 5.7. Using the reference signal (the command angular displacement of the control surface), measured current in the phase windings *i*, mechanical angular velocity ω_{rm}, and actual mechanical angular displacement θ_{rm}, the controller develops signal-level signals which drive high-frequency switches of the power amplifier. The magnitude and frequency of the applied voltage to the phase winding is controlled by the PWM power amplifier (see Figure 5.7).

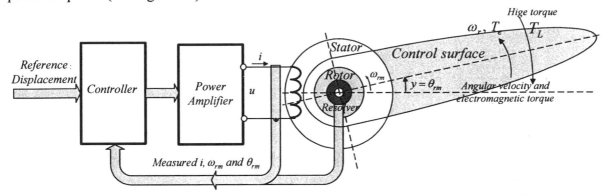

Figure 5.7. Fly-by-wire flight servo with electric motor and PWM power amplifier

The electromechanical flight servo-system integrates electromechanical motion devices (actuator and resolver) and power amplifier. These components must be modeled and then simulated and analyzed in the MATLAB environment. In fact, the analysis performed illustrates that the designer must develop accurate mathematical models integrating all components of complex multivariable real-world dynamic systems. The state and control variables must be defined, and differential equations (mathematical models) must be found with a minimum level of simplifications and assumptions. As the mathematical model is developed, the dynamic systems can be simulated and analyzed using MATLAB.

5.2. Mathematical Model Developments and
MATLAB Applications

The equations to model the dynamics of mechanical systems can be straightforwardly found using Newton's second law of motion

$$\sum \vec{F}(\bar{x},t) = m\vec{a},$$

where $\vec{F}(\bar{x},t)$ is the vector sum of all forces applied to the body; $\vec{a}$ is the vector of acceleration of the body with respect to an inertial reference frame; m is the mass.

Hence, in the Cartesian system, or any other coordinate systems, the forces, acceleration, velocity, and displacement in one, two, or three dimensions (x, y, and z axes in the three-dimensional Cartesian system) are examined. One obtains

$$\sum \vec{F}(\bar{\mathbf{x}},t) = m\vec{a} = m\frac{d\bar{\mathbf{x}}^2}{dt^2} = m\begin{bmatrix} \dfrac{d\bar{x}^2}{dt^2} \\ \dfrac{d\bar{y}^2}{dt^2} \\ \dfrac{d\bar{z}^2}{dt^2} \end{bmatrix}.$$

Example 5.2.1.
Consider a body of mass m in the xy plane (two-dimensional systems). Derive the equations of motion assuming that the external force $\vec{F}_a$ is applied in the x direction ($\vec{F}_a(t,x) = 10v\cos 100t = 10\dfrac{dx}{dt}\cos 100t$) and the viscous friction force is $F_{fr} = B_v\dfrac{dx}{dt}$; B_v is the viscous friction coefficient.

Solution.
The free-body diagram is illustrated in Figure 5.8.

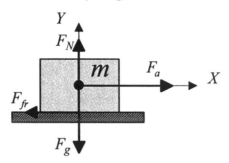

Figure 5.8. Free-body diagram

The *net* force acting in the x direction is found using the time-varying applied force $\vec{F}_a$ and the friction force $\vec{F}_{fr}$. In particular,
$$\sum \vec{F}_X = \vec{F}_a - \vec{F}_{fr}.$$
Hence, the second-order differential equation of motion in the x direction is
$$\vec{F}_a - \vec{F}_{fr} = ma_x = m\frac{d^2x}{dt^2}.$$
We obtain the following second-order differential equation to model the body dynamics in the x direction $\dfrac{d^2x}{dt^2} = \dfrac{1}{m}\left(F_a - B_v\dfrac{dx}{dt}\right)$. Using the velocity in the x direction $v = \dfrac{dx}{dt}$, a set of two first-order differential equations results, and
$$\frac{dx}{dt} = v,$$
$$\frac{dv}{dt} = \frac{1}{m}\left(F_a - B_v\frac{dx}{dt}\right) = \frac{1}{m}\left(10v\cos 100t - B_vv\right).$$
The sum of the forces acting in the y direction is
$$\sum \vec{F}_Y = \vec{F}_N - \vec{F}_g,$$
where $\vec{F}_g = mg$ is the gravitational force; $\vec{F}_N$ is the normal force (equal and opposite to the gravitational force, e.g., $\vec{F}_N = -\vec{F}_g$).

The equation of motion in the y direction is
$$\vec{F}_N - \vec{F}_g = 0 = ma_y = m\frac{d^2y}{dt^2}. \qquad \square$$

Newton's second law of rotational motion is

$$\sum M = J\alpha = J\frac{d^2\theta}{dt^2},$$

where $\sum M$ is the sum of all moments about the center of mass of a body; J is the moment of inertia about the center of mass; α is the angular acceleration, $\alpha = \dfrac{d^2\theta}{dt^2}$; θ is the angular displacement.

In the next example we illustrate the application of the rotational Newtonian mechanics in the model developments.

Example 5.2.2.

Figure 5.9 illustrates a simple pendulum (point mass m) suspended by a massless unstretchable string of length l. Derive the equations of motion (mathematical model in the form of differential equations) assuming that the friction force is a linear function of the angular velocity (e.g., $T_f = B_m\omega$); B_m is the viscous friction coefficient.

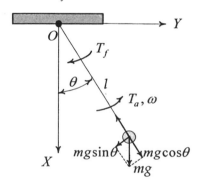

Figure 5.9. Simple pendulum

Solution.

The restoring force is $F_{rest} = -mg\sin\theta$.

Thus, the *net* moment about the pivot point O is

$$\sum M = T_{rest} + T_a - T_f = -mgl\sin\theta + T_a - B_m\omega,$$

where T_a is the applied torque.

We have the following second-order differential equation to model the pendulum motion

$$J\alpha = J\frac{d^2\theta}{dt^2} = -mgl\sin\theta + T_a - B_m\omega, \text{ or } \frac{d^2\theta}{dt^2} = \frac{1}{J}\left(-mgl\sin\theta + T_a - B_m\omega\right)$$

where J is the moment of inertial of the mass about the point O.

Taking note of $\dfrac{d\theta}{dt} = \omega$, one obtains a set of two first-order differential equations

$$\frac{d\omega}{dt} = \frac{1}{J}\left(-mgl\sin\theta + T_a - B_m\omega\right),$$

$$\frac{d\theta}{dt} = \omega.$$

The moment of inertia is $J = ml^2$. Thus, we have two linear differential equations

$$\frac{d\omega}{dt} = -\frac{B_m}{ml^2}\omega - \frac{g}{l}\sin\theta + \frac{1}{ml^2}T_a,$$

$$\frac{d\theta}{dt} = \omega.$$

This set of differential equations can be numerically simulated in MATLAB using two m-files as illustrated in the examples. The pendulum parameters (B_m, m, and l) should be assigned. The simulation of a simple pendulum is performed in Chapter 6 (see Example 6.1.2).

□

Example 5.2.3.

A body is suspended from a spring with coefficient k_s, and the viscous friction coefficient is B_v (see Figure 5.10). Derive the mathematical model in the form of differential equations.

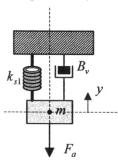

Figure 5.10.

Solution.

Using Newton's second law, one finds the resulting second-order differential equation

$$m\frac{d^2y}{dt^2} + B_v\frac{dy}{dt} + k_s y = F_a,$$

which models the body dynamics and, therefore, represents the mathematical model. □

The circuitry mathematical models to simulate and analyze the circuitry dynamics are found using Kirchhoff's voltage and current laws. The following examples illustrate the application of Kirchhoff's laws.

Example 5.2.4.

An electric circuit is documented in Figure 5.11. Find the mathematical model in the form of integro-differential equations.

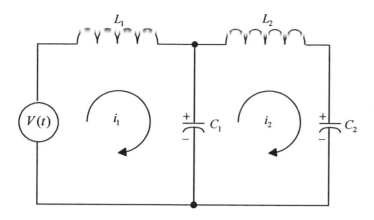

Figure 5.11. Two-mesh circuit

Solution.

Using Kirchhoff's law, we find

$$L_1 \frac{di_1}{dt} + \frac{1}{C_1} \int (i_1 - i_2) dt = V \quad \text{and} \quad L_2 \frac{di_2}{dt} - \frac{1}{C_1} \int (i_1 - i_2) dt + \frac{1}{C_2} \int i_2 dt = 0.$$

Thus, the integro-differential equations to model the circuit are found. □

Example 5.2.5.

A *buck (step-down)* switching converter is documented in Figure 5.12 [3, 4]. In this converter, switch *S*, inductor *L*, and capacitor *C* have resistances. These resistances are denoted as r_s, r_L, and r_c. The resistive–inductive load with the *back emf* E_a is formed by the resistor r_a and inductor L_a. Derive the mathematical model and study the converter dynamics through numerical simulations.

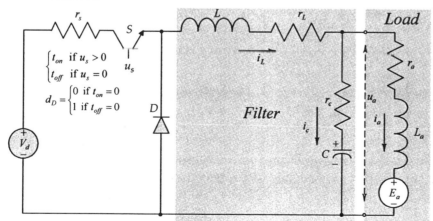

Figure 5.12. Switching converter

Solution.

The voltage is regulated by opening and closing the switch *S*. Thus, this switch, which is a high-frequency transistor, open and closed. Correspondingly, differential equations must be found for these two switch "states." One concludes that the voltage at the load is regulated by using a pulse-width-modulation (PWM) switching. For lossless switch (if $r_s = 0$), the voltage across the diode D is equal to the supplied voltage V_d when the switch is closed, and the voltage is zero if the switch is open. The voltage applied to the load u_a is regulated by controlling the switching *on* and *off* durations (t_{on} and t_{off}). The switching frequency is $\dfrac{1}{t_{on} + t_{off}}$. These *on* and *off* durations are controlled by u_s. If $u_s = 0$, the switch is closed, while if $u_s > 0$, the switch is open.

Making use of the duty ratio $d_D = \dfrac{t_{on}}{t_{on} + t_{off}}$, $d_D = \begin{cases} 0 \text{ if } t_{on} = 0 \\ 1 \text{ if } t_{off} = 0 \end{cases}$, $d_D \in [0 \ \ 1]$, using the *averaging* concept, if $r_s = 0$ we have $u_{dN} = \dfrac{t_{on}}{t_{on} + t_{off}} V_d = d_D V_d$.

Using Kirchhoff's laws the following sets of differential equations are derived.

- Switch is closed:
  When the switch is closed, the diode is reverse biased. For $t_{off} = 0$, $d_D = 1$, we have

$$\frac{du_C}{dt} = \frac{1}{C}(i_L - i_a),$$

$$\frac{di_L}{dt} = \frac{1}{L}\left(-u_C - (r_L + r_c)i_L + r_c i_a - r_s i_L + V_d\right),$$

$$\frac{di_a}{dt} = \frac{1}{L_a}\left(u_C + r_c i_L - (r_a + r_c)i_a - E_a\right).$$

- Switch is open:
  If the switch is open, the diode is forward biased. For $d_D = 0$ ($t_{on} = 0$), we find

$$\frac{du_C}{dt} = \frac{1}{C}(i_L - i_a),$$

$$\frac{di_L}{dt} = \frac{1}{L}\left(-u_C - (r_L + r_c)i_L + r_c i_a\right),$$

$$\frac{di_a}{dt} = \frac{1}{L_a}\left(u_C + r_c i_L - (r_a + r_c)i_a - E_a\right).$$

When the switch is closed, the duty ratio is 1. In contrast, if the switch is open, the duty ratio is 0. Therefore, $d_D = \begin{cases} 0 \text{ if } t_{on} = 0 \\ 1 \text{ if } t_{off} = 0 \end{cases}$.

Assuming that the switching frequency is high, one uses the duty ratio to find the following augmented set of differential equations to model the converter transients. In particular,

$$\frac{du_C}{dt} = \frac{1}{C}(i_L - i_a),$$

$$\frac{di_L}{dt} = \frac{1}{L}\left(-u_C - (r_L + r_c)i_L + r_c i_a - r_s i_L d_D + V_d d_D\right),$$

$$\frac{di_a}{dt} = \frac{1}{L_a}\left(u_C + r_c i_L - (r_a + r_c)i_a - E_a\right).$$

Thus, the *buck* converter dynamics is modeled by a set of derived nonlinear differential equations. Our next step is to numerically solve these differential equations using MATLAB. By making use of a set of differential equations, two m-files are written to perform simulations and visualize the converter dynamics. The following parameters are used:

r_s = 0.025 ohm, r_L = 0.05 ohm, r_c = 0.05 ohm, r_a = 2.5 ohm, C = 0.05 F, L = 0.005 H, L_a = 0.05 H, V_d = 40 V, E_a = 5 V and d_D = 0.5.

The initial conditions are assigned to be $\begin{bmatrix} u_{C0} \\ i_{L0} \\ i_{a0} \end{bmatrix} = \begin{bmatrix} 10 \\ 5 \\ -5 \end{bmatrix}$.

MATLAB script (c5_2_5a.m):

```
echo on; clear all
t0=0; tfinal=0.4; tspan=[t0 tfinal]; % initial and final time
y0=[10 5 -5]';                       % initial conditions
[t,y]=ode45('c5_2_5b',tspan,y0);     % ode45 MATLAB solver
% Plot of the time history found by solving
% three differential equations assigned in the file c5_2_5b.m
% 3-D plot using x1, x2 and x3 as the variables
plot3(y(:,1),y(:,2),y(:,3))
xlabel('x1'), ylabel('x2'), zlabel('x3')
text(10,5,-5,'x0 Initial')
v=axis
pause
% 3-D plot using x1, x3 and time as the variables
plot3(y(:,1),y(:,3),t)
xlabel('x1'), ylabel('x3'), zlabel('time')
text(10,-5,0,'x0 Initial')
v=axis
pause
% 2-D plots
subplot(2,2,1); plot(t,y);
xlabel('Time (seconds)');
title('Dynamics of the state variables');
subplot(2,2,2); plot(t,y(:,1),'-');
xlabel('Time (seconds)'); title('Voltage uc (x1), [V]');
subplot(2,2,3); plot(t,y(:,2),'--');
xlabel('Time (seconds)'); title('Current iL (x2), [A]');
subplot(2,2,4); plot(t,y(:,3),':');
xlabel('Time (seconds)'); title('Current ia (x3), [A]');
disp('END');
```

MATLAB script (c5_2_5b.m):

```
function yprime=difer(t,y);
% converter parameters
rs=0.025; rl=0.05; rc=0.05; ra=2.5; C=0.05; L=0.005; La=0.05;
% voltage applied, back emf and duty ratio
Vd=50; Ea=5; D=0.5;
% three differential equations to model a buck converter
yprime=[(y(2,:)-y(3,:))/C;...
(-y(1,:)-(rl+rc)*y(2,:)+rc*y(3,:)-rs*y(2,:)*D+Vd*D)/L;...
(y(1,:)+rc*y(2,:)-(rc+ra)*y(3,:)-Ea)/La];
```

Three-dimensional plots using $x_1(t)$, $x_2(t)$, and $x_3(t)$ as well as $x_1(t)$, $x_3(t)$, and t as the variables are shown in Figure 5.13. Figure 5.13 also illustrates two-dimensional plots reporting the transient dynamics for three state variables $u_C(t)$, $i_L(t)$, and $i_a(t)$ which are $x_1(t)$, $x_2(t)$, and $x_3(t)$. We conclude that we performed numerical simulations and visualized the results using plotting statements.

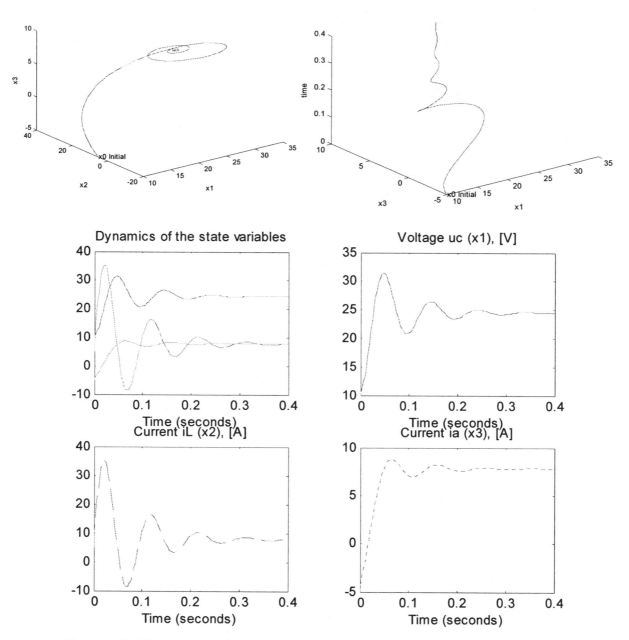

Figure 5.13. Evolution of the variables (in three dimensions) and transient dynamics

Making note of the output equation $u_a = u_C + r_c i_L - r_c i_a$, the voltage at the load terminal u_a can be plotted. We type in the Command Window

```
»rc=0.05;plot(t,y(:,1)+rc*y(:,2)-rc*y(:,3),'-');xlabel('Time (seconds)');title('Voltage ua, [V]');
```

The resulting plot for $u_a(t)$ is shown in Figure 5.14.

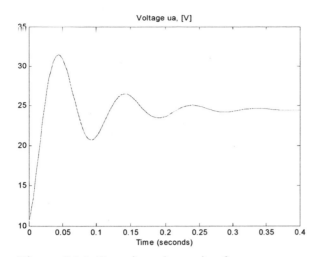

Figure 5.14. Transient dynamics for u_a, $u_a = u_C + r_c i_L - r_c i_a$ □

Example 5.2.6.

A one-quadrant *boost* (*step-up*) switching converter is documented in Figure 5.15 [3, 4]. The converter parameters are: $r_s = 0.025$ ohm, $r_L = 0.05$ ohm, $r_c = 0.05$ ohm, $r_a = 2.5$ ohm, $C = 0.05$ F, $L = 0.005$ H, $L_a = 0.05$ H, $V_d = 40$ V, $E_a = 5$ V and $d_D = 0.25$.

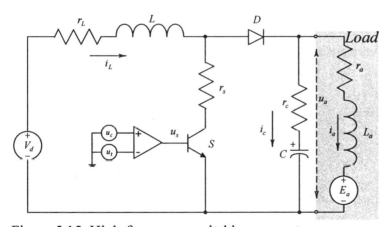

Figure 5.15. High-frequency switching converter

Solution.

When the switch is closed, the diode is reverse biased. Correspondingly, the following set of differential equations results:

$$\frac{du_C}{dt} = -\frac{1}{C}i_a, \quad \frac{di_L}{dt} = \frac{1}{L}\left(-\left(r_L + r_s\right)i_L + V_d\right), \quad \frac{di_a}{dt} = \frac{1}{L_a}\left(u_C - \left(r_a + r_c\right)i_a - E_a\right).$$

If the switch is open, the diode is forward biased due to the fact that the direction of the inductor current i_L does not change instantly. Hence, we have the differential equations

$$\frac{du_C}{dt} = \frac{1}{C}\left(i_L - i_a\right), \quad \frac{di_L}{dt} = \frac{1}{L}\left(-u_C - \left(r_L + r_c\right)i_L + r_c i_a + V_d\right), \quad \frac{di_a}{dt} = \frac{1}{L_a}\left(u_C + r_c i_L - \left(r_a + r_c\right)i_a - E_a\right).$$

Using the duty ratio d_D (which can vary from 0 to 1), we find the resulting model, and

$$\frac{du_C}{dt} = \frac{1}{C}\left(i_L - i_a - i_L d_D\right),$$

$$\frac{di_L}{dt} = \frac{1}{L}\left(-u_C - (r_L + r_c)i_L + r_c i_a + u_C d_D + (r_c - r_s)i_L d_D - r_c i_a d_D + V_d\right),$$

$$\frac{di_a}{dt} = \frac{1}{L_a}\left(u_C + r_c i_L - (r_a + r_c)i_a - r_c i_L d_D - E_a\right).$$

Our goal is to simulate the *boost* converter, and initial conditions and parameters must be assigned. Let the initial conditions be $\begin{bmatrix} u_{C0} \\ i_{L0} \\ i_{a0} \end{bmatrix} = \begin{bmatrix} 10 \\ 5 \\ -5 \end{bmatrix}$.

Taking note of the differential equations, the following m-files are written to solve differential equations with the assigned initial conditions, converter parameters, and duty ratio.

MATLAB script (c5_2_6a.m):

```
echo on; clear all
t0=0; tfinal=0.4; tspan=[t0 tfinal]; % initial and final time
y0=[10 5 -5]';                        % initial conditions
[t,y]=ode45('c5_2_6b',tspan,y0);      % ode45 MATLAB solver
% Plot of the time history found by solving
% three differential equations assigned in the file c5_2_5b.m
% 3-D plot using x1, x2 and x3 as the variables
plot3(y(:,1),y(:,2),y(:,3))
xlabel('x1'), ylabel('x2'), zlabel('x3')
text(10,5,-5,'x0 Initial')
v=axis
pause
% 3-D plot using x1, x3 and time as the variables
plot3(y(:,1),y(:,3),t)
xlabel('x1'), ylabel('x3'), zlabel('time')
text(10,-5,0,'x0 Initial')
v=axis
pause
% 2-D plots
subplot(2,2,1); plot(t,y);
xlabel('Time (seconds)');
title('Dynamics of the state variables');
subplot(2,2,2); plot(t,y(:,1),'-');
xlabel('Time (seconds)'); title('Voltage uc (x1), [V]');
subplot(2,2,3); plot(t,y(:,2),'--');
xlabel('Time (seconds)'); title('Current iL (x2), [A]');
subplot(2,2,4); plot(t,y(:,3),':');
xlabel('Time (seconds)'); title('Current ia (x3), [A]');
disp('END');
```

MATLAB script (c5_2_6b.m):

```
function yprime=difer(t,y);
% converter parameters
rs=0.025; rl=0.05; rc=0.05; ra=2.5; C=0.05; L=0.005; La=0.05;
% voltage applied, back emf and duty ratio
Vd=50; Ea=5; D=0.25;
% three differential equations to model a boost converter
yprime=[(y(2,:)-y(3,:)-y(2,:)*D)/C; ...

(-y(1,:)-(rl+rc)*y(2,:)+rc*y(3,:)+y(1,:)*D+(rc-rs)*y(2,:)*D-
rc*y(3,:)*D+Vd)/L; ...
(y(1,:)+rc*y(2,:)-(ra+rc)*y(3,:)-rc*y(2,:)*D-Ea)/La];
```

Two three-dimensional plots $[x_1(t), x_2(t), x_3(t)]$ and $[x_1(t), x_3(t), t]$ are illustrated in Figure 5.16. The converter transient dynamics for $x_1(t), x_2(t), x_3(t)$ are reported in Figure 5.16.

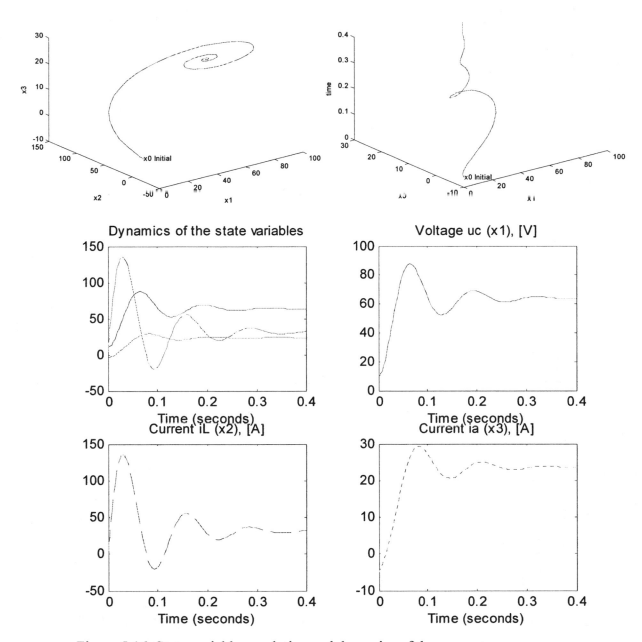

Figure 5.16. State variables evolution and dynamics of the converter

We conclude that numerical simulations and visualization were performed. In particular, the evolution of three state variables $u_C(t)$, $i_L(t)$, and $i_a(t)$ is documented, and the analysis can be performed. □

5.3. Modeling and Computing Using MATLAB

It was illustrated that differential equations result as one applies the fundamental laws to electrical and mechanical systems. It has been shown that the transient dynamics of electrical and mechanical systems are described by linear and nonlinear differential equations. To illustrate the similarity of results, and to visualize the results, the equations of motion for some electromechanical system elements are shown in Table 5.1 [3].

Table 5.1. Basic Elements of Electromechanical Systems

Electromechanical System	Variables Used	Equation
Resistance, R [ohm]	Applied voltage $u_a(t)$ [V] Current $i(t)$ [A]	$u_a(t) = Ri(t)$ $i(t) = \dfrac{1}{R}u_a(t)$
Inductance, L [H]	Applied voltage $u_a(t)$ [V] Current $i(t)$ [A]	$u_a(t) = L\dfrac{di(t)}{dt}$ $i(t) = \dfrac{1}{L}\displaystyle\int_{t_0}^{t} u_a(\tau)d\tau$
Capacitance, C [F]	Applied voltage $u_a(t)$ [V] Current $i(t)$ [A]	$u_a(t) = \dfrac{1}{C}\displaystyle\int_{t_0}^{t} i(\tau)d\tau$ $i(t) = C\dfrac{du_a(t)}{dt}$
Translational damper, B_v [N-sec]	Applied force $F_a(t)$ [N] Linear velocity $v(t)$ [m/sec] Linear position $x(t)$ [m]	$F_a(t) = B_m v(t)$ $v(t) = \dfrac{1}{B_m}F_a(t)$ and $F_a(t) = B_m v(t) = B_m\dfrac{dx(t)}{dt}$ $x(t) = \dfrac{1}{B_v}\displaystyle\int_{t_0}^{t} F_a(\tau)d\tau$

Translational spring, k_s [N]	Applied force $F_a(t)$ [N] Linear velocity $v(t)$ [m/sec] Linear position $x(t)$ [m]	$F_a(t) = k_s x(t)$ $x(t) = \dfrac{1}{k_s} F_a(t)$ and $v(t) = \dfrac{dx(t)}{dt} = \dfrac{1}{k_s}\dfrac{dF_a(t)}{dt}$ $F_a(t) = k_s \displaystyle\int_{t_0}^{t} v(\tau)d\tau$
Mass (grounded), m [kg]	Applied force $F_a(t)$ [N] Linear velocity $v(t)$ [m/sec] Linear position $x(t)$ [m]	$F_a(t) = m\dfrac{dv}{dt} = m\dfrac{d^2 x(t)}{dt^2}$ $v(t) = \dfrac{1}{m}\displaystyle\int_{t_0}^{t} F_a(\tau)d\tau$
Rotational damper, B_m [N-m-sec/rad]	Applied torque $T_a(t)$ [N-m] Angular velocity $\omega(t)$ [rad/sec] Angular displacement $\theta(t)$ [rad]	$T_a(t) = B_m \omega(t)$ $\omega(t) = \dfrac{1}{B_m} T_a(t)$ and $T_a(t) = B_m \omega(t) = B_m \dfrac{d\theta(t)}{dt}$ $\theta(t) = \dfrac{1}{B_m}\displaystyle\int_{t_0}^{t} T_a(\tau)d\tau$
Rotational spring, k_s [N-m-sec/rad]	Applied torque $T_a(t)$ [N-m] Angular velocity $\omega(t)$ [rad/sec] Angular displacement $\theta(t)$ [rad]	$T_a(t) = k_s \theta(t)$ $\theta(t) = \dfrac{1}{k_s} T_a(t)$ and $\omega(t) = \dfrac{d\theta(t)}{dt} = \dfrac{1}{k_s}\dfrac{dT_a(t)}{dt}$ $T_a(t) = k_s \displaystyle\int_{t_0}^{t} \omega(\tau)d\tau$
Rotational mass (grounded), J [kg-m^2]	Applied torque $T_a(t)$ [N-m] Angular velocity $\omega(t)$ [rad/sec] Angular displacement $\theta(t)$ [rad]	$T_a(t) = J\dfrac{d\omega}{dt} = J\dfrac{d^2\theta(t)}{dt^2}$ $\omega(t) = \dfrac{1}{J}\displaystyle\int_{t_0}^{t} T_a(\tau)d\tau$

The similarity of equations of motion is evident as one compares the derived dynamics, which is given by the corresponding differential equations. Consider the translational and rotational (torsional) mechanical systems shown in Figure 5.17.

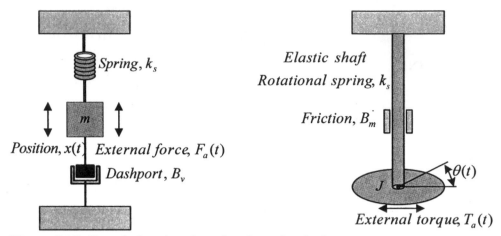

Figure 5.17. Translational and torsional mechanical systems

From Newton's second law, the second-order differential equations of translational and torsional dynamics are found to be

1. Translational dynamics: $\qquad m\dfrac{d^2x}{dt^2} + B_v\dfrac{dx}{dt} + k_sx = F_a(t)$,

2. Torsional dynamics: $\qquad J\dfrac{d^2\theta}{dt^2} + B_m\dfrac{d\theta}{dt} + k_s\theta = T_a(t)$,

where $F_a(t)$ and $T_a(t)$ are the time-varying applied force and torque; B_v and B_m are the viscous friction coefficients; k_s is the translational and rotational (elasticity) spring coefficient.

Consider two *RLC* circuits illustrated in Figure 5.18.

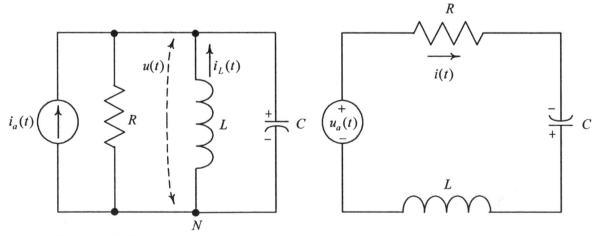

Figure 5.18. Parallel and series *RLC* circuits

The energy is stored in the inductor and the capacitor. The integro-differential equation (an integral as well as a derivative of the dependent variables appears) for the parallel circuit is obtained by summing the currents away from the top node

$$\frac{u}{R} + \frac{1}{L}\int_{t_0}^{t} u(\tau)d\tau - i_L(t_0) + C\frac{du}{dt} = i_a(t),$$

while the integro-differential equation for the series circuit is found by summing the voltages around the closed path. In particular,

$$Ri + \frac{1}{C}\int_{t_0}^{t} i(\tau)d\tau - v_C(t_0) + L\frac{di}{dt} = u_a(t).$$

By differentiating these equations with respect to time and using the fact that $i_L(t_0)$ and $v_C(t_0)$ are constants, we have

$$C\frac{d^2u}{dt^2} + \frac{1}{R}\frac{du}{dt} + \frac{1}{L}u = \frac{di_a}{dt}, \text{ or } \frac{d^2u}{dt^2} + \frac{1}{RC}\frac{du}{dt} + \frac{1}{LC}u = \frac{1}{C}\frac{di_a}{dt},$$

and

$$L\frac{d^2i}{dt^2} + R\frac{di}{dt} + \frac{1}{C}i = \frac{du_a}{dt}, \text{ or } \frac{d^2i}{dt^2} + \frac{R}{L}\frac{di}{dt} + \frac{1}{LC}i = \frac{1}{L}\frac{du_a}{dt}.$$

Parallel and series *RLC* circuits lead to the second-order differential equations. It is evident that these linear differential equations can be numerically modeled in MATLAB using the ode solvers that were illustrated.

It was shown that the mechanical systems and the *RLC* circuits considered are modeled by the second-order differential equations. The analytical solution of linear differential equations with constant coefficients can be easily derived. The general solution of the second-order linear differential equations is found by using the roots of the characteristic equation. The damping coefficient ξ and the resonant frequency ω_0 are given by

$$\xi = \frac{1}{2RC}, \omega_0 = \frac{1}{\sqrt{LC}} \text{ and } \xi = \frac{R}{2L}, \omega_0 = \frac{1}{\sqrt{LC}}$$

for the parallel and series *RLC* circuits (for mechanical systems, $\xi = \frac{B_m}{2\sqrt{k_s m}}$ and $\omega_0 = \sqrt{\frac{k_s}{m}}$).

We write the differential equation as

$$\frac{d^2x}{dt^2} + 2\xi\frac{dx}{dt} + x = f(t)$$

to find three possible solutions examining the characteristic equation

$$s^2 + 2\xi s + \omega_0^2 = (s - s_1)(s - s_2) = 0.$$

This characteristic equation was found by making use the Laplace operator $s = \frac{d}{dt}$. Furthermore,

$$s^2 = \frac{d^2}{dt^2}.$$ The characteristic roots (eigenvalues) are given as

$$s_{1,2} = -\xi \pm \sqrt{\xi^2 - \omega_0^2}.$$

Case 1. If $\xi^2 > \omega_0^2$, the real distinct characteristic roots s_1 and s_2 result.

The general solution is $x(t) = ae^{s_1 t} + be^{s_2 t} + c_f$, where coefficients a and b are obtained using the initial conditions, c_f is the solution due to the *forcing* function f (for the *RLC* circuits f is $i_a(t)$ and $u_a(t)$).

Case 2. For $\xi^2 = \omega_0^2$, the characteristic roots are real and identical, e.g.,

$$s_1 = s_2 = -\xi.$$

The solution of the second-order differential equation is given as

$$x(t) = (a+b)e^{-\xi t} + c_f.$$

Case 3. If $\xi^2 < \omega_0^2$, the complex distinct characteristic roots are found as

$$s_{1,2} = -\xi \pm j\sqrt{\omega_0^2 - \xi^2}.$$

Hence, the general solution is

$$x(t) = e^{-\xi t}\left[a\cos\left(\sqrt{\omega_0^2 - \xi^2}\,t\right) + b\sin\left(\sqrt{\omega_0^2 - \xi^2}\,t\right)\right] + c_f = e^{-\xi t}\sqrt{a^2 + b^2}\cos\left[\left(\sqrt{\omega_0^2 - \xi^2}\,t\right) + \tan^{-1}\left(\frac{-b}{a}\right)\right] + c_f.$$

Example 5.3.1.

For the series *RLC* circuit, find the analytical solutions. Derive and plot the transient response due to the unit step input with initial conditions. Assign the following parameters: $R = 0.4$ ohm, $L = 0.5$ H, $C = 2$ F, $a = 2$ and $b = -2$.

Solution.

For the series *RLC* circuit, the following differential equation was obtained:

$$\frac{d^2 i}{dt^2} + \frac{R}{L}\frac{di}{dt} + \frac{1}{LC}i = \frac{1}{L}\frac{du_a}{dt}.$$

The characteristic equation is $s^2 + \frac{R}{L}s + \frac{1}{LC} = 0$. Therefore, the characteristic roots are

$$s_1 = -\frac{R}{2L} - \sqrt{\left(\frac{R}{2L}\right)^2 - \frac{1}{LC}} \quad \text{and} \quad s_2 = -\frac{R}{2L} + \sqrt{\left(\frac{R}{2L}\right)^2 - \frac{1}{LC}}.$$

If $\left(\frac{R}{2L}\right)^2 > \frac{1}{LC}$, then the characteristic roots are real and distinct.

If $\left(\frac{R}{2L}\right)^2 = \frac{1}{LC}$, then the characteristic roots are real and identical.

If $\left(\frac{R}{2L}\right)^2 < \frac{1}{LC}$, then the characteristic roots are complex.

Making use of the assigned values for R, L, and C, one concludes that the underdamped series dynamics are given by

$$x(t) = e^{-\xi t}\left[a\cos\left(\sqrt{\omega_0^2 - \xi^2}\,t\right) + b\sin\left(\sqrt{\omega_0^2 - \xi^2}\,t\right)\right] + c_f,$$

where $\xi = \frac{R}{2L} = 0.4$ and $\omega_0 = \frac{1}{\sqrt{LC}} = 1$.

In the Command Window we type the following statements:

```
>> t=0:.01:15; a=2; b=-2; cf=1; e=0.4; w0=1;
>> x=exp(-e*t).*(a*cos(sqrt(w0^2-e^2)*t)+b*sin(sqrt(w0^2-e^2)*t))+cf;plot(t,x)
```

The resulting circuitry dynamics are documented in Figure 5.19.

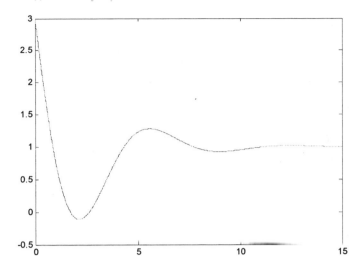

Figure 5.19. Circuitry dynamics due to the unit step input and initial conditions   □

We have used Newton's and Kichhoff's laws to find the differential equations to perform the analysis of mechanical systems and electric circuits. Mathematical models of electromechanical systems can be derived integrating differential equations found for electrical and mechanical subsystems. Furthermore, the application of MATLAB was illustrated to perform numerical simulations. It must be emphasized that the MATLAB environment can be used to derive the analytical solution as demonstrated by the following example.

Example 5.3.2.
Analytically solve the third-order differential equation

$$\frac{d^3x}{dt^3} + 2\frac{dx}{dt} + 3x = 4f$$

using the Symbolic Math Toolbox.

Solution.
Using the `dsolve` solver, we type in the Command Window
```
>> x=dsolve('D3x+2*Dx+3*x=4*f')
```
The resulting solution is
```
x =
4/3*f+C1*exp(-t)+C2*exp(1/2*t)*cos(1/2*11^(1/2)*t)+C3*exp(1/2*t)*sin(1/2*11^(1/2)*t)
```
Using the `pretty` function, we find
```
>> pretty(x)
                                           1/2
  4/3 f + C1 exp(-t) + C2 exp(1/2 t) cos(1/2 11    t)

                          1/2
      + C3 exp(1/2 t) sin(1/2 11    t)
```
Thus, the solution is

$$x(t) = \frac{4}{3}f + c_1 e^{-t} + c_2 e^{0.5t} co\left(\tfrac{1}{2}\sqrt{11}t\right) + c_3 e^{0.5t} \sin\left(\tfrac{1}{2}\sqrt{11}t\right).$$

Using the initial conditions, the unknown constants are found. As an example, let us assign the following initial conditions $\left(\dfrac{d^2x}{dt^2}\right)_0 = 5, \left(\dfrac{dx}{dt}\right)_0 = 0$ and $x_0 = -5$. We have

```
>> x=dsolve('D3x+2*Dx+3*x=4*f','D2x(0)=5','Dx(0)=0','x(0)=-5'); pretty(x)
```

```
                                                                 1/2
    4/3 f + (- 4/5 f - 2) exp(-t) + (- 8/15 f - 3) exp(1/2 t) cos(1/2 11    t)

                      1/2                      1/2
        - 1/165 (16 f + 15) 11    exp(1/2 t) sin(1/2 11    t)
```

Hence, $c_1 = -\dfrac{4}{5}f - 2$, $c_2 = -\dfrac{8}{15}f - 3$, and $c_3 = -\dfrac{1}{165}(16f + 15)\sqrt{11}$.

If the forcing function is time-varying, the analytical solution of

$$\frac{d^3x}{dt^3} + 2\frac{dx}{dt} + 3x = 4f(t)$$

is found as

```
>> x=dsolve('D3x+2*Dx+3*x=4*f(t)'); pretty(x)
```

```
        /     /
        |     |
  4/55  |11   |    exp(t) f(t) dt exp(- 3/2 t)
        |     |
        \    /
              /
              |                        1/2
        +     |    -3 exp(- 1/2 t) f(t) 11    %1 - 11 exp(- 1/2 t) f(t) %2 dt %2
              |
             /
              /                                                                 \
              |                        1/2                                      |
        +     |    3 exp(- 1/2 t) f(t) 11    %2 - 11 exp(- 1/2 t) f(t) %1 dt %1  |
              |                                                                 |
             /                                                                 /
            exp(1/2 t) + C1 exp(-t) + C2 exp(1/2 t) %2 + C3 exp(1/2 t) %1
                      1/2
    %1 := sin(1/2 11    t)

                      1/2
    %2 := cos(1/2 11    t)
```

Letting $f(t) = \sin(t)$ and assuming $\left(\dfrac{d^2x}{dt^2}\right)_0 = 5, \left(\dfrac{dx}{dt}\right)_0 = 0$ and $x_0 = -5$, we have

```
>> x=dsolve('D3x+2*Dx+3*x=4*sin(t)','D2x(0)=5','Dx(0)=0','x(0)=-5'); pretty(x)
```

```
                                                                         1/2
    2/5 %2 sin(%4) - 2/5 %2 sin(%3) - 2/5 %1 cos(%4) - 2/55 %1 sin(%3) 11

                       1/2                      1/2
        + 2/55 %1 sin(%4) 11    + 2/55 %2 cos(%4) 11

                       1/2                      1/2
        - 4/55 %2 sin(%3) 11    - 4/55 %2 sin(%4) 11

                       1/2                      1/2
        + 4/55 %1 cos(%4) 11    + 4/55 %1 cos(%3) 11    + 2/5 %1 cos(%3)

                                               1/2
        - 2/5 cos(t) + 2/5 sin(t) - 2/55 %2 cos(%3) 11    - 8/5 exp(-t)

                          13   1/2
        - 3 exp(1/2 t) %2 - -- 11    exp(1/2 t) %1
                          55
                      1/2
    %1 := sin(1/2 11    t)
```

```
                   1/2
%2 := cos(1/2 11   t)

              1/2
%3 := 1/2 (-2 + 11   ) t

              1/2
%4 := 1/2 (2 + 11   ) t
```

Thus, the Symbolic Math Toolbox allows us to find the analytical solutions for differential equations.

☐

Example 5.3.3.

Consider the series *RLC* circuit given in Figure 5.20. Find the analytical solution using MATLAB. Plot the circuitry dynamics assigning circuitry parameters and setting initial conditions.

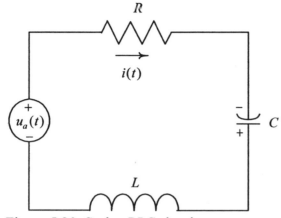

Figure 5.20. Series *RLC* circuit

Solution.

The state and control (*forcing* function) variables are used in the development of the mathematical model. Using the voltage across the capacitor and the current through the inductor as the state variables, and the supplied voltage $u_a(t)$ as the control, we have the following set of first-order differential equations:

$$C\frac{du_C}{dt} = i, \quad L\frac{di}{dt} = -u_C - Ri + u_a(t).$$

Hence, we have

$$\frac{du_C}{dt} = \frac{1}{C}i, \quad \frac{di}{dt} = \frac{1}{L}\left(-u_C - Ri + u_a(t)\right).$$

The analytical solution is found using the Symbolic Math Toolbox. In particular, for time-varying $u_a(t)$, we obtain

```
>> [V,I]=dsolve('DV=I/C','DI=(-V-R*I+Va(t))/L')

V =
-(-C*int(diff(Va(t),t)*exp(1/2/L*t*R)*exp(-1/2/C/L*t*(R^2*C^2-4*C*L)^(1/2)),t)*exp(-
1/2/L*t*R+1/2/C/L*t*(R^2*C^2-
4*C*L)^(1/2))+C*int(diff(Va(t),t)*exp(1/2/L*t*R)*exp(1/2/C/L*t*(R^2*C^2-
4*C*L)^(1/2)),t)*exp(-1/2/L*t*R-1/2/C/L*t*(R^2*C^2-4*C*L)^(1/2))-C1*exp(-
```

```
1/2/L*t*R+1/2/C/L*t*(R^2*C^2-4*C*L)^(1/2))*(R^2*C^2-4*C*L)^(1/2)-C2*exp(-1/2/L*t*R-
1/2/C/L*t*(R^2*C^2-4*C*L)^(1/2))*(R^2*C^2-4*C*L)^(1/2))/(R^2*C^2-4*C*L)^(1/2)

I =
-1/2*(int(diff(Va(t),t)*exp(1/2/L*t*R)*exp(-1/2/C/L*t*(R^2*C^2-
4*C*L)^(1/2)),t)*R*C*exp(-1/2/L*t*R+1/2/C/L*t*(R^2*C^2-4*C*L)^(1/2))-
int(diff(Va(t),t)*exp(1/2/L*t*R)*exp(1/2/C/L*t*(R^2*C^2-4*C*L)^(1/2)),t)*R*C*exp(-
1/2/L*t*R-1/2/C/L*t*(R^2*C^2-
4*C*L)^(1/2))+int(diff(Va(t),t)*exp(1/2/L*t*R)*exp(1/2/C/L*t*(R^2*C^2-
4*C*L)^(1/2)),t)*exp(-1/2/L*t*R-1/2/C/L*t*(R^2*C^2-4*C*L)^(1/2))*(R^2*C^2-
4*C*L)^(1/2)+exp(-1/2/L*t*R+1/2/C/L*t*(R^2*C^2-
4*C*L)^(1/2))*int(diff(Va(t),t)*exp(1/2/L*t*R)*exp(-1/2/C/L*t*(R^2*C^2-
4*C*L)^(1/2)),t)*(R^2*C^2-4*C*L)^(1/2)-2*Va(t)*(R^2*C^2-4*C*L)^(1/2)+C1*R*exp(-
1/2/L*t*R+1/2/C/L*t*(R^2*C^2-4*C*L)^(1/2))*(R^2*C^2-4*C*L)^(1/2)+C1*R^2*C*exp(-
1/2/L*t*R+1/2/C/L*t*(R^2*C^2-4*C*L)^(1/2))-4*C1*L*exp(-1/2/L*t*R+1/2/C/L*t*(R^2*C^2-
4*C*L)^(1/2))+C2*R*exp(-1/2/L*t*R-1/2/C/L*t*(R^2*C^2-4*C*L)^(1/2))*(R^2*C^2-
4*C*L)^(1/2)-C2*R^2*C*exp(-1/2/L*t*R-1/2/C/L*t*(R^2*C^2-4*C*L)^(1/2))+4*C2*L*exp(-
1/2/L*t*R-1/2/C/L*t*(R^2*C^2-4*C*L)^(1/2)))/(R^2*C^2-4*C*L)^(1/2)
```

If the applied voltage (forcing function) is constant $u_a(t) = const$, we have

```
>> [V,I]=dsolve('DV=I/C','DI=(-V-R*I+Va)/L')

V =
C1*exp(-1/2/L*t*R+1/2/C/L*t*(R^2*C^2-4*C*L)^(1/2))
+C2*exp(-1/2/L*t*R-1/2/C/L*t*(R^2*C^2-4*C*L)^(1/2))

I =
-1/2*(-2*Va*C+C1*R*exp(-1/2/L*t*R+1/2/C/L*t*(R^2*C^2-4*C*L)^(1/2))*C
+C1*(R^2*C^2-4*C*L)^(1/2)*exp(-1/2/L*t*R+1/2/C/L*t*(R^2*C^2-4*C*L)^(1/2))
+C2*R*exp(-1/2/L*t*R-1/2/C/L*t*(R^2*C^2-4*C*L)^(1/2))*C
-C2*(R^2*C^2-4*C*L)^(1/2)*exp(-1/2/L*t*R-1/2/C/L*t*(R^2*C^2-4*C*L)^(1/2)))/C
```

Assigning the values of the resistance, inductance, and capacitance to be $R = 50$ ohm, $L = 0.25$ H, and $C = 0.01$ F, for $u_a(t) = 10$ V, we obtain

```
>> % [V,I]=dsolve('DV=I/C','DI=(-V-R*I+Va)/L')
>> R=50, L=0.25, C=0.01, Va=10, [V,I]=dsolve('DV=I/0.01','DI=(-V-50*I+10)/0.25')

R =
    50
L =
    0.2500
C =
    0.0100
Va =
    10

V =
1/2*C1*exp(-20*(5+2*6^(1/2))*t)
-5/24*C1*6^(1/2)*exp(20*(-5+2*6^(1/2))*t)
+5/24*C1*6^(1/2)*exp(-20*(5+2*6^(1/2))*t)+1/2*C1*exp(20*(-5+2*6^(1/2))*t)-
1/120*C2*6^(1/2)*exp(20*(-5+2*6^(1/2))*t)+1/120*C2*6^(1/2)*exp(-20*(5+2*6^(1/2))*t)
I =
-10/(5+2*6^(1/2))/(-5+2*6^(1/2))-1/24*(5*C1*6^(1/2)*exp(20*(-5+2*6^(1/2))*t)
-5*C1*6^(1/2)*exp(-20*(5+2*6^(1/2))*t)+12*C2*exp(-20*(5+2*6^(1/2))*t)
+5*C2*6^(1/2)*exp(20*(-5+2*6^(1/2))*t)
-5*C2*6^(1/2)*exp(-20*(5+2*6^(1/2))*t)
+12*C2*exp(20*(-5+2*6^(1/2))*t))/(5+2*6^(1/2))/(-5+2*6^(1/2))
```

where the constants $C1$ and $C2$ must be found by using the initial conditions.

The initial conditions can be easily incorporated. Assigning the initial conditions to be $[25, -5]^T$, we obtain

```
>> % [V,I]=dsolve('DV=I/C','DI=(-V-R*I+Va)/L'); R=50; L=0.25; C=0.01; Va=10;
>> [V,I]=dsolve('DV=I/0.01','DI=(-V-50*I+10)/0.25', 'V(0)=25, I(0)=-5')

V =
-5/2*exp(-20*(5+2*6^(1/2))*t)+11/12*6^(1/2)*exp(20*(-5+2*6^(1/2))*t)-
11/12*6^(1/2)*exp(-20*(5+2*6^(1/2))*t)-5/2*exp(20*(-5+2*6^(1/2))*t)

I =
-10/(5+2*6^(1/2))/(-5+2*6^(1/2))-1/24*(50*6^(1/2)*exp(20*(-5+2*6^(1/2))*t)-
50*6^(1/2)*exp(-20*(5+2*6^(1/2))*t)+180*exp(-20*(5+2*6^(1/2))*t)
```

```
1180*exn(20*(-5+2*6^(1/2))*t))/(5+2*6^(1/2))/(-5+2*6^(1/2))
```
The derived expressions can be simplified using the simplify function. In particular, simplify(V) and simplify(I) are used as demonstrated here:
```
>> V simplify=simplify(V), I simplify=simplify(I)

V simplify =
-5/2*exp(-20*(5+2*6^(1/2))*t)+11/12*6^(1/2)*exp(20*(-5+2*6^(1/2))*t)-
11/12*6^(1/2)*exp(-20*(5+2*6^(1/2))*t)-5/2*exp(20*(-5+2*6^(1/2))*t)

I simplify =
5/12*(-24-5*6^(1/2)*exp(20*(-5+2*6^(1/2))*t)+5*6^(1/2)*exp(-20*(5+2*6^(1/2))*t)-
18*exp(-20*(5+2*6^(1/2))*t)-18*exp(20*(-5+2*6^(1/2))*t))/(5+2*6^(1/2))/(-5+2*6^(1/2))
```
The derived expression for $u_C(t)$ is

$$u_C(t) = -\frac{5}{2}e^{-20(5+2\sqrt{6})t} + \frac{11}{12}\sqrt{6}e^{20(-5+2\sqrt{6})t} - \frac{11}{12}\sqrt{6}e^{-20(5+2\sqrt{6})t} - \frac{5}{2}e^{20(-5+2\sqrt{6})t}.$$

Figure 5.21 documents the plots for $u_C(t)$ and $i(t)$ which are found using the following statement:
```
t=0:0.001:3;
I_simplify=5/12*(-24-5*6^(1/2)*exp(20*(-5+2*6^(1/2))*t)
+5*6^(1/2)*exp(-20*(5+2*6^(1/2))*t)-18*exp(-20*(5+2*6^(1/2))*t)
-18*exp(20*(-5+2*6^(1/2))*t))/(5+2*6^(1/2))/(-5+2*6^(1/2));
plot(t,I_simplify); hold;
V_simplify=-5/2*exp(-20*(5+2*6^(1/2))*t)
+11/12*6^(1/2)*exp(20*(-5+2*6^(1/2))*t)
-11/12*6^(1/2)*exp(-20*(5+2*6^(1/2))*t)-5/2*exp(20*(-5+2*6^(1/2))*t);
plot(t,V_simplify)
```

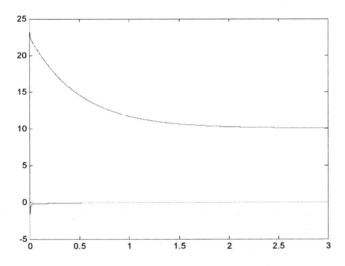

Figure 5.21. Dynamics for $u_C(t)$ and $i(t)$ □

The state-space modeling concept is widely used in simulation and analysis. The state, control (forcing function), and output variables are used. The state-space techniques are commonly applied in simulation and analysis of dynamic systems in the MATLAB environment. Mathematical models of dynamic systems are found in the form of linear and nonlinear differential equations. In general, a set of n first-order linear ordinary differential equations with n states $x \in \mathbb{R}^n$ and m controls (forcing functions) $u \in \mathbb{R}^m$ is written as [4]

$$\frac{dx}{dt} = \begin{bmatrix} \dfrac{dx_1}{dt} \\ \dfrac{dx_2}{dt} \\ \vdots \\ \dfrac{dx_{n-1}}{dt} \\ \dfrac{dx_n}{dt} \end{bmatrix} = \begin{bmatrix} a_{11} & a_{12} & \cdots & a_{1\,n-1} & a_{1n} \\ a_{21} & a_{22} & \cdots & a_{2\,n-1} & a_{2n} \\ \vdots & \vdots & \ddots & \vdots & \vdots \\ a_{n-1\,1} & a_{n-1\,2} & \cdots & a_{n-1\,n-1} & a_{n-1\,n} \\ a_{n1} & a_{n2} & \cdots & a_{n\,n-1} & a_{nn} \end{bmatrix} \begin{bmatrix} x_1 \\ x_2 \\ \vdots \\ x_{n-1} \\ x_n \end{bmatrix} + \begin{bmatrix} b_{11} & b_{12} & \cdots & b_{1\,m-1} & b_{1m} \\ b_{21} & b_{22} & \cdots & b_{2\,m-1} & b_{2m} \\ \vdots & \vdots & \ddots & \vdots & \vdots \\ b_{n-1\,1} & b_{n-1\,2} & \cdots & b_{n-1\,m-1} & b_{n-1\,m} \\ b_{n1} & b_{n2} & \cdots & b_{n\,m-1} & b_{nm} \end{bmatrix} \begin{bmatrix} u_1 \\ u_2 \\ \vdots \\ u_{m-1} \\ u_m \end{bmatrix} = Ax + Bu,$$

where $A \in \mathbb{R}^{n \times m}$ and $B \in \mathbb{R}^{n \times m}$ are the matrices of coefficients.

The output equation is expressed as

$$y = Hx + Du,$$

where $H \in \mathbb{R}^{b \times n}$ and $D \in \mathbb{R}^{b \times m}$ are the matrices of coefficients.

Nonlinear multivariable dynamic systems are modeled by a set of n first-order nonlinear differential equations

$$\frac{dx}{dt} = F(t,x,u),\ x(t_0) = x_0,$$

where t is the time; $F(t,x,u)$ is the nonlinear function.

In the first section of this chapter we considered the aircraft. The aircraft outputs are the Euler angles, and the fighter is controlled by deflecting the control surfaces. The multi-input (eight control surfaces) - multi-output (three Euler angles θ, ϕ, and ψ to be controlled) nature is obvious. The pilot assigns the desired Euler angles r_θ, r_ϕ, and r_ψ (pedal and stick reference commands). Using the errors between the reference vector $r = \begin{bmatrix} r_\theta \\ r_\phi \\ r_\psi \end{bmatrix}$ and output vector $y = \begin{bmatrix} \theta \\ \phi \\ \psi \end{bmatrix}$, as

defined by $e = r - y = \begin{bmatrix} r_\theta \\ r_\phi \\ r_\psi \end{bmatrix} - \begin{bmatrix} \theta \\ \phi \\ \psi \end{bmatrix}$, the controller $u = \Pi(e,x)$ calculates the control inputs (control

surface deflections). The aircraft outputs (θ, ϕ and ψ) can be obtained by using the state variables (v, α, q, θ, β, p, r, ϕ and ψ).

Figure 5.22 shows the block diagram representation of the multivariable aircraft with nine states $x \in \mathbb{R}^9$ ($v, \alpha, q, \theta, \beta, p, r, \phi, \psi$), eight control surfaces $u \in \mathbb{R}^8$ (right and left horizontal stabilizers, right and left leading- and trailing-edge flaps, right and left rudders), three outputs $y \in \mathbb{R}^3$ (θ, ϕ, ψ), and three reference inputs $r \in \mathbb{R}^3$ (r_θ, r_ϕ, r_ψ) [4].

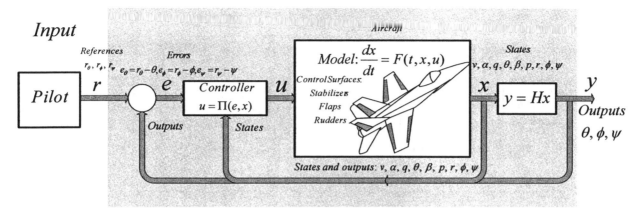

Figure 5.22. Block diagram representation of a multi-input/multi-output aircraft

The functional block diagram of nonlinear multivariable dynamic systems (n states, m controls, b reference inputs, and b outputs), which are described by

state-space equation $\quad \dfrac{dx}{dt} = F(t,x,u), x(t_0) = x_0$

output equation $\quad\quad y = Hx$,

is illustrated in Figure 5.23.

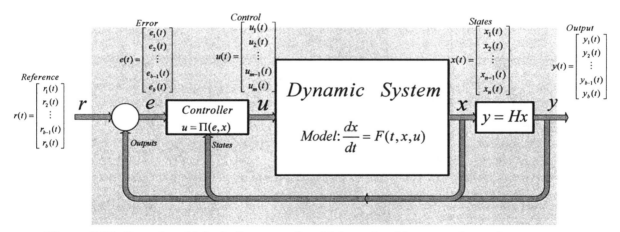

Figure 5.23. Functional block diagram of multi-input/multi-output dynamic systems

Example 5.3.4.
Consider the aircraft described by the sate-space differential equations
$\dot{x} = Ax + Bu$, $y = Hx + Du$,

$$\frac{dx}{dt} = \begin{bmatrix} \dfrac{dx_1}{dt} \\ \dfrac{dx_2}{dt} \\ \dfrac{dx_3}{dt} \\ \dfrac{dx_4}{dt} \\ \dfrac{dx_5}{dt} \\ \dfrac{dx_6}{dt} \end{bmatrix} = Ax + Bu = A\begin{bmatrix} x_1 \\ x_2 \\ x_3 \\ x_4 \\ x_5 \\ x_6 \end{bmatrix} + Bu, \ y = Hx + Du = H\begin{bmatrix} x_1 \\ x_2 \\ x_3 \\ x_4 \\ x_5 \\ x_6 \end{bmatrix} + Du$$

where

$$A = \begin{bmatrix} -20 & -150 & -1000 & -5000 & -12500 & -15000 \\ 1 & 0 & 0 & 0 & 0 & 0 \\ 0 & 1 & 0 & 0 & 0 & 0 \\ 0 & 0 & 1 & 0 & 0 & 0 \\ 0 & 0 & 0 & 1 & 0 & 0 \\ 0 & 0 & 0 & 0 & 1 & 0 \end{bmatrix}, B = \begin{bmatrix} 1 \\ 0 \\ 0 \\ 0 \\ 0 \\ 0 \end{bmatrix}, H = \begin{bmatrix} 0 & 0 & 0 & 0 & 0 & 1 \end{bmatrix} \text{and } D = [0]$$

Perform numerical simulations using the lsim MATLAB solver.

Solution.

The description of the lsim solver is given below.

```
>> help lsim
 LSIM   Simulate time response of LTI models to arbitrary inputs.

    LSIM(SYS,U,T) plots the time response of the LTI model SYS to the
    input signal described by U and T.  The time vector T consists of
    regularly spaced time samples and U is a matrix with as many columns
    as inputs and whose i-th row specifies the input value at time T(i).
    For example,
            t = 0:0.01:5;   u = sin(t);   lsim(sys,u,t)
    simulates the response of a single-input model SYS to the input
    u(t)=sin(t) during 5 seconds.

    For discrete-time models, U should be sampled at the same rate as SYS
    (T is then redundant and can be omitted or set to the empty matrix).
    For continuous-time models, choose the sampling period T(2)-T(1) small
    enough to accurately describe the input U.  LSIM issues a warning when
    U is undersampled and hidden oscillations may occur.

    LSIM(SYS,U,T,X0) specifies the initial state vector X0 at time T(1)
    (for state-space models only).  X0 is set to zero when omitted.

    LSIM(SYS1,SYS2,...,U,T,X0) simulates the response of multiple LTI
    models SYS1,SYS2,... on a single plot.  The initial condition X0
    is optional.  You can also specify a color, line style, and marker
    for each system, as in
       lsim(sys1,'r',sys2,'y--',sys3,'gx',u,t).

    Y = LSIM(SYS,U,T) returns the output history Y.  No plot is drawn on
    the screen.  The matrix Y has LENGTH(T) rows and as many columns as
    outputs in SYS.  For state-space models,
       [Y,T,X] = LSIM(SYS,U,T,X0)
    also returns the state trajectory X, a matrix with LENGTH(T) rows
    and as many columns as states.

    For continuous-time models,
       LSIM(SYS,U,T,X0,'zoh')  or  LSIM(SYS,U,T,X0,'foh')
    explicitly specifies how the input values should be interpolated
```

```
between samples (zero-order hold or linear interpolation).  By
default, LSIM selects the interpolation method automatically based
on the smoothness of the signal U.

See also GENSIG, STEP, IMPULSE, INITIAL, LTIMODELS.
```

Using this description, we download four matrices, e.g.,

```
A=[-15 -150 -1100 -4500 -12500 -15000;
     1    0     0     0      0      0;
     0    1     0     0      0      0;
     0    0     1     0      0      0;
     0    0     0     1      0      0;
     0    0     0     0      1      0];
B=[1 0 0 0 0 0]';
H=[0 0 0 0 0 1];
D=[0];
```

enter the simulation duration as 5 seconds, assign the step input (command), and letting the initial conditions for six variables be $[1\ 5\ 0\ -5\ -10\ -20\ ]^T$

```
t=0:.01:5; u=ones(size(t)); x0=[0 10 50 100 -50 -10];
```

Typing In the Command Window

```
>> [y,x]=lsim(A,B,H,D,u,t,x0); plot(t,x)
```

and pressing the Enter key, the transient dynamics of the aircraft result. Figure 5.24 represents the aircraft's state variable behavior. If one needs to plot the output transient, it can be done using the following statement:

```
>> plot(t,y)
```

The resulting plot is illustrated in Figure 5.24.

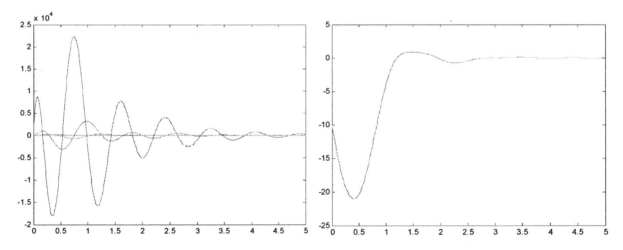

Figure 5.24. State variables and output evolutions due to step input and initial conditions

The "system" methodology is illustrated for the example under consideration. In particular, we use the help lsim. The user can define the "system" with six state variables, one control, and one output. Then, using the lsim solver, we numerically simulate the "systems" and find the output responses due to the initial conditions and unit step input.

```
States={'x1' 'x2' 'x3' 'x4' 'x5' 'x6'}
Control={'u'}
Output={'y'}
A=[-15 -150 -1100 -4500 -12500 -15000;
     1    0     0     0      0      0;
```

```
        0    1    0    0    0    0;
        0    0    1    0    0    0;
        0    0    0    1    0    0;
        0    0    0    0    1    0];
B=[1 0 0 0 0 0]';
H=[0 0 0 0 0 1];
D=[0];
System=ss(A,B,H,D,'statename',States,'inputname',Control,'outputname',Output);
System
t=0:.01:5; u=ones(size(t)); x0=[0 10 50 100 -50 -10];
lsim(System,u,t);plot(t,y); pause
step(System); % step response with zero initial conditions
```

The following system description results in the Command Window

```
States =
    'x1'    'x2'    'x3'    'x4'    'x5'    'x6'

Control =
    'u'

Output =
    'y'

a =
                x1          x2          x3          x4          x5          x6
    x1         -15        -150       -1100       -4500   -1.25e+004   -1.5e+004
    x2           1           0           0           0           0           0
    x3           0           1           0           0           0           0
    x4           0           0           1           0           0           0
    x5           0           0           0           1           0           0
    x6           0           0           0           0           1           0

b =
        u
    x1  1
    x2  0
    x3  0
    x4  0
    x5  0
    x6  0

c =
        x1 x2 x3 x4 x5 x6
    y    0  0  0  0  0  1

d =
        u
    y   0
```

Continuous-time model.

The resulting dynamics are documented in Figure 5.25.

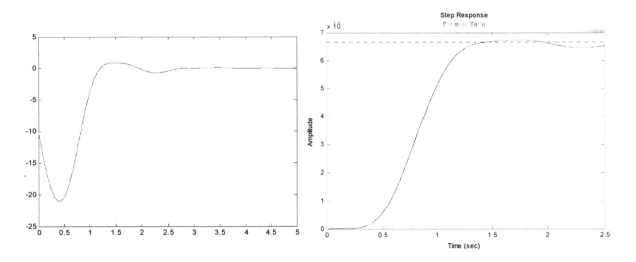

Figure 5.25. Output dynamics due to initial conditions and unit step input

Example 5.3.5.

Using the state-space concept, develop the state-space model of the series *RLC* circuit illustrated in Figure 5.26. The voltage across the capacitor is the circuit output. Find matrices *A*, *B*, *H*, and *D* of the state-space model and the output equation. Perform numerical simulations in MATLAB assigning the following parameters: $R = 1$ ohm, $L = 0.1$ H, and $C = 0.5$ F.

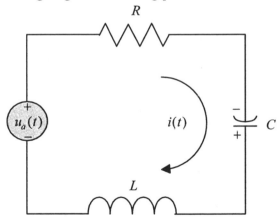

Figure 5.26. *RLC* circuit

Solution.

Using Kirchhoff's law, which gives the following equations

$$C\frac{du_C}{dt} = i \ \text{ and } \ L\frac{di}{dt} = -u_C - Ri + u_a(t),$$

a set of two first-order differential equations to model the circuitry dynamics is found to be

$$\frac{du_C}{dt} = \frac{1}{C}i,$$

$$\frac{di}{dt} = \frac{1}{L}\big(-u_C - Ri + u_a(t)\big).$$

The state and control variables are denoted as
$$x_1(t) = u_C(t),\ x_2(t) = i(t)\ \text{and}\ u(t) = u_a(t).$$
Thus, we have

$$\frac{dx}{dt} = \begin{bmatrix} \dfrac{dx_1}{dt} \\ \dfrac{dx_2}{dt} \end{bmatrix} = \begin{bmatrix} \dfrac{du_C}{dt} \\ \dfrac{di}{dt} \end{bmatrix} = \begin{bmatrix} 0 & \dfrac{1}{C} \\ -\dfrac{1}{L} & -\dfrac{R}{L} \end{bmatrix} \begin{bmatrix} u_C \\ i \end{bmatrix} + \begin{bmatrix} 0 \\ \dfrac{1}{L} \end{bmatrix} u_a = Ax + Bu.$$

The matrices of coefficients are found to be $A = \begin{bmatrix} 0 & \dfrac{1}{C} \\ -\dfrac{1}{L} & -\dfrac{R}{L} \end{bmatrix}$ and $B = \begin{bmatrix} 0 \\ \dfrac{1}{L} \end{bmatrix}$.

The voltage across the capacitor is the output. Hence, $y(t) = u_C(t)$. The output equation is

$$y = \begin{bmatrix} 1 & 0 \end{bmatrix} \begin{bmatrix} u_C \\ i \end{bmatrix} = [0]u_a = Hx + Du,$$

where $H = \begin{bmatrix} 1 & 0 \end{bmatrix}$ and $D = [0]$.

The simulation is performed assigning R = 1 ohm, L = 0.1 H, and C = 0.5 F. Correspondingly, we find the numerical values for matrices to be

$$A = \begin{bmatrix} 0 & \dfrac{1}{C} \\ -\dfrac{1}{L} & -\dfrac{R}{L} \end{bmatrix} = \begin{bmatrix} 0 & 2 \\ -10 & -10 \end{bmatrix},\ B = \begin{bmatrix} 0 \\ \dfrac{1}{L} \end{bmatrix} = \begin{bmatrix} 0 \\ 10 \end{bmatrix},\ H = \begin{bmatrix} 1 & 0 \end{bmatrix},\ \text{and}\ D = [0].$$

To perform numerical simulations, we download these four matrices:
```
>> A=[0 2; -10 -10], B=[0 10]', H=[1 0], D=[0]
```
These matrices are stored in the memory, and the following matrices are displayed:
```
A =
       0      2
     -10    -10
B =
       0
      10
H =
       1      0
D =
       0
```
Assigning the simulation duration to be 2 seconds, assigning the step input (command) with the magnitude 10, and letting the initial conditions be $[-5\ -10\ ]^T$, we type
```
>> t=0:.001:2; u=10*ones(size(t)); x0=[-5 -10];
```
Typing in the Command Window
```
>> [y,x]=lsim(A,B,H,D,u,t,x0); plot(t,x)
```
and pressing the Enter key, the transient dynamics of the circuit result. Figure 5.27 represents the states variable behavior. If we need to plot the output transient (*y*) and the input command (*u*), the user types the following statements:
```
>> plot(t,y), hold, plot(t,u,'+')
```
or
```
>> plot(t,y,t,u,'+')
```
The plots are shown in Figure 5.27.

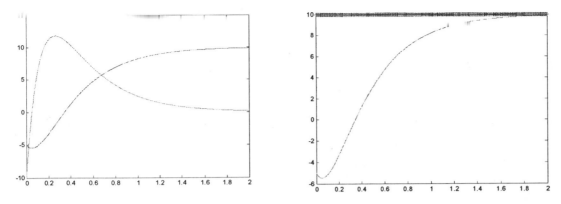

Figure 5.27. State variables and output behavior due to input function and initial conditions

□

Example 5.3.6. Mathematical model of permanent-magnet direct-current motors

Develop a mathematical model and build an *s*-domain block diagram for permanent-magnet DC motors. A schematic diagram of a permanent-magnet DC machine (motor and generator operation) is illustrated in Figure 5.28 [3]. Perform numerical simulations for a permanent-magnet DC motor in MATLAB assigning the following motor parameters: $r_a = 1$ ohm, $k_a = 0.1$, $L_a = 0.01$ H, $B_m = 0.005$ and $J = 0.001$ kg-m^2.

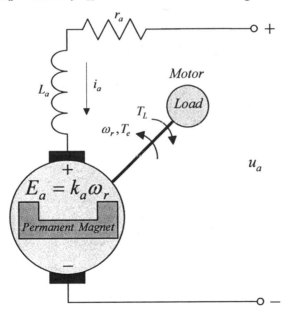

Figure 5.28. Schematic diagram of a permanent-magnet DC motor

Solution.

The flux, established by the permanent magnets, is constant. Applying Kirchhoff's voltage and Newton's second laws, the differential equations for permanent-magnet DC motors are derived using the motor representation documented in Figure 5.28. Denoting the *back emf* and *torque* constants as k_a, we have the following differential equations describing the armature winding and *torsional-mechanical* dynamics [3, 4]:

$$\frac{di_a}{dt} = -\frac{r_a}{L_a}i_a - \frac{k_a}{L_a}\omega_r + \frac{1}{L_a}u_a, \quad \text{(motor circuitry dynamics)}$$

$$\frac{d\omega_r}{dt} = \frac{k_a}{J}i_a - \frac{B_m}{J}\omega_r - \frac{1}{J}T_L. \quad \text{(\textit{torsional-mechanical} dynamics)}$$

Augmenting these two first-order differential equations, in the state-space form we have

$$\begin{bmatrix} \dfrac{di_a}{dt} \\ \dfrac{d\omega_r}{dt} \end{bmatrix} = \begin{bmatrix} -\dfrac{r_a}{L_a} & -\dfrac{k_a}{L_a} \\ \dfrac{k_a}{J} & -\dfrac{B_m}{J} \end{bmatrix} \begin{bmatrix} i_a \\ \omega_r \end{bmatrix} + \begin{bmatrix} \dfrac{1}{L_a} \\ 0 \end{bmatrix} u_a - \begin{bmatrix} 0 \\ \dfrac{1}{J} \end{bmatrix} T_L.$$

An *s*-domain block diagram of permanent-magnet DC motors is developed and shown in Figure 5.29 (this block-diagram is of particular importance if we use SIMULINK).

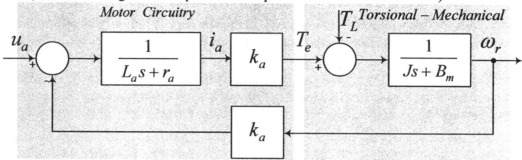

Figure 5.29. Block diagram of permanent-magnet DC motors

As assigned, the simulation is performed assuming the following parameters: $r_a = 1$, $k_a = 0.1$, $L_a = 0.01$, $B_m = 0.005$ and $J = 0.001$. Taking note that the motor output is the angular velocity, we use the following matrices:

$$A = \begin{bmatrix} -100 & -10 \\ 100 & -5 \end{bmatrix}, \ B = \begin{bmatrix} 100 \\ 0 \end{bmatrix}, \ H = \begin{bmatrix} 0 & 1 \end{bmatrix} \text{ and } D = [0].$$

To perform numerical simulations, we download these matrices:

```
>> A=[-100 -10; 100 5], B=[100 0]', H=[0 1], D=[0]
```

Assigning the simulation duration to be 1 second, letting the applied voltage be 10 V ($u_a = 10$ V), and setting the initial conditions for two variables to be $[0 \ 0]^T$ ($i_a = 0$ A and $\omega_r = 0$ rad/sec), we type in the Command Window

```
>> t=0:.001:1; u=10*ones(size(t)); x0=[0 0];
>> [y,x]=lsim(A,B,H,D,u,t,x0);
>> plot(t,x); xlabel('Time (seconds)'); title('Angular velocity and current');
```

The motor state variables are plotted in Figure 5.30, e.g., two states $i_a(t)$ and $\omega_r(t)$ are documented. The simulation results illustrate that the motor reaches the angular velocity 200 rad/sec within 1 sec.

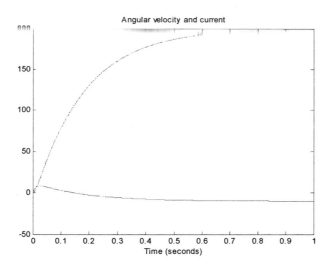

Figure 5.30. Motor state variables dynamical behavior of $i_a(t)$ and $\omega_r(t)$ states

The simulation of permanent-magnet DC motors is also reported in Examples 6.2.2 and 6.2.6 using SIMULINK.   □

REFERENCES

1. *MATLAB 6.5 Release 13,* CD-ROM, MathWorks, Inc., 2002.
2. Kuo, B. C., *Automatic Control Systems*, Prentice Hall, Englewood Cliffs, NJ, 1995.
3. Lyshevski, S. E., *Electromechanical Systems, Electric Machines, and Applied Mechatronics*, CRC Press, Boca Raton, FL, 2000.
4. Lyshevski, S. E., *Control Systems Theory with Engineering Applications*, Birchauser, Boston, MA, 2002.
5. Ogata, K., *Modern Control Engineering*, Prentice-Hall, Upper Saddle River, NJ, 2001.

Chapter 6

SIMULINK

6.1. Introduction to SIMULINK

SIMULINK (interactive computing package for simulating and analyzing differential equations, mathematical models, and dynamic systems) is a part of the MATLAB environment [1]. SIMILINK is a graphical mouse-driven program that allows one to numerically simulate and analyze systems by developing and manipulating blocks and diagrams. It is applied to linear, nonlinear, continuous-time, discrete-time, multivariable, multirate, and hybrid equations and systems. Blocksets are built-in blocks in SIMULINK that provide a full comprehensive block library for different system components, and C-code from block diagrams is generated using the Real-time Workshop Toolbox. SIMULINK is widely used for nonlinear simulations and data-intensive analysis of continuous-time (analog), discrete-time (discrete), and hybrid systems. Using a mouse-driven block-diagram interface, the SIMULINK diagrams (models) are created and edited. These block diagrams (`mdl` models) represent systems modeled in the form of linear and nonlinear differential and difference equations which describe the system dynamics [1 - 5]. Hybrid and discrete-even systems are straightforwardly simulated, analyzed, and visualized. The distinct advantage is that SIMULINK provides a graphical user interface (GUI) for building models (block diagrams) using "click-and-drag" mouse-based operations.

A comprehensive and complete block library of sinks, sources, linear and nonlinear components (elements), connectors, as well as customized blocks (S-functions) provide great flexibility, immense interactability, superior efficiency, robustness, and excellent prototyping features making use of both top-down and bottom-up approaches. For example, complex system can be built using high- and low-level blocks (double-clicking on blocks provides access to the low-level blocks). It was illustrated in the previous chapter that systems can be numerically simulated (solving differential equations) using a wide choice of methods applying the `ode` solvers. Different methods and algorithms can be used in SIMULINK as well. However, one interacts using the SIMULINK menus rather than entering the commands and functions in MATLAB Command Window. The easy-to-use SIMULINK menus are particularly convenient for interactive design, simulations, analysis, and visualization.

To run SIMULINK, we type in the Command Window

```
>> simulink
```

and presses the Enter key.

Alternatively, click on the SIMULINK icon .

The window shown in Figure 6.1 appears.

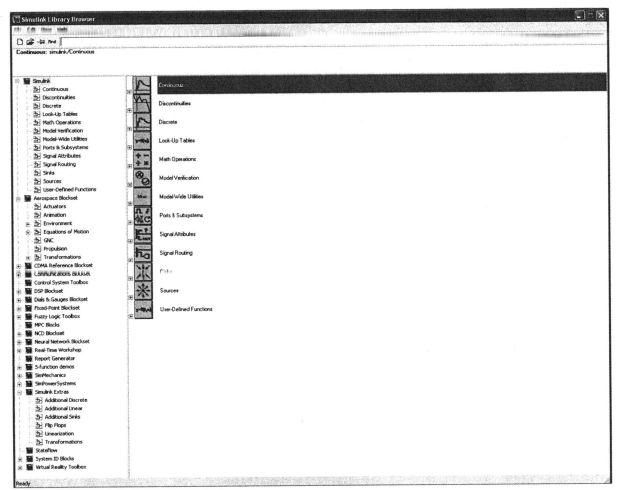

Figure 6.1. SIMULINK window

To run SIMULINK demonstration programs, type

```
>> demo simulink
```

The SIMULINK demo window is documented in Figure 6.2.

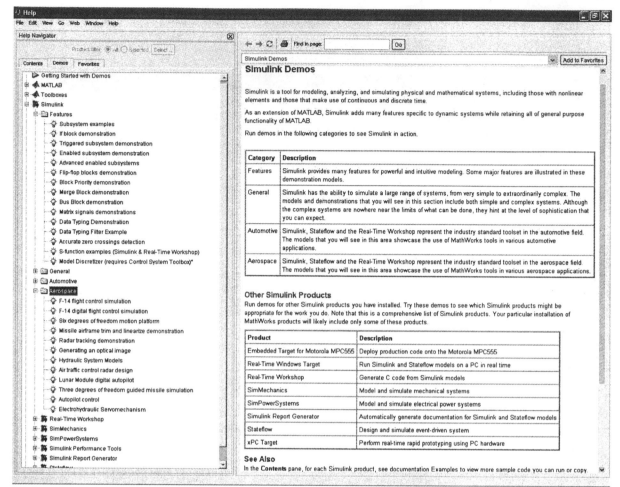

Figure 6.2. SIMULINK demo window

To analyze, model, and simulate continuous- and discrete-time dynamic systems (described by nonlinear differential and difference equations) block diagrams are used, and SIMULINK notably extends the MATLAB environment. SIMULINK offers a large variety of ready-to-use building blocks to build mathematical models. One can learn and explore SIMULINK using the SIMULINK and MATLAB Demos. Users who do not have enough experience within SIMULINK will find a great deal of help using these MATLAB and SIMULINK Demos. After double-clicking Simulink in the MATLAB Demos, the subtopics become available as shown in Figure 6.2. It must be emphasized that different MATLAB and SIMULINK releases are available and accessible to users. Figures 6.1 and 6.2 represent SIMULINK windows for MATLAB 6.5, while Figure 6.3 represents the MATLAB 6.1 release. Though there are some differences, the similarity and coherence should be appreciated.

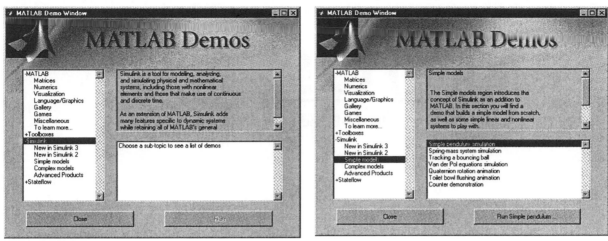

Figure 6.3. MATLAB 6.1 demos: SIMULINK package

The SIMULINK documentation and user manuals are available in the Portable Document Format (pdf). The the `help` folder C:\MATLAB6p5\help\pdf_doc\simulink includes the user manuals. The pdf files (SIMULINK manuals) in the `simulink` subfolder are shown in Figure 6.4.

Figure 6.4. SIMULINK user manuals in the `simulink` subfolder

These user-friendly manuals can be accessed and printed, and this chapter does not attempt to rewrite the excellent SIMULINK user manuals. For example, a *SIMULINK: Model-Based and System-Based Design* user manual consists of 476 pages. The front page of the manual is documented in Figure 6.5 [1].

Model-Based and System-Based Design

Modeling

Simulation

Implementation

Using Simulink

Version 5

Figure 6.5. Front page of the *SIMULINK: Model-Based and System-Based Design* user manual

With the ultimate goal of providing supplementary coverage and educating the reader in how to solve practical problems, our introduction to SIMULINK has step-by-step instructions as well as practical examples. A good starting point is simple models (see Figure 6.1). Simple pendulum and spring-mass system simulations, tracking a bouncing ball, van der Pol equations simulations (covered in Chapter 5 using the MATLAB ode solvers), as well as other examples are available. Many examples have been already examined in this book. Therefore, let us start with a familiar example, in particular, van der Pol equations.

Example 6.1.1. Van der Pol differential equations simulations in SIMULINK
In SIMULINK simulate the van der Pol oscillator which is described by the second-order nonlinear differential equation

$$\frac{d^2x}{dt^2} - k\left(1 - x^2\right)\frac{dx}{dt} + x = d(t),$$

where $d(t)$ is the forcing function.

Let $k = 10$, $d(t) = 10\mathrm{rect}(2t)$, and $x_0 = \begin{bmatrix} x_{10} \\ x_{20} \end{bmatrix} = \begin{bmatrix} -2 \\ 2 \end{bmatrix}$.

Solution.

The second-order van der Pol differential equation is rewritten as a system of coupled first-order differential equations

$$\frac{dx_1(t)}{dt} = x_2, x_1(t_0) = x_{10},$$

$$\frac{dx_2(t)}{dt} = -x_1 + kx_2 - kx_1^2 x_2 + d(t), x_2(t_0) = x_{20}.$$

It should be emphasized that differential equations for the van der Pol oscillator used in Chapter 5

$$\frac{dx_1(t)}{dt} = x_2, x_1(t_0) = x_{10}, \frac{dx_2(t)}{dt} = \mu\left[(1 - x_1^2)x_2 - x_1\right], x_2(t_0) = x_{20},$$

correspond to this example.

The SIMULINK block diagram (`mdl` model) is built using the following blocks: Signal Generator, Gain, Integrator, Sum, and Scope (Figure 6.6).

Simulation of the transient dynamics was performed assigning $k = 10$ and $d(t) = 10\mathrm{rect}(2t)$. The coefficient, forcing function, and initial conditions must be downloaded.

The coefficient k can be assigned by double-clicking the Gain block and entering the value needed, or typing k in the Gain block as illustrated in Figure 6.6.

By double-clicking the Signal Generator block we select the square function and assign the corresponding magnitude 10 and frequency 2 Hz (Figure 6.6).

The initial conditions $x_0 = \begin{bmatrix} x_{10} \\ x_{20} \end{bmatrix} = \begin{bmatrix} -2 \\ 2 \end{bmatrix}$ are assigned by double-clicking the Integrator

blocks and typing x10 and x20 (the specified values for x10 and x20 are convenient to download in the Command Window). Hence, in the Command Window we type
```
>> k=10; x10=-2; x20=2;
```
Specifying the simulation time to be 15 seconds (see Figure 6.6 where the simulation

parameters window is illustrated), the SIMULINK `mdl` model is run by clicking the ▶ icon.

The simulation results are illustrated in Figure 6.6 (behaviors of two variables are displayed by two Scopes).

The plotting statements can be used, and in the Scopes we use the Data history and Scope properties assigning the variable names. We use the following variables: x1 and x2. Then, the designer types
```
>> plot(x(:,1),x(:,2))
>> plot(x1(:,1),x1(:,2))
```
The resulting plots are illustrated in Figure 6.7.

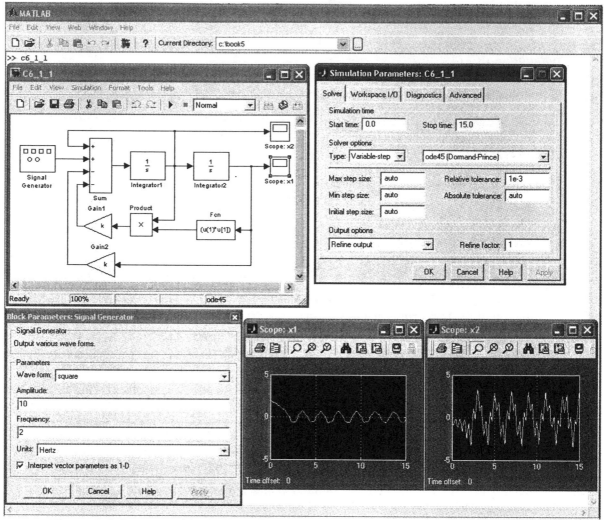

Figure 6.6. SIMULINK block diagram (c6_1_1.mdl)

Transient behavior for x_1 Transient behavior for x_2

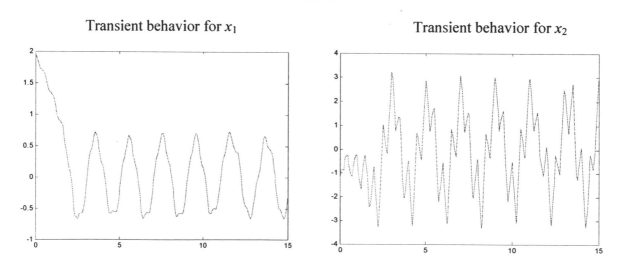

Figure 6.7. Dynamics of the state variables

Many illustrative and valuable examples are given in the MATLAB and SIMULINK demos, and the van der Pol equations simulations are covered. By double-clicking the van der Pol equations simulation, the SIMULINK block diagram appears as shown in Figure 6.8. In particular, we simulate the following differential equations:

$$\frac{dx_1(t)}{dt} = x_2, \quad \frac{dx_2(t)}{dt} = -x_1 + x_2 - x_1^2 x_2.$$

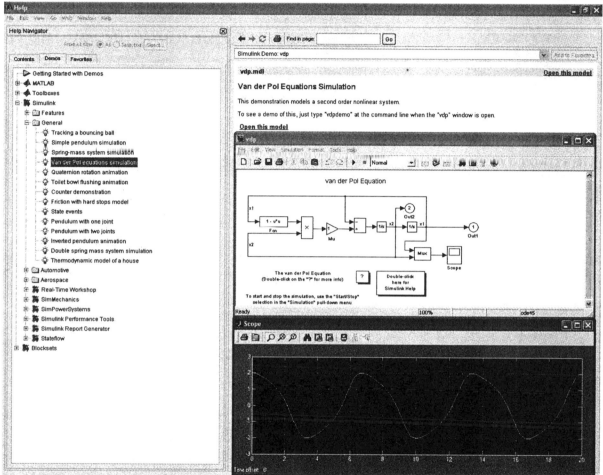

Figure 6.8. SIMULINK demo window, block diagram to simulate the van der Pol equations, and scope with the simulation results

Example 6.1.2. Simple pendulum
Simulate a simple pendulum, studied in Example 5.2.2, using the SIMULINK demo.
Solution.
Double clicking the simple pendulum simulation in the SIMULINK demo library, the SIMULINK block diagram (model window that contains this system) appears. This `mdl` model (block diagram) is documented in Figure 6.9.

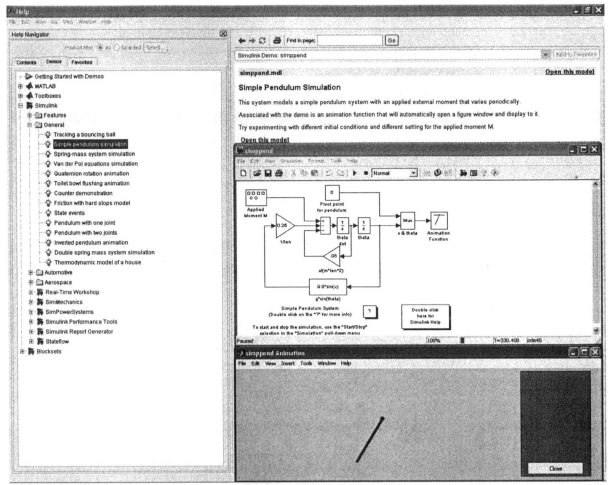

Figure 6.9. SIMULINK demo window and block diagram to simulate a simple pendulum as well as perform animation

The equations of motion for a simple pendulum were derived in Example 5.2.2 using Newton's second law of rotational motion. In particular, we found that the following two first-order differential equations describe the pendulum dynamics:

$$\frac{d\omega}{dt} = \frac{1}{J}\left(-mgl\sin\theta + T_a - B_m\omega\right),\ \frac{d\theta}{dt} = \omega\ .$$

The moment of inertia is given by $J = ml^2$. Hence, we have

$$\frac{d\omega}{dt} = -\frac{g}{l}\sin\theta + \frac{1}{ml^2}T_a,$$

$$\frac{d\theta}{dt} = \omega\ .$$

These equations are clearly used in the SIMULINK block diagram documented in Figure 6.9. We simulate the pendulum by clicking Simulation, and then clicking Start (Start button on the SIMULINK toolbar) or clicking the ▶ icon. As the simulation runs, the animation that visualizes the pendulum swing becomes available (Figure 6.9).

All demo SIMULINK models can be modified. For example, since we use the differential equations, which simulate the pendulum dynamics, the state variables (angular velocity ω and displacement θ) can be plotted. We use two `Scopes` and `XY Graph` blocks (Sinks SIMULINK blocks), and the resulting modified SIMULINK block diagram is documented in Figure 6.10. As illustrated in Figure 6.10, we set the "Stop time" to be 60 seconds.

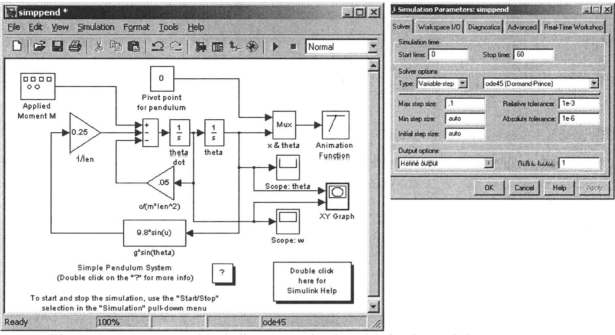

Figure 6.10. SIMULINK block diagram to simulate the simple pendulum

The resulting dynamics and the xy plot are illustrated by the two `Scopes` and `XY Graph` blocks. In particular, the simulation results are shown in Figure 6.11.

Scope: theta (θ)   Scope: w (ω)   XY Graph

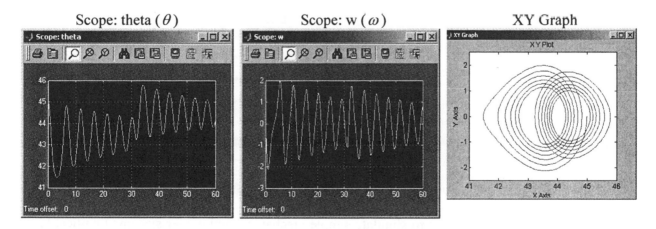

Figure 6.11. Simulation results for the simple pendulum

To start, stop or pause the simulation, the Start, Stop, and Pause buttons are available in the Simulation menu (Start, Stop, and Pause buttons can be clicked on the toolbar as well).

One can open SIMULINK, Aerospace, CDMA, Communication, DSP, other Blocksets, as well as the Control System Toolbox, Fuzzy Logic Toolbox, Real-Time Workshop, SIMULINK Extra, System ID (identification) Blocks, etc. Figure 6.12 documents the SIMULINK Library Browser accessible by clicking the Continuous, Math Operation, and Sinks SIMULINK libraries.

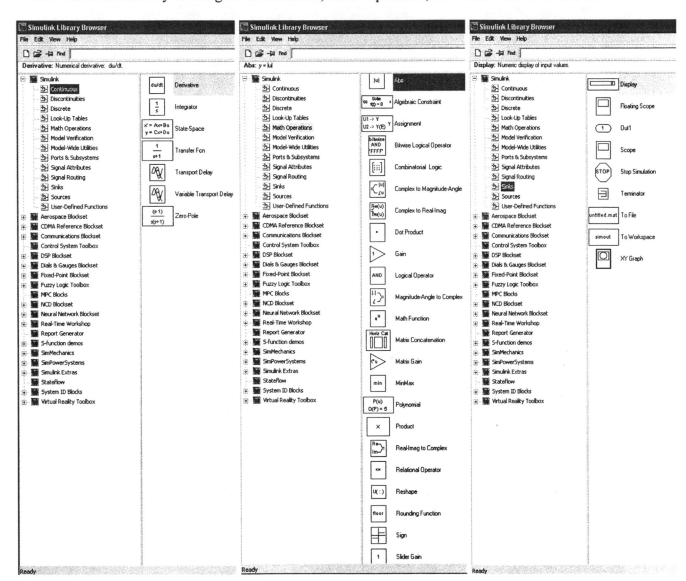

Figure 6.12. Continuous, Math Operation, and Sinks SIMULINK libraries

The SIMULINK libraries to simulate simple mechanical and power systems (applicable for educational purposes) are available: see SimMechanics (Sensors & Actuators) and SimPowerSystems (Elements) illustrated in Figure 6.13.

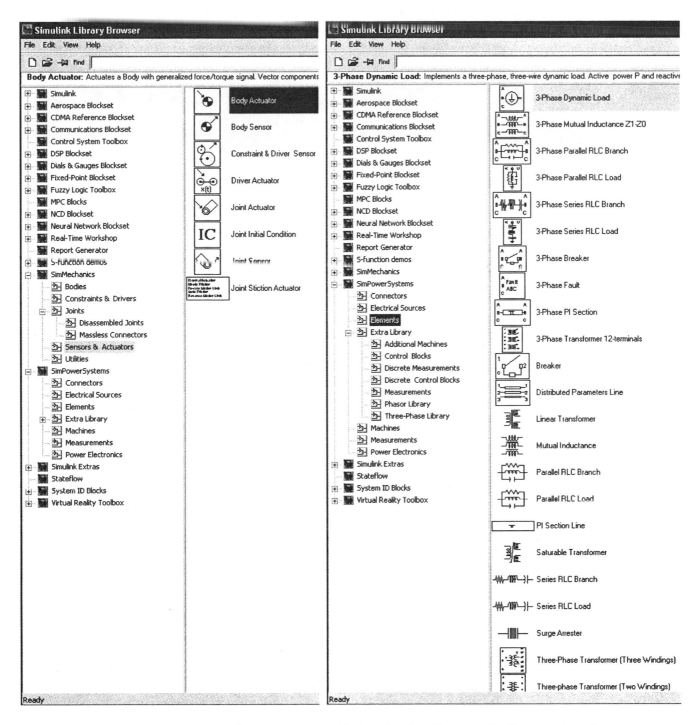

Figure 6.13. SIMULINK Library Browser: SimMechanics (Sensors & Actuators) and SimPowerSystems (Elements)

It was emphasized that the SIMULINK windows are different for distinct MATLAB releases. Figure 6.14 illustrates MATLAB 6.1. By clicking on Simulink and Simulink extra, and then opening the Continuous, one has SIMULINK Library Browsers as documented in Figures 6.14.

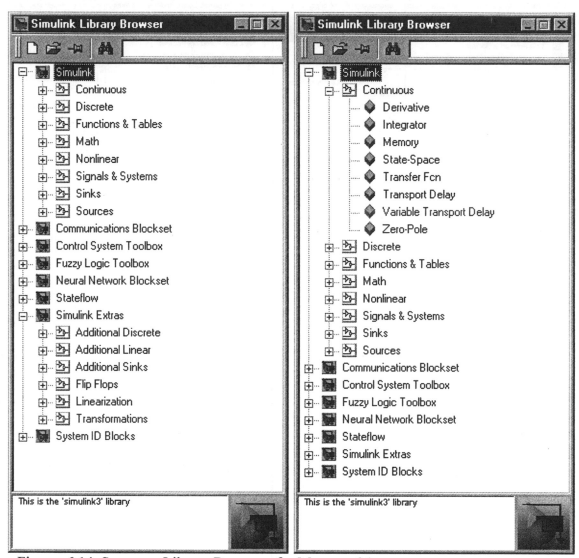

Figures 6.14. SIMULINK Library Browsers for MATLAB 6.1

In addition to Continuous, the designer can open the Discrete, Function & Tables, Math, Nonlinear, Signal & Systems, Sinks, Sources, and other block libraries by double-clicking the corresponding icon. Ready-to-use building blocks commonly applied in analysis and design of dynamic systems become available.

6.2. Engineering and Scientific Computations Using SIMULINK with Examples

To demonstrate how to effectively use SIMULINK, this section covers examples in numerical simulations of dynamic systems. We start with the illustrative examples in aerospace and automotive applications available in the SIMULINK demos illustrated in Figures 6.15 (MATLAB 6.5) and 6.16 (MATLAB 6.1), which can be accessed by typing `demo simulink` in the Command Window and pressing the Enter key.

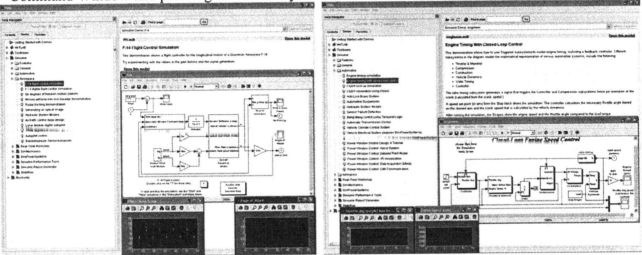

Figure 6.15. SIMULINK demo with automotive and aerospace applications examples: MATLAB 6.5

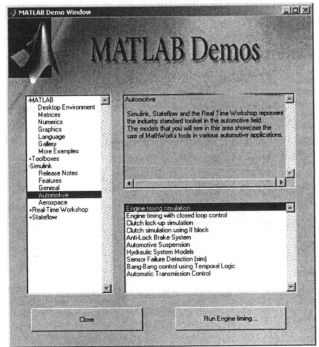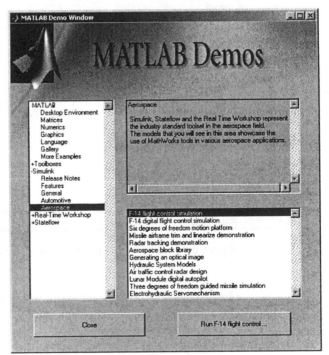

Figure 6.16. SIMULINK demo with automotive and aerospace applications examples: MATLAB 6.1

By double-clicking on the `F14 flight control simulation`, the SIMULINK block diagram (`mdl` model) illustrated in Figure 6.15 is displayed. The simulation results are documented in Figure 6.15. This SIMULINK block diagram was developed using the differential equations which describe the aircraft dynamics. Having emphasized the importance of the demonstration features, let us master SIMULINK through illustrative examples.

Illustrative Example: Simple problem
In SIMULINK simulate the system modeled by the following two linear differential equations:

$$\frac{dx_1(t)}{dt} = -k_1 x_1(t) + u(t), \ x_1(t_0) = x_{10},$$

$$\frac{dx_2(t)}{dt} = k_2 x_1 - x_2, \ x_2(t_0) = x_{20} = 0.$$

The input $u(t)$ is a sinusoidal signal with magnitude 50 and frequency 2 Hz. The coefficients and an initial condition are $k_1 = 5$, $k_2 = 10$, $x_{10} = 20$, and $x_{20} = 0$.

Solution.
We use the Signal Generator, Sum, Gain, Integrator, Transfer Function, and Scope blocks. These blocks are dragged from the SIMULINK block libraries to the untitled `mdl` window model, positioned (placed), and connected using the signal lines shown in Figure 6.17. That is, by connecting the blocks, the SIMULINK block diagram to be used for simulations results.

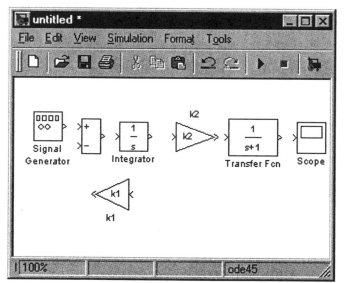 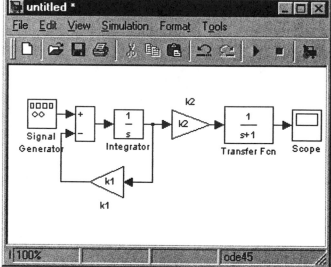

Figure 6.17. SIMULINK block diagram to model $\dfrac{dx_1(t)}{dt} = -k_1 x_1(t) + u(t)$, $\dfrac{dx_2(t)}{dt} = k_2 x_1 - x_2$

The differential equations parameters and initial conditions must be downloaded. In the Command window we type
```
>> k1=5; k2=10; x10=20; x20=0;
```
to download (input) two coefficients and initial condition. The Signal Generator block is used to generate the sinusoidal input, and we specify the amplitude and frequency as illustrated in Figure 6.18.

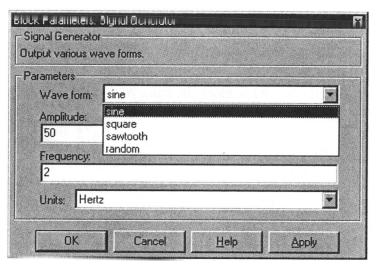

Figure 6.18. Block Parameters: Signal Generator

Initial conditions are set in the Integrator block. Specifying the simulation time to be 10 seconds, the transient behavior of the state $x_2(t)$ is plotted in the Scope (Figure 6.19).

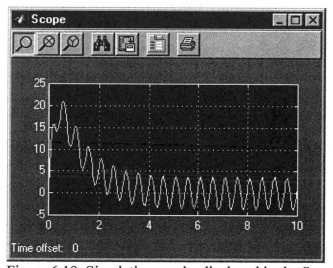

Figure 6.19. Simulation results displayed in the Scope

Example 6.2.1. Simulation of permanent-magnet DC motors
Numerically simulate permanent-magnet DC motors [4] in SIMULINK. The motor parameters (coefficient of differential equations) are: r_a = 1 ohm, L_a = 0.02 H, k_a = 0.3 V-sec/rad, J = 0.0001 kg-m^2, and B_m=0.000005 N-m-sec/rad. The applied armature voltage is u_a=40rect(t) V and the load torque is T_L=0.2rect($2t$) N-m. Initial conditions must be used.
Solution.
Two linear differential equations must be used to model and then simulate the motor dynamics. Model developments were reported in Example 5.3.6. The following differential equations were found:

$$\frac{di_a}{dt} = -\frac{r_a}{L_a}i_a - \frac{k_a}{L_a}\omega_r + \frac{1}{L_a}u_a,$$

$$\frac{d\omega_r}{dt} = \frac{k_a}{J}i_a - \frac{B_m}{J}\omega_r - \frac{1}{J}T_L.$$

The next problem is to develop the SIMULINK block diagram. An *s*-domain block diagram for permanent-magnet DC motors was developed in Example 5.3.6. This block diagram is documented in Figure 6.20.

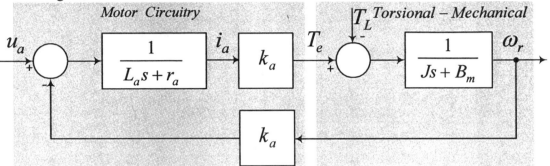

Figure 6.20. Block diagram of permanent-magnet DC motors

Making use of the *s*-domain block diagram of permanent-magnet DC motors, the corresponding SIMULINK block diagram (`mdl` model) is built and represented in Figure 6.21. The initial conditions $x_0 = \begin{bmatrix} x_{10} \\ x_{20} \end{bmatrix} = \begin{bmatrix} -1 \\ 1 \end{bmatrix}$ are downloaded (see "Initial conditions" in the `Integrator 1` and `Integrator 2` blocks as shown in Figure 6.21).

The `Signal Generator` block is used to set the applied voltage to be $u_a = 40\text{rect}(t)$ V.

As was emphasized, the motor parameters should be assigned symbolically using equations rather than using numerical values (this allows us to attain the greatest level of flexibility and adaptability). Two `Gain` blocks used are illustrated in Figure 6.21.

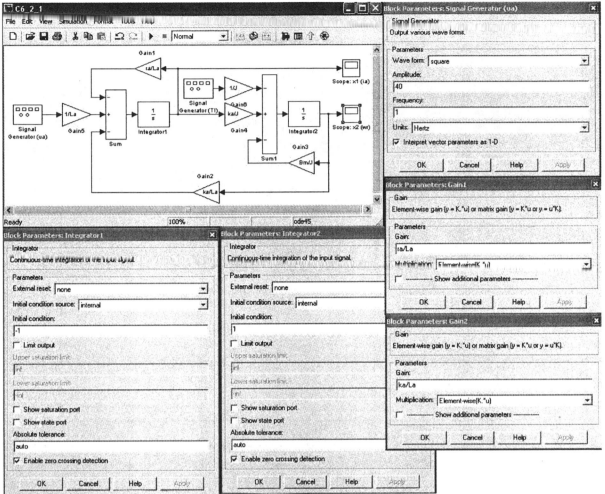

Figure 6.21. SIMULINK block diagram to simulate permanent-magnet DC motors
(`c6_2_1.mdl`)

To perform simulations, the motor parameters are downloaded (we input the coefficients of the differential equations). We download the motor parameters in the Command window by typing

```
>> ra=1; La=0.02; ka=0.3; J=0.0001; Bm=0.000005;
```

The transient responses for the state variables (armature current $x_1 = i_a$ and angular velocity $x_2 = \omega_r$) are illustrated in Figure 6.22. It should be emphasized that `plot` was used. In particular, to plot the motor dynamics we use

```
>> plot(x(:,1),x(:,2)); xlabel('Time (seconds)'); title('Armature current ia, [A]');
>> plot(x1(:,1),x1(:,2)); xlabel('Time (seconds)'); title('Velocity wr, [rad/sec]');
```

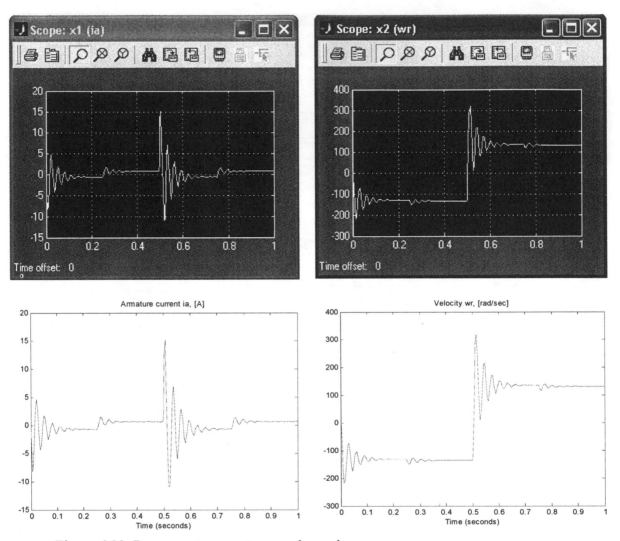

Figure 6.22. Permanent-magnet motor dynamics

This example illustrates the application of the SIMULINK package to simulate dynamic systems and visualize the results. ☐

Example 6.2.2.
In SIMULINK, numerically simulate the second-order dynamic system [5]
$$\frac{dx_1(t)}{dt} = x_2, \, x_1(t_0) = x_{10},$$
$$\frac{dx_2(t)}{dt} = -x_1 + kx_2 - kk_1x_1^2x_2, \, x_2(t_0) = x_{20}.$$
assigning the following coefficients:

- *Case 1*: $k = 5$ and $k_1 = 1$;
- *Case 2*: $k = 100$ and $k_1 = 1$;
- *Case 3*: $k = 100$ and $k_1 = 0$.

The initial conditions are $x_0 = \begin{bmatrix} x_{10} \\ x_{20} \end{bmatrix} = \begin{bmatrix} 1 \\ -1 \end{bmatrix}$.

Solution

The SIMULINK block diagram (which allow us to perform numerical simulations for three cases) is developed and illustrated in Figure 6.23.

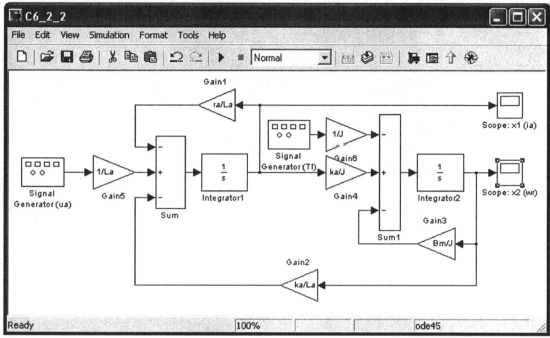

Figure 6.23. SIMULINK block diagram (`c6_2_2.mdl`)

The transient dynamic waveforms, which are displayed by double-clicking the `Scope` blocks, if $k = 5$ and $k_1 = 1$ are shown in Figure 6.24.

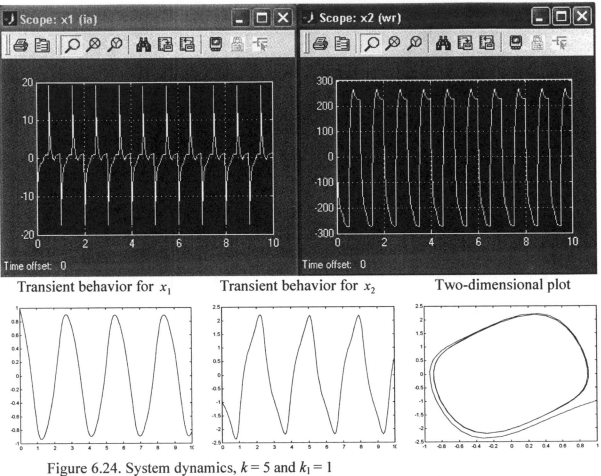

Figure 6.24. System dynamics, $k = 5$ and $k_1 = 1$

Assigning $k = 100$ and $k_1 = 1$, the simulated responses are plotted in Figure 6.25.

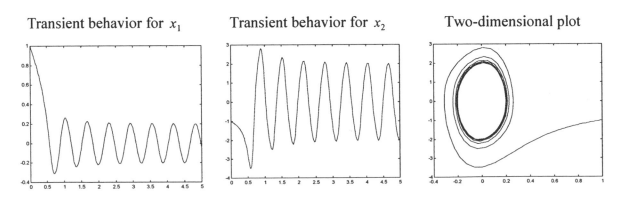

Figure 6.25. System dynamics, $k = 100$ and $k_1 = 1$

For $k = 100$ and $k_1 = 0$, we simulate $\dfrac{dx_1(t)}{dt} = x_2, \, x_1(t_0) = 1, \; \dfrac{dx_2(t)}{dt} = -x_1 + 100x_2, \, x_2(t_0) = -1$.

The system behavior is plotted in Figure 6.26.

Transient behavior for x_1	Transient behavior for x_2	Two-dimensional plot

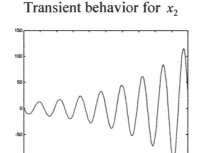 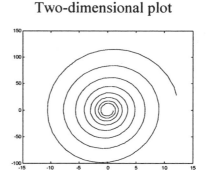

Figure 6.26. System dynamics, $k = 100$ and $k_1 = 0$

This example illustrates that dynamic systems can be efficiently simulated and analyzed using SIMULINK (system can be stable and unstable if $k = 100$ and $k_1 = 0$). □

Example 6.2.3. Simulation of single-phase reluctance motors

The nonlinear differential equations to model synchronous reluctance motors are [4, 5]

$$\frac{di_{as}}{dt} = -\frac{r_s}{L_{ls}+\overline{L}_m-L_{\Delta m}\cos2\theta_r}i_{as} - \frac{2L_{\Delta m}}{L_{ls}+\overline{L}_m-L_{\Delta m}\cos2\theta_r}i_{as}\omega_r\sin2\theta_r + \frac{1}{L_{ls}+\overline{L}_m-L_{\Delta m}\cos2\theta_r}u_{as},$$

$$\frac{d\omega_r}{dt} = \frac{1}{J}\left(L_{\Delta m}i_{as}^2\sin2\theta_r - B_m\omega_r - T_L\right),$$

$$\frac{d\theta_r}{dt} = \omega_r.$$

Simulate the motor in the SIMULINK assigning parameters as: $r_s = 2$ ohm, $L_{md} = 0.5$ H, $L_{mq} = 0.02$ H, $L_{ls} = 0.004$ H, $J = 0.00001$ kg-m^2, and $B_m = 0.000004$ N-m-sec/rad.

The voltage applied to the stator winding is $u_{as} = 20\sin(2\theta_r - 0.62)$. The load torque is $T_L = 0$ N-m.

Solution.

The motor parameters are downloaded by using the data m-file.

```
% synchronous reluctance motor
P=2; rs=2; Lmd=0.5; Lmq=0.02; Lls=0.004; J=0.00001; Bm=0.000004;
Lmb=(Lmq+Lmd)/3; Ldm=(Lmd-Lmq)/3;
%rms value of the voltage
um=20;
%load torque
Tl=0;
```

We must run this data m-file or just type the parameter values in the Command Window before running the SIMULINK mdl model. The SIMULINK block diagram is documented in Figure 6.27.

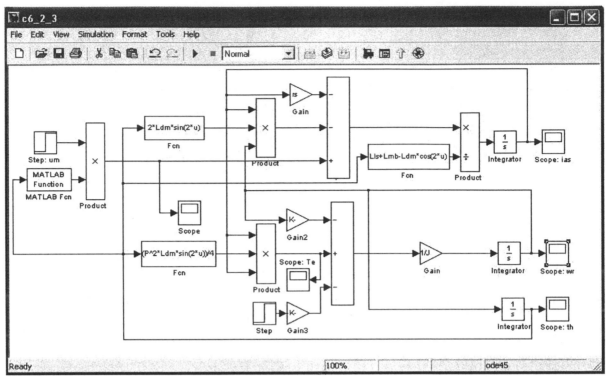

Figure 6.27. SIMULINK block diagram for simulation elementary reluctance motors
(`c6_2_3.mdl`)

The transient responses for the angular velocity $\omega_r(t)$ and the phase current $i_{as}(t)$ are plotted in Figures 6.28.

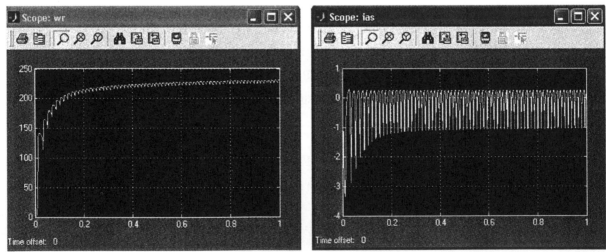

Figures 6.28. Transient responses for the motor variables (ω_r and i_{as})

We conclude that SIMULINK was applied to model a single-phase reluctance motor. Changing the motor parameters, the user can examine electromechanical motion device dynamics in the time domain. □

Example 6.2.4. Simulation of three-phase squirrel-cage induction motors

In SIMULINK simulate induction motors. The mathematical model of three-phase induction motors is governed by a set of the following nonlinear differential equations [4, 5]:

$$u_{as} = r_s i_{as} + (L_{ls} + L_{ms})\frac{di_{as}}{dt} - \frac{1}{2}L_{ms}\frac{di_{bs}}{dt} - \frac{1}{2}L_{ms}\frac{di_{cs}}{dt} + L_{ms}\frac{d(i'_{ar}\cos\theta_r)}{dt} + L_{ms}\frac{d\left(i'_{br}\cos\left(\theta_r + \frac{2\pi}{3}\right)\right)}{dt} + L_{ms}\frac{d\left(i'_{cr}\cos\left(\theta_r - \frac{2\pi}{3}\right)\right)}{dt},$$

$$u_{bs} = r_s i_{bs} - \frac{1}{2}L_{ms}\frac{di_{as}}{dt} + (L_{ls} + L_{ms})\frac{di_{bs}}{dt} - \frac{1}{2}L_{ms}\frac{di_{cs}}{dt} + L_{ms}\frac{d\left(i'_{ar}\cos\left(\theta_r - \frac{2\pi}{3}\right)\right)}{dt} + L_{ms}\frac{d\left(i'_{br}\cos\theta_r\right)}{dt} + L_{ms}\frac{d\left(i'_{cr}\cos\left(\theta_r + \frac{2\pi}{3}\right)\right)}{dt},$$

$$u_{cs} = r_s i_{cs} - \frac{1}{2}L_{ms}\frac{di_{as}}{dt} - \frac{1}{2}L_{ms}\frac{di_{bs}}{dt} + (L_{ls} + L_{ms})\frac{di_{cs}}{dt} + L_{ms}\frac{d\left(i'_{ar}\cos\left(\theta_r + \frac{2\pi}{3}\right)\right)}{dt} + L_{ms}\frac{d\left(i'_{br}\cos\left(\theta_r - \frac{2\pi}{3}\right)\right)}{dt} + L_{ms}\frac{d\left(i'_{cr}\cos\theta_r\right)}{dt},$$

$$u'_{ar} = r'_r i'_{ar} + L_{ms}\frac{d(i_{as}\cos\theta_r)}{dt} + L_{ms}\frac{d\left(i_{bs}\cos\left(\theta_r - \frac{2\pi}{3}\right)\right)}{dt} + L_{ms}\frac{d\left(i_{cs}\cos\left(\theta_r + \frac{2\pi}{3}\right)\right)}{dt} + (L'_{lr} + L_{ms})\frac{di'_{ar}}{dt} - \frac{1}{2}L_{ms}\frac{di'_{br}}{dt} - \frac{1}{2}L_{ms}\frac{di'_{cr}}{dt},$$

$$u'_{br} = r'_r i'_{br} + L_{ms}\frac{d\left(i_{as}\cos\left(\theta_r + \frac{2\pi}{3}\right)\right)}{dt} + L_{ms}\frac{d(i_{bs}\cos\theta_r)}{dt} + L_{ms}\frac{d\left(i_{cs}\cos\left(\theta_r - \frac{2\pi}{3}\right)\right)}{dt} - \frac{1}{2}L_{ms}\frac{di'_{ar}}{dt} + (L'_{lr} + L_{ms})\frac{di'_{br}}{dt} - \frac{1}{2}L_{ms}\frac{di'_{cr}}{dt},$$

$$u'_{cr} = r'_r i'_{cr} + L_{ms}\frac{d\left(i_{as}\cos\left(\theta_r - \frac{2\pi}{3}\right)\right)}{dt} + L_{ms}\frac{d\left(i_{bs}\cos\left(\theta_r + \frac{2\pi}{3}\right)\right)}{dt} + L_{ms}\frac{d(i_{cs}\cos\theta_r)}{dt} - \frac{1}{2}L_{ms}\frac{di'_{ar}}{dt} - \frac{1}{2}L_{ms}\frac{di'_{br}}{dt} + (L'_{lr} + L_{ms})\frac{di'_{cr}}{dt},$$

$$\frac{d\omega_r}{dt} = -\frac{P^2}{4J}L_{ms}\left\{\left[i_{as}\left(i'_{ar} - \tfrac{1}{2}i'_{br} - \tfrac{1}{2}i'_{cr}\right) + i_{bs}\left(i'_{br} - \tfrac{1}{2}i'_{ar} - \tfrac{1}{2}i'_{cr}\right) + i_{cs}\left(i'_{cr} - \tfrac{1}{2}i'_{br} - \tfrac{1}{2}i'_{ar}\right)\right]\sin\theta_r \right.$$
$$\left. + \frac{\sqrt{3}}{2}\left[i_{as}\left(i'_{br} - i'_{cr}\right) + i_{bs}\left(i'_{cr} - i'_{ar}\right) + i_{cs}\left(i'_{ar} - i'_{br}\right)\right]\cos\theta_r\right\} - \frac{B_m}{J}\omega_r - \frac{P}{2J}T_L,$$

$$\frac{d\theta_r}{dt} = \omega_r.$$

The induction motor to be numerically simulated has the following parameters: $r_s = 0.3$ ohm, $r_r = 0.2$ ohm, $L_{ms} = 0.035$ H, $L_{ls} = 0.001$ H, $L_{lr} = 0.001$ H, $J = 0.025$ kg-m^2, and $B_m = 0.004$ N-m-sec/rad.

Solution.

Using the differential equations, one must build the SIMULINK block diagram. From the differential equations given above, we obtain the following set of equations to be used in the SIMULINK `mdl` model:

$$\frac{di_{as}}{dt} = \frac{1}{L_{ls}+L_{ms}}\left[-r_s i_{as} + \frac{1}{2}L_{ms}\frac{di_{bs}}{dt} + \frac{1}{2}L_{ms}\frac{di_{cs}}{dt} - L_{ms}\frac{d(i'_{ar}\cos\theta_r)}{dt} - L_{ms}\frac{d(i'_{br}\cos(\theta_r+\frac{2\pi}{3}))}{dt} - L_{ms}\frac{d(i'_{cr}\cos(\theta_r-\frac{2\pi}{3}))}{dt} + u_{as}\right],$$

$$\frac{di_{bs}}{dt} = \frac{1}{L_{ls}+L_{ms}}\left[-r_s i_{bs} + \frac{1}{2}L_{ms}\frac{di_{as}}{dt} + \frac{1}{2}L_{ms}\frac{di_{cs}}{dt} - L_{ms}\frac{d(i'_{ar}\cos(\theta_r-\frac{2\pi}{3}))}{dt} - L_{ms}\frac{d(i'_{br}\cos\theta_r)}{dt} - L_{ms}\frac{d(i'_{cr}\cos(\theta_r+\frac{2\pi}{3}))}{dt} + u_{bs}\right],$$

$$\frac{di_{cs}}{dt} = \frac{1}{L_{ls}+L_{ms}}\left[-r_s i_{cs} + \frac{1}{2}L_{ms}\frac{di_{as}}{dt} + \frac{1}{2}L_{ms}\frac{di_{bs}}{dt} - L_{ms}\frac{d(i'_{ar}\cos(\theta_r+\frac{2\pi}{3}))}{dt} - L_{ms}\frac{d(i'_{br}\cos(\theta_r-\frac{2\pi}{3}))}{dt} - L_{ms}\frac{d(i'_{cr}\cos\theta_r)}{dt} + u_{cs}\right],$$

$$\frac{di'_{ar}}{dt} = \frac{1}{L'_{lr}+L_{ms}}\left[-r'_r i'_{ar} - L_{ms}\frac{d(i_{as}\cos\theta_r)}{dt} - L_{ms}\frac{d(i_{bs}\cos(\theta_r-\frac{2\pi}{3}))}{dt} - L_{ms}\frac{d(i_{cs}\cos(\theta_r+\frac{2\pi}{3}))}{dt} + \frac{1}{2}L_{ms}\frac{di'_{br}}{dt} + \frac{1}{2}L_{ms}\frac{di'_{cr}}{dt} + u'_{ar}\right],$$

$$\frac{di'_{br}}{dt} = \frac{1}{L'_{lr}+L_{ms}}\left[-r'_r i'_{br} - L_{ms}\frac{d(i_{as}\cos(\theta_r+\frac{2\pi}{3}))}{dt} - L_{ms}\frac{d(i_{bs}\cos\theta_r)}{dt} - L_{ms}\frac{d(i_{cs}\cos(\theta_r-\frac{2\pi}{3}))}{dt} + \frac{1}{2}L_{ms}\frac{di'_{ar}}{dt} + \frac{1}{2}L_{ms}\frac{di'_{cr}}{dt} + u'_{br}\right],$$

$$\frac{di'_{cr}}{dt} = \frac{1}{L'_{lr}+L_{ms}}\left[-r'_r i'_{cr} - L_{ms}\frac{d(i_{as}\cos(\theta_r-\frac{2\pi}{3}))}{dt} - L_{ms}\frac{d(i_{bs}\cos(\theta_r+\frac{2\pi}{3}))}{dt} - L_{ms}\frac{d(i_{cs}\cos\theta_r)}{dt} + \frac{1}{2}L_{ms}\frac{di'_{ar}}{dt} + \frac{1}{2}L_{ms}\frac{di'_{br}}{dt} + u'_{cr}\right],$$

$$\frac{d\omega_r}{dt} = -\frac{P^2}{4J}L_{ms}\left\{\left[i_{as}\left(i'_{ar}-\frac{1}{2}i'_{br}-\frac{1}{2}i'_{cr}\right) + i_{bs}\left(i'_{br}-\frac{1}{2}i'_{ar}-\frac{1}{2}i'_{cr}\right) + i_{cs}\left(i'_{cr}-\frac{1}{2}i'_{br}-\frac{1}{2}i'_{ar}\right)\right]\sin\theta_r\right.$$

$$\left.+\frac{\sqrt{3}}{2}\left[i_{as}\left(i'_{br}-i'_{cr}\right) + i_{bs}\left(i'_{cr}-i'_{ar}\right) + i_{cs}\left(i'_{ar}-i'_{br}\right)\right]\cos\theta_r\right\} - \frac{B_m}{J}\omega_r - \frac{P}{2J}T_L,$$

$$\frac{d\theta_r}{dt} = \omega_r.$$

To guarantee the balanced operating condition, the following phase voltages should be applied to the induction motor windings:

$$u_{as}(t) = \sqrt{2}u_M\cos(\omega_f t),$$

$$u_{bs}(t) = \sqrt{2}u_M\cos(\omega_f t - \tfrac{2}{3}\pi),$$

$$u_{cs}(t) = \sqrt{2}u_M\cos(\omega_f t + \tfrac{2}{3}\pi).$$

The SIMULINK block diagram to simulate three-phase squirrel-cage induction motors is developed and illustrated in Figure 6.29. The `Derivative` blocks are used.

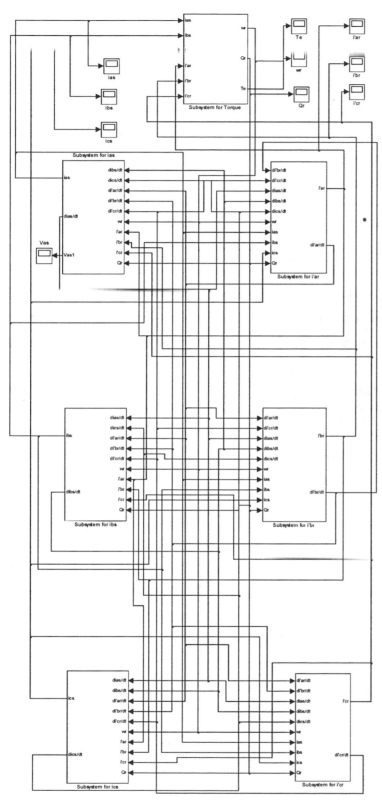

Figure 6.29. SIMULINK block diagram to simulate squirrel-cage induction motors (c6_2_4.mdl)

The induction motor parameters r_s = 0.3 ohm, r_r = 0.2 ohm, L_{ms} = 0.035 H, L_{ls} = 0.001 H, L_{lr} = 0.001 H, J = 0.025 kg-m^2, and B_m = 0.004 N-m-sec/rad are downloaded. In particular, in the Command Window, the designer inputs the motor parameters as

```
» P=2; Rs=0.3; Rr=0.2; Lms=0.035; Lls=0.001; Llr=0.001; Bm=0.004; J=0.025;
```

Nonlinear simulations were performed, and transient dynamics of the stator and rotor currents in the *as, bs, cs, ar, br,* and *cr* windings $i_{as}(t), i_{bs}(t), i_{cs}(t), i'_{ar}(t), i'_{br}(t),$ and $i'_{cr}(t)$ as well as the rotor angular velocity $\omega_{rm}(t)$, are documented in Figures 6.30 and 6.31. The statement to plot the evolution of $\omega_{rm}(t)$ is

```
>> plot(wr(:,1),wr(:,2)); xlabel('Time (seconds)'); title('Angular velocity wr, [rad/sec]');
```

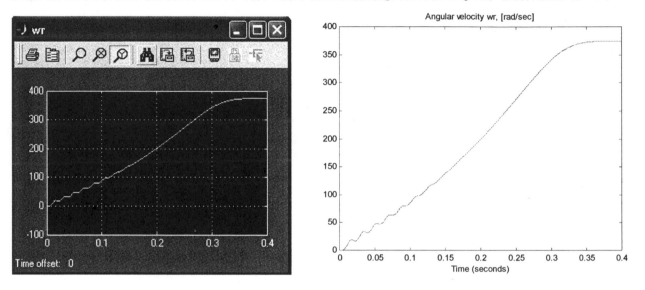

Figure 6.30. Transient dynamic for the angular velocity $\omega_{rm}(t)$

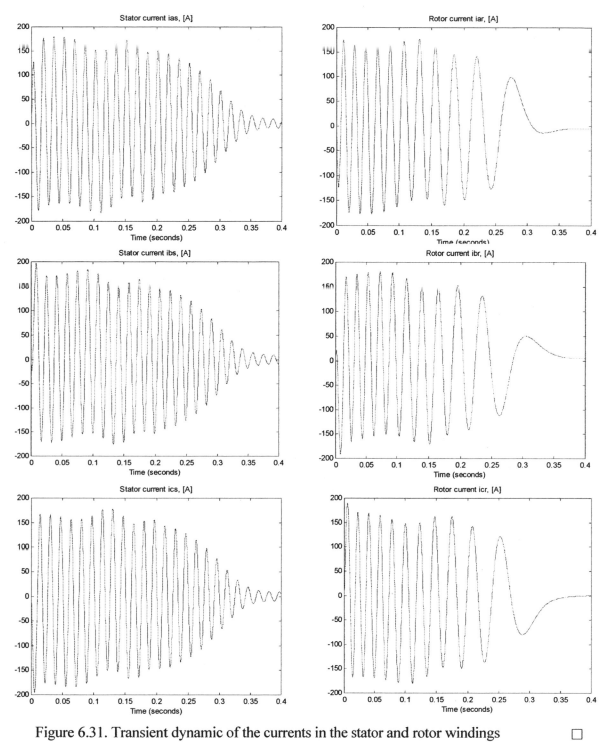

Figure 6.31. Transient dynamic of the currents in the stator and rotor windings

Example 6.2.5. Simulation of permanent-magnet synchronous motors

In SIMULINK simulate three-phase permanent-magnet synchronous motors described by five nonlinear differential equations [4]:

$$\frac{di_{as}}{dt} = -\frac{r_s\left(2L_{ss}-\overline{L}_m\right)}{2L_{ss}^2 - L_{ss}\overline{L}_m - \overline{L}_m^2}i_{as} - \frac{r_s\overline{L}_m}{2L_{ss}^2 - L_{ss}\overline{L}_m - \overline{L}_m^2}i_{bs} - \frac{r_s\overline{L}_m}{2L_{ss}^2 - L_{ss}\overline{L}_m - \overline{L}_m^2}i_{cs}$$

$$-\frac{\psi_m\left(2L_{ss}-\overline{L}_m\right)}{2L_{ss}^2 - L_{ss}\overline{L}_m - \overline{L}_m^2}\omega_r\cos\theta_r - \frac{\psi_m\overline{L}_m}{2L_{ss}^2 - L_{ss}\overline{L}_m - \overline{L}_m^2}\omega_r\cos\left(\theta_r - \tfrac{2}{3}\pi\right) - \frac{\psi_m\overline{L}_m}{2L_{ss}^2 - L_{ss}\overline{L}_m - \overline{L}_m^2}\omega_r\cos\left(\theta_r + \tfrac{2}{3}\pi\right)$$

$$+\frac{2L_{ss}-\overline{L}_m}{2L_{ss}^2 - L_{ss}\overline{L}_m - \overline{L}_m^2}u_{as} + \frac{\overline{L}_m}{2L_{ss}^2 - L_{ss}\overline{L}_m - \overline{L}_m^2}u_{bs} + \frac{\overline{L}_m}{2L_{ss}^2 - L_{ss}\overline{L}_m - \overline{L}_m^2}u_{cs},$$

$$\frac{di_{bs}}{dt} = -\frac{r_s\overline{L}_m}{2L_{ss}^2 - L_{ss}\overline{L}_m - \overline{L}_m^2}i_{as} - \frac{r_s\left(2L_{ss}-\overline{L}_m\right)}{2L_{ss}^2 - L_{ss}\overline{L}_m - \overline{L}_m^2}i_{bs} - \frac{r_s\overline{L}_m}{2L_{ss}^2 - L_{ss}\overline{L}_m - \overline{L}_m^2}i_{cs}$$

$$-\frac{\psi_m\overline{L}_m}{2L_{ss}^2 - L_{ss}\overline{L}_m - \overline{L}_m^2}\omega_r\cos\theta_r - \frac{\psi_m\left(2L_{ss}-\overline{L}_m\right)}{2L_{ss}^2 - L_{ss}\overline{L}_m - \overline{L}_m^2}\omega_r\cos\left(\theta_r - \tfrac{2}{3}\pi\right) - \frac{\psi_m\overline{L}_m}{2L_{ss}^2 - L_{ss}\overline{L}_m - \overline{L}_m^2}\omega_r\cos\left(\theta_r + \tfrac{2}{3}\pi\right)$$

$$+\frac{\overline{L}_m}{2L_{ss}^2 - L_{ss}\overline{L}_m - \overline{L}_m^2}u_{as} + \frac{2L_{ss}-\overline{L}_m}{2L_{ss}^2 - L_{ss}\overline{L}_m - \overline{L}_m^2}u_{bs} + \frac{\overline{L}_m}{2L_{ss}^2 - L_{ss}\overline{L}_m - \overline{L}_m^2}u_{cs},$$

$$\frac{di_{cs}}{dt} = -\frac{r_s\overline{L}_m}{2L_{ss}^2 - L_{ss}\overline{L}_m - \overline{L}_m^2}i_{as} - \frac{r_s\overline{L}_m}{2L_{ss}^2 - L_{ss}\overline{L}_m - \overline{L}_m^2}i_{bs} - \frac{r_s\left(2L_{ss}-\overline{L}_m\right)}{2L_{ss}^2 - L_{ss}\overline{L}_m - \overline{L}_m^2}i_{cs}$$

$$-\frac{\psi_m\overline{L}_m}{2L_{ss}^2 - L_{ss}\overline{L}_m - \overline{L}_m^2}\omega_r\cos\theta_r - \frac{\psi_m\overline{L}_m}{2L_{ss}^2 - L_{ss}\overline{L}_m - \overline{L}_m^2}\omega_r\cos\left(\theta_r - \tfrac{2}{3}\pi\right) - \frac{\psi_m\left(2L_{ss}-\overline{L}_m\right)}{2L_{ss}^2 - L_{ss}\overline{L}_m - \overline{L}_m^2}\omega_r\cos\left(\theta_r + \tfrac{2}{3}\pi\right)$$

$$+\frac{\overline{L}_m}{2L_{ss}^2 - L_{ss}\overline{L}_m - \overline{L}_m^2}u_{as} + \frac{\overline{L}_m}{2L_{ss}^2 - L_{ss}\overline{L}_m - \overline{L}_m^2}u_{bs} + \frac{2L_{ss}-\overline{L}_m}{2L_{ss}^2 - L_{ss}\overline{L}_m - \overline{L}_m^2}u_{cs},$$

$$\frac{d\omega_r}{dt} = \frac{P^2\psi_m}{4J}\left(i_{as}\cos\theta_r + i_{bs}\cos\left(\theta_r - \tfrac{2}{3}\pi\right) + i_{cs}\cos\left(\theta_r + \tfrac{2}{3}\pi\right)\right) - \frac{B_m}{J}\omega_r - \frac{P}{2J}T_L,$$

$$\frac{d\theta_r}{dt} = \omega_r.$$

The following phase voltages are applied to guarantee the balance motor operation:

$$u_{as}(t) = \sqrt{2}u_M\cos\theta_r, \quad u_{bs}(t) = \sqrt{2}u_M\cos\left(\theta_r - \tfrac{2}{3}\pi\right) \text{ and } u_{cs}(t) = \sqrt{2}u_M\cos\left(\theta_r + \tfrac{2}{3}\pi\right).$$

The motor parameters are:

u_M = 40 V, r_s = 1 ohm, L_{ss} = 0.002 H, L_{ls} = 0.0002 H, $\overline{L}_m$ = 0.0012 H, ψ_m = 0.08 V-sec/rad, ψ_m = 0.08 N-m/A, B_m = 0.000008 N-m-sec/rad, and J = 0.00004 kg-m^2.

Solution.

As the differential equations are known, one can develop the SIMULINK block diagram (mdl model) to simulate permanent-magnet synchronous motors. The resulting SIMULINK block diagram is illustrated in Figure 6.32.

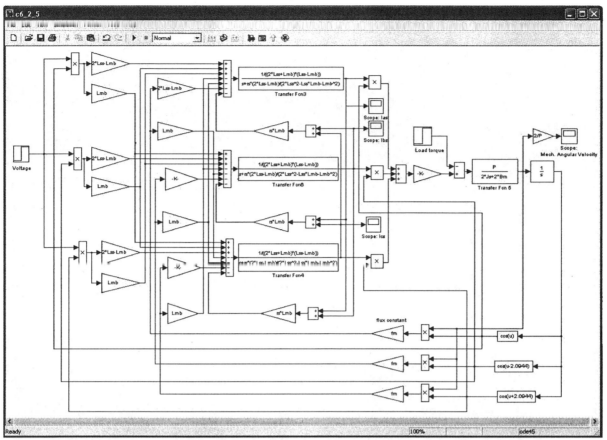

Figure 6.32. SIMULINK block diagram to simulate permanent-magnet synchronous motors (c6_2_5.mdl)

The transient dynamics are studied as the motor accelerates and the rated voltage is supplied to the stator windings. In particular,

$$u_{as}(t) = \sqrt{2}\,40\cos\theta_r, \; u_{bs}(t) = \sqrt{2}\,40\cos\left(\theta_r - \tfrac{2}{3}\pi\right) \text{ and } u_{cs}(t) = \sqrt{2}\,40\cos\left(\theta_r + \tfrac{2}{3}\pi\right).$$

The motor parameters are downloaded using the following statement typed in the Command Window:

```
% Parameters of the permanent-magnet synchronous motor
P=4; um=40; rs=1; Lss=0.002; Lls=0.0002; fm=0.08; Bm=0.000008; J=0.00004;
Lmb=2*(Lss-Lls)/3;
```

The motor accelerates from stall, and the load torque 0.5 N-m is applied at 0 sec.

Figure 6.33 illustrates the evolution of four states for the three-phase permanent-magnet synchronous motor.

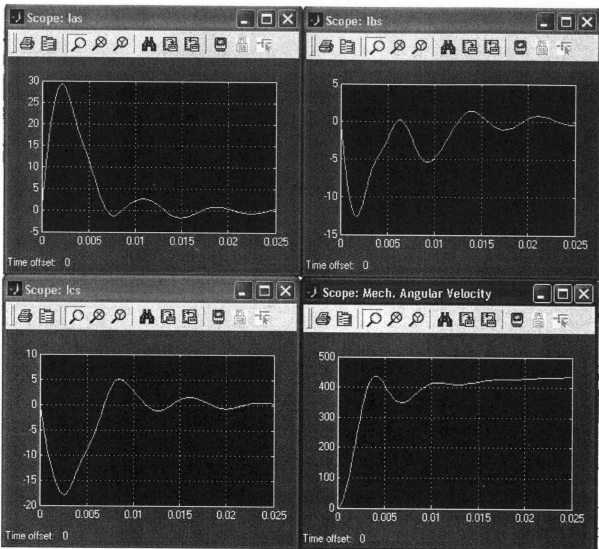

Figure 6.33. Transient dynamics of the permanent-magnet synchronous motor variables

These state variables can be plotted using `plot`. In particular, the following m-file can be used to plot the transient data:

```
% Plots of the transient dynamics of the permanent-magnet synchronous motor
plot(Ias(:,1),Ias(:,2)); xlabel('Time (seconds)'); title('Current Ias, [A]'); pause
plot(Ibs(:,1),Ibs(:,2)); xlabel('Time (seconds)'); title('Current Ibs, [A]'); pause
plot(Ics(:,1),Ics(:,2)); xlabel('Time (seconds)'); title('Current Ics, [A]'); pause
plot(wrm(:,1),wrm(:,2)); xlabel('Time (seconds)');title('Angular velocity wrm, [rad/sec]'); pause
```

□

Example 6.2.6. Simulation of permanent-magnet DC motors using the state-space model

Simulate permanent-magnet DC motors in SIMULINK using the state-space form. The linear differential equations to model permanent-magnet DC motors are (see Examples 5.3.6 and 6.2.1)

$$\frac{di_a}{dt} = -\frac{r_a}{L_a}i_a - \frac{k_a}{L_a}\omega_r + \frac{1}{L_a}u_a,$$

$$\frac{d\omega_r}{dt} = \frac{k_a}{J}i_a - \frac{B_m}{J}\omega_r - \frac{1}{J}T_L.$$

The motor parameters to be used in numerical simulations are: $r_a = 1$ ohm, $L_a = 0.02$ H, $k_a = 0.3$ V-sec/rad, $J = 0.0001$ kg-m^2, and $B_m = 0.000005$ N-m-sec/rad. The applied voltage is $u_a = 25\text{rect}(t)$ V. The initial conditions to be used are $\begin{bmatrix} i_{a0} \\ \omega_{r0} \end{bmatrix} = \begin{bmatrix} x_{10} \\ x_{20} \end{bmatrix} = \begin{bmatrix} 1 \\ 10 \end{bmatrix}$.

Solution.

Using the differential equations which model permanent-magnet DC motors we obtain the model in the state-space form as

$$\begin{bmatrix} \dfrac{di_a}{dt} \\ \dfrac{d\omega_r}{dt} \end{bmatrix} = \begin{bmatrix} -\dfrac{r_a}{L_a} & -\dfrac{k_a}{L_a} \\ \dfrac{k_a}{J} & -\dfrac{B_m}{J} \end{bmatrix} \begin{bmatrix} i_a \\ \omega_r \end{bmatrix} + \begin{bmatrix} \dfrac{1}{L_a} \\ 0 \end{bmatrix} u_a.$$

Denoting the state and control variables to be $x_1 = i_a$, $x_2 = \omega_r$ and $u = u_a$, we find

$$\begin{bmatrix} \dfrac{dx}{dt} \end{bmatrix} = \begin{bmatrix} \dfrac{dx_1}{dt} \\ \dfrac{dx_2}{dt} \end{bmatrix} = \begin{bmatrix} -\dfrac{r_a}{L_a} & -\dfrac{k_a}{L_a} \\ \dfrac{k_a}{J} & -\dfrac{B_m}{J} \end{bmatrix} \begin{bmatrix} x_1 \\ x_2 \end{bmatrix} + \begin{bmatrix} \dfrac{1}{L_a} \\ 0 \end{bmatrix} u \text{ with initial conditions } \begin{bmatrix} i_{a0} \\ \omega_{r0} \end{bmatrix} = \begin{bmatrix} x_{10} \\ x_{20} \end{bmatrix}.$$

In general, we have $\dfrac{dx}{dt} = \begin{bmatrix} \dfrac{dx_1}{dt} \\ \vdots \\ \dfrac{dx_n}{dt} \end{bmatrix} = A \begin{bmatrix} x_1 \\ \vdots \\ x_n \end{bmatrix} + Bu$.

For our example, $x = \begin{bmatrix} x_1 \\ x_2 \end{bmatrix}$, $A = \begin{bmatrix} -\dfrac{r_a}{L_a} & -\dfrac{k_a}{L_a} \\ \dfrac{k_a}{J} & -\dfrac{B_m}{J} \end{bmatrix}$ and $B = \begin{bmatrix} \dfrac{1}{L_a} \\ 0 \end{bmatrix}$.

The output equation is $y = \omega_r$.

Hence, we have the following state-space model for permanent-magnet DC motors:

$$y = \omega_r = Cx + Du = \begin{bmatrix} 0 & 1 \end{bmatrix} \begin{bmatrix} i_a \\ \omega_r \end{bmatrix} + \begin{bmatrix} 0 \end{bmatrix} u_a = \begin{bmatrix} 0 & 1 \end{bmatrix} \begin{bmatrix} x_1 \\ x_2 \end{bmatrix} + \begin{bmatrix} 0 \end{bmatrix} u, \quad C = \begin{bmatrix} 0 & 1 \end{bmatrix} \text{ and } D = \begin{bmatrix} 0 \end{bmatrix}.$$

Using the `State-Space` block, the simulation can be performed. To attain flexibility, symbolic notations are used. The `State-Space` block is illustrated in Figure 6.34.

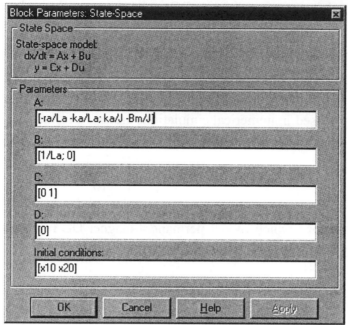

Figure 6.34. `State-Space` block with parameters of permanent-magnet DC motors

The developed SIMULINK `mdl` model is documented in Figure 6.35.

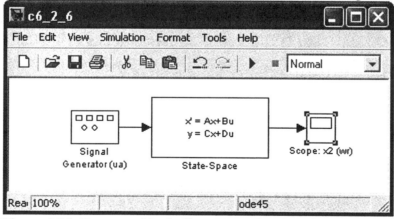

Figure 6.35. SIMULINK block diagram to simulate the motor dynamics (`c6_2_6.mdl`)

The simulations are performed assigning the motor parameters and initial conditions. In particular, the motor parameters ($r_a = 1$ ohm, $L_a = 0.02$ H, $k_a = 0.3$ V-sec/rad, $J = 0.0001$ kg-m^2, and $B_m = 0.000005$ N-m-sec/rad), applied voltage $u_a = 25\text{rect}(t)$ V, and the initial conditions $[1\ 10]^T$ are downloaded. We input the following in the Command Window:

```
>> ra=1; La=0.02; ka=0.3; J=0.0001; Bm=0.000005; x10=1; x20=10;
```

Running the simulation and using the following plotting statement

```
>> plot(x(:,1),x(:,2)); xlabel('Time (seconds)'); title('Angular velocity wr, [rad/sec]')
```

the dynamics of the motor angular velocity result (Figures 6.36).

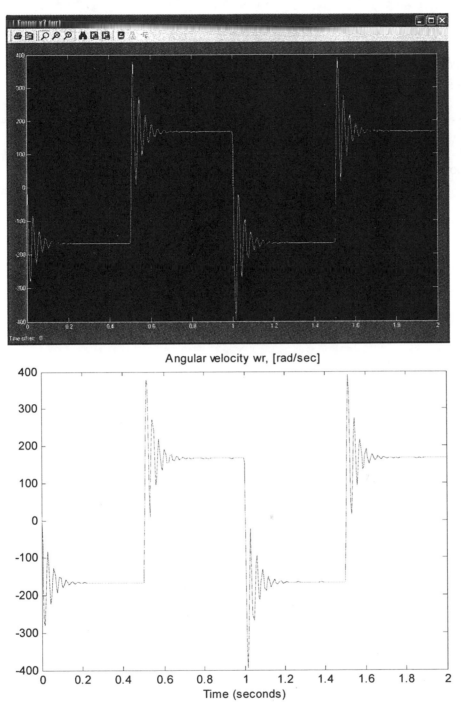

Figure 6.36. Angular velocity dynamics if $u_a = 40\text{rect}(t)$ V $\qquad$ □

Again it should be emphasized that different illustrative educational examples in aerospace and automotive applications are readily available. These examples with the corresponding SIMULINK block diagrams can be easily accessed and used to master the MATLAB environment.

REFERENCES

1. *MATLAB 6.5 Release 13,* CD-ROM, MathWorks, Inc., 2002.
2. Dabney, J. B. and Harman, T. L., *Mastering SIMULINK 2*, Prentice Hall, Upper Saddle River, NJ, 1998.
3. *User's Guide. The Student Edition of MATLAB: The Ultimate Computing Environment for Technical Education*, MathWorks, Inc., Prentice Hall, Upper Saddle River, NJ, 1995.
4. Lyshevski, S. E., *Electromechanical Systems, Electric Machines, and Applied Mechatronics*, CRC Press, Boca Raton, FL, 2000.
5. Lyshevski, S. E., *Control Systems Theory with Engineering Applications*, Birkhauser, Boston, MA, 2002.

APPENDIX

MATLAB Functions, Operators, Characters, Commands, and Solvers [1]

Table A.1. Operators and Special Characters

+	Plus (addition operator)
−	Minus (subtraction operator)
*	Scalar and matrix multiplication (multiplication operator)
.*	Array multiplication (multiplication operator)
^	Scalar and matrix exponentiation operator (power)
.^	Array exponentiation operator (power)
kron	Kronecker tensor product
\	Left division operator
/	Right division operator
./ and .\	Array division (right and left operators)
:	Colon (generates equally spaced arrays - rows and columns)
( )	Parentheses
[ ]	Brackets (encloses array and matrix elements and entries)
{ }	Curly braces
.	Decimal point
...	Continuation (line continuation operator)
,	Comma (separates statements and elements)
;	Semicolon
%	Percent sign (comment)
!	Exclamation point
'	Transpose operator and quote sign
.'	Nonconjugated transpose operator
=	Assignment (replacement) operator
==	Equality (equal to) operator
<	Relational operators (less than)
<=	Relational operators (less than or equal to)
>	Relational operators (greater than)
>=	Relational operators (greater than or equal to)
~=	Relational operators (not equal to)
&	AND (logical operator)
|	OR (logical operator)
~	NOT (logical operator)
xor	EXECUTIVE OR (logical operator)

Table A.2. Logical Functions

all	Test to determine if all elements are nonzero
any	Test for any nonzeros
exist	Check if a variable or file exists
find	Find indices and values of nonzero elements
is*	Detect state
isa	Detect an object of a given class
iskeyword	Test if string is a MATLAB keyword
isvarname	Test if string is a valid variable name

`logical`	Convert numeric values to logical
`mislocked`	True if M-file cannot be cleared

Table A.3. Language Constructs and Debugging
Table A.3.1. MATLAB as a Programming Language

`builtin`	Execute built-in function from overloaded method
`eval`	Interpret strings containing MATLAB expressions
`evalc`	Evaluate MATLAB expression with capture
`evalin`	Evaluate expression in workspace
`feval`	Function evaluation
`function`	Function m-files
`global`	Define global variables
`nargchk`	Check number of input arguments
`persistent`	Define persistent variable
`script`	Script m-files

Table A.3.2. Control Flow

`break`	Terminate execution of "`for`" or "`while`" loop
`case`	Case switch
`catch`	Begin catch block
`continue`	Pass control to the next iteration of "`for`" or "`while`" loop
`else`	Conditionally execute statements
`elseif`	Conditionally execute statements
`end`	Terminate `for`, `while`, `switch`, `try`, and `if` statements or indicate last index
`error`	Display error messages
`for`	Repeat statements a specific number of times
`if`	Conditionally execute statements
`otherwise`	Default part of switch statement
`return`	Return to the invoking function
`switch`	Switch among several cases based on expression
`try`	Begin try block
`warning`	Display warning message
`while`	Repeat statements an indefinite number of times

Table A.3.3. Interactive Input

`input`	Request user input
`keyboard`	Invoke the keyboard in an m-file
`menu`	Generate a menu of choices for user input
`pause`	Halt execution temporarily (until any key will be pressed)

Table A.3.4. Object-Oriented Programming

`class`	Create object or return class of object
`double`	Convert to double precision
`inferiorto`	Inferior class relationship
`inline`	Construct an inline object
`int8, int16, int32`	Convert to signed integer
`isa`	Detect an object of a given class
`loadobj`	Extends the load function for user objects

saveobj	Save filter for objects
single	Convert to single precision
superiorto	Superior class relationship
uint8, uint16, uint32	Convert to unsigned integer

Table A.3.5. Debugging

dbclear	Clear breakpoints
dbcont	Resume execution
dbdown	Change local workspace context
dbmex	Enable MEX-file debugging
dbquit	Quit debug mode
dbstack	Display function call stack
dbstatus	List all breakpoints
dbstep	Execute one or more lines from a breakpoint
dbstop	Set breakpoints in an m-file function
dbtype	List m-file with line numbers
dbup	Change local workspace context

Table A.3.6. Function Handles

function_handle	MATLAB data type that is a handle to a function
functions	Return information about a function handle
func2str	Constructs a function name string from a function handle
str2func	Constructs a function handle from a function name string

Table A.4. Character String Functions

Table A.4.1. General

Abs	Absolute value and complex magnitude
Eval	Interpret strings containing MATLAB expressions
Real	Real part of complex number
Strings	MATLAB string handling

Table A.4.2. String to Function Handle Conversion

func2str	Constructs a function name string from a function handle
str2func	Constructs a function handle from a function name string

Table A.4.3. String Manipulation

Deblank	Strip trailing blanks from the end of a string
Findstr	Find one string within another
Lower	Convert string to lowercase
Strcat	String concatenation
Strcmp	Compare strings
Strcmpi	Compare strings, ignoring case
strjust	Justify a character array
strmatch	Find possible matches for a string
strncmp	Compare the first n characters of strings
strncmpi	Compare the first n characters of strings, ignoring case
strrep	String search and replace
strtok	First token in string

strvcat	Vertical concatenation of strings
symvar	Determine symbolic variables in an expression
texlabel	Produce the TeX format from a character string
upper	Convert string to uppercase

Table A.4.4. String to Number Conversion

char	Create character array (string)
int2str	Integer to string conversion
mat2str	Convert a matrix into a string
num2str	Number to string conversion
Sprintf	Write formatted data to a string
Sscanf	Read string under format control
str2double	Convert string to double-precision value
str2mat	String to matrix conversion
str2num	String to number conversion

Table A.4.5. Radix Conversion

bin2dec	Binary to decimal number conversion
dec2bin	Decimal to binary number conversion
dec2hex	Decimal to hexadecimal number conversion
hex2dec	Hexadecimal to decimal number conversion
hex2num	Hexadecimal to double number conversion

Table A.5. Bit-Wise Functions

bitand	Bit-wise and
bitcmp	Complement bits
bitor	Bit-wise or
bitmax	Maximum floating-point integer
bitset	Set bit
bitshift	Bit-wise shift
bitget	Get bit
bitxor	Bit-wise xor

Table A.6. Structure Functions

fieldnames	Field names of a structure
getfield	Get field of structure array
rmfield	Remove structure fields
setfield	Set field of structure array
struct	Create structure array
struct2cell	Structure to cell array conversion

Table A.7. MATLAB Object Functions

class	Create object or return class of object
isa	Detect an object of a given class
methods	Display method names
methodsview	Displays information on all methods implemented by a class
subsasgn	Overloaded method for A(I)=B, A{I}=B, and A.field=B
subsindex	Overloaded method for X(A)
subsref	Overloaded method for A(I), A{I}, and A.field

Table A.8. Cell Array Functions

cell	Create cell array
cellfun	Apply a function to each element in a cell array
cellstr	Create cell array of strings from character array
cell2struct	Cell array to structure array conversion
celldisp	Display cell array contents
cellplot	Graphically display the structure of cell arrays
num2cell	Convert a numeric array into a cell array

Table A.9. Multidimensional Array Functions

cat	Concatenate arrays
flipdim	Flip array along a specified dimension
ind2sub	Subscripts from linear index
ipermute	Inverse permute the dimensions of a multidimensional array
ndgrid	Generate arrays for multidimensional functions and interpolation
ndims	Number of array dimensions
permute	Rearrange the dimensions of a multidimensional array
reshape	Reshape array
shiftdim	Shift dimensions
squeeze	Remove singleton dimensions
sub2ind	Single index from subscripts

Table A.10. MATLAB Functions

Table A.10.1. Mathematics: Elementary Mathematical Functions

abs	Absolute value and complex magnitude
acos, acosh	Inverse cosine and inverse hyperbolic cosine
acot, acoth	Inverse cotangent and inverse hyperbolic cotangent
acsc, acsch	Inverse cosecant and inverse hyperbolic cosecant
angle	Phase angle
asec, asech	Inverse secant and inverse hyperbolic secant
asin, asinh	Inverse sine and inverse hyperbolic sine
atan, atanh	Inverse tangent and inverse hyperbolic tangent
atan2	Four-quadrant inverse tangent
ceil	Round toward infinity
complex	Construct complex data from real and imaginary components
conj	Complex conjugate
cos, cosh	Cosine and hyperbolic cosine
cot, coth	Cotangent and hyperbolic cotangent
csc, csch	Cosecant and hyperbolic cosecant
exp	Exponential
fix	Round toward zero
floor	Round toward minus infinity
gcd	Greatest common divisor
imag	Imaginary part of a complex number
lcm	Least common multiple
log	Natural logarithm
log2	Base 2 logarithm and dissect floating-point numbers into exponent and mantissa
log10	Common (base 10) logarithm

mod	Modulus (signed remainder after division)
nchoosek	Binomial coefficient or all combinations
real	Real part of complex number
rem	Remainder after division
round	Round to nearest integer
sec, sech	Secant and hyperbolic secant
sign	Signum function
sin, sinh	Sine and hyperbolic sine
sqrt	Square root
tan, tanh	Tangent and hyperbolic tangent

Table A.10.2. Plotting and Data Visualization

Table A.10.2.1. Basic Plots and Graphs

bar	Vertical bar chart
barh	Horizontal bar chart
hist	Plot histograms
histc	Histogram count
hold	Hold current graph
loglog	Plot using loglog scales
pie	Pie plot
plot	Plot vectors or matrices.
polar	Polar coordinate plot
semilogx	Semi-log scale plot
semilogy	Semi-log scale plot
subplot	Create axes in tiled positions

Table A.10.2.2. Three-Dimensional Plotting

bar3	Vertical 3D bar chart
bar3h	Horizontal 3D bar chart
comet3	3D comet plot
cylinder	Generate cylinder
fill3	Draw filled 3D polygons in three-space
plot3	Plot lines and 3D points (in three-dimensional space)
quiver3	3D quiver (or velocity) plot
slice	Volumetric slice plot
sphere	Generate sphere
stem3	Plot discrete surface data
waterfall	Waterfall plot

Table A.10.2.3. Plot Annotation and Grids

clabel	Add contour labels to a contour plot
datetick	Date formatted tick labels
grid	Grid lines for 2D and 3D plots
gtext	Place text on a 2D graph using a mouse
legend	Graph legend for lines and patches
plotyy	Plot graphs with Y tick labels on the left and right
title	Titles for 2D and 3D plots
xlabel	X-axis labels for 2D and 3D plots

ylabel	Y-axis labels for 2D and 3D plots
zlabel	Z-axis labels for 3D plots

Table A.10.2.4. Surface, Mesh, and Contour Plots

contour	Contour (level curves) plot
contourc	Contour computation
contourf	Filled contour plot
hidden	Mesh hidden line removal mode
meshc	Combination mesh/contourplot
mesh	3D mesh with reference plane
peaks	A sample function of two variables
surf	3D shaded surface graph
surface	Create surface low-level objects
surfc	Combination surf/contourplot
surfl	3D shaded surface with lighting
trimesh	Triangular mesh plot
trisurf	Triangular surface plot

Table A.10.3. Volume Visualization

coneplot	Plot velocity vectors as cones in 3D vector field
contourslice	Draw contours in volume slice plane
curl	Compute the curl and angular velocity of a vector field
divergence	Compute the divergence of a vector field
flow	Generate scalar volume data
interpstreamspeed	Interpolate streamline vertices from vector-field magnitudes
isocaps	Compute isosurface end-cap geometry
isocolors	Compute the colors of isosurface vertices
isonormals	Compute normals of isosurface vertices
isosurface	Extract isosurface data from volume data
reducepatch	Reduce the number of patch faces
reducevolume	Reduce number of elements in volume data set
shrinkfaces	Reduce the size of patch faces
slice	Draw slice planes in volume
smooth3	Smooth 3D data
stream2	Compute 2D streamline data
stream3	Compute 3D streamline data
streamline	Draw streamlines from two- or three-dimensional vector data
streamparticles	Draws stream particles from vector volume data
streamribbon	Draws stream ribbons from vector volume data
streamslice	Draws well-spaced streamlines from vector volume data
streamtube	Draws stream tubes from vector volume data
surf2patch	Convert surface data to patch data
subvolume	Extract subset of volume data set
volumebounds	Return coordinate and color limits for volume (scalar and vector)

Table A.10.4. Domain Generation

griddata	Data gridding and surface fitting
meshgrid	Generation of X and Y arrays for 3D plots

Table A.10.5. Specialized Plotting

area	Area plot
box	Axis box for 2D and 3D plots
comet	Comet plot
compass	Compass plot
errorbar	Plot graph with error bars
ezcontour	Easy-to-use contour plotter
ezcontourf	Easy-to-use filled contour plotter
ezmesh	Easy-to-use 3D mesh plotter
ezmeshc	Easy-to-use combination mesh/contour plotter
ezplot	Easy-to-use function plotter
ezplot3	Easy-to-use 3D parametric curve plotter
ezpolar	Easy-to-use polar coordinate plotter
ezsurf	Easy-to-use 3D colored surface plotter
ezsurfc	Easy-to-use combination surface/contour plotter
feather	Feather plot
fill	Draw filled 2D polygons
fplot	Plot a function
pareto	Pareto char
pie3	3D pie plot
plotmatrix	Scatter plot matrix
pcolor	Pseudocolor (checkerboard) plot
rose	Plot rose or angle histogram
quiver	Quiver (or velocity) plot
ribbon	Ribbon plot
stairs	Stairstep graph
scatter	Scatter plot
scatter3	3D scatter plot
stem	Plot discrete sequence data
convhull	Convex hull
delaunay	Delaunay triangulation
dsearch	Search Delaunay triangulation for nearest point
inpolygon	True for points inside a polygonal region
polyarea	Area of polygon
tsearch	Search for enclosing Delaunay triangle
voronoi	Voronoi diagram

Table A.10.6. View Control

camdolly	Move camera position and target
camlookat	View specific objects
camorbit	Orbit about camera target
campan	Rotate camera target about camera position
campos	Set or get camera position
camproj	Set or get projection type
camroll	Rotate camera about viewing axis
camtarget	Set or get camera target
camup	Set or get camera up-vector
camva	Set or get camera view angle
camzoom	Zoom camera in or out

daspect	Set or get data aspect ratio
pbaspect	Set or get plot box aspect ratio
view	3-D graph viewpoint specification.
viewmtx	Generate view transformation matrices
xlim	Set or get the current x-axis limits
ylim	Set or get the current y-axis limits
zlim	Set or get the current z-axis limits

Table A.10.7. Lighting

camlight	Cerate or position Light
light	Light object creation function
lighting	Lighting mode
lightangle	Position light in spherical coordinates
material	Material reflectance mode

Table A.10.8. Transparency

Alpha	Set or query transparency properties for objects in current axes
Alphamap	Specify the figure alphamap
Alim	Set or query the axes alpha limits

Table A.10.9. Color Operations

Brighten	Brighten or darken colormap
Caxis	Pseudocolor axis scaling
Colorbar	Display color bar (color scale)
Colordef	Set up color defaults
Colormap	Set the color look-up table (list of colormaps)
Graymon	Graphics figure defaults set for grayscale monitor
hsv2rgb	Hue-saturation-value to red-green-blue conversion
rgb2hsv	RGB to HSV conversion
Rgbplot	Plot colormap
Shading	Color shading mode
Spinmap	Spin the colormap
Surfnorm	3D surface normals
Whitebg	Change axes background color for plots

Table A.10.10. Colormaps

Autumn	Shades of red and yellow colormap
bone	Gray-scale with a tinge of blue colormap
contrast	Gray colormap to enhance image contrast
cool	Shades of cyan and magenta colormap
copper	Linear copper-tone colormap
flag	Alternating red, white, blue, and black colormap
gray	Linear gray-scale colormap
hot	Black-red-yellow-white colormap
hsv	Hue-saturation-value (HSV) colormap
jet	Variant of HSV
lines	Line color colormap
prism	Colormap of prism colors
spring	Shades of magenta and yellow colormap

summer	Shades of green and yellow colormap
winter	Shades of blue and green colormap

Table A.10.11. Printing

orient	Hardcopy paper orientation
pagesetupdlg	Page position dialog box
print	Print graph or save graph to file
printdlg	Print dialog box
printopt	Configure local printer defaults
saveas	Save figure to graphic file

Table A.10.12. Handle Graphics, General

allchild	Find all children of specified objects
copyobj	Make a copy of a graphics object and its children
findall	Find all graphics objects (including hidden handles)
findobj	Find objects with specified property values
gcbo	Return object whose callback is currently executing
gco	Return handle of current object
get	Get object properties
rotate	Rotate objects about specified origin and direction
ishandle	True for graphics objects
set	Set object properties

Table A.10.13. Working with Application Data

getappdata	Get value of application data
isappdata	True if application data exists
rmappdata	Remove application data
setappdata	Specify application data

Table A.10.14. Handle Graphics and Object Creation

axes	Create Axes object
figure	Create Figure (graph) windows
image	Create Image (2D matrix)
light	Create Light object (illuminates Patch and Surface)
line	Create Line object (3D polylines)
patch	Create Patch object (polygons)
rectangle	Create Rectangle object (2D rectangle)
surface	Create Surface (quadrilaterals)
text	Create Text object (character strings)
uicontextmenu	Create context menu (popup associated with object)

Table A.10.15. Handle Graphics, Figure Windows

capture	Screen capture of the current figure
clc	Clear figure window
clf	Clear figure
close	Close specified window
closereq	Default close request function
gcf	Get current figure handle
newplot	Graphics M-file preamble for NextPlot property

refresh	Refresh figure
saveas	Save figure or model to desired output format

Table A.10.16. Handle Graphics, Axes

axis	Plot axis scaling and appearance
cla	Clear Axes
gca	Get current Axes handle

Table A.10.17. Object Manipulation

Reset	Reset axis or figure
rotate3d	Interactively rotate the view of a 3D plot
Selectmoveresize	Interactively select, move, or resize objects

Table A.10.18. Interactive User Input

ginput	Graphical input from a mouse or cursor
zoom	Zoom in and out on a 2D plot

Table A.10.19. Region of Interest

Dragrect	Drag XOR rectangles with mouse
Drawnow	Complete any pending drawing
Rbbox	Rubberband box

Table A.11. Polynomial and Interpolation Functions

Table A.11.1. Polynomials

conv	Convolution and polynomial multiplication
deconv	Deconvolution and polynomial division
poly	Polynomial with specified roots
polyder	Polynomial derivative
polyeig	Polynomial eigenvalue problem
polyfit	Polynomial curve fitting
polyint	Analytic polynomial integration
polyval	Polynomial evaluation
polyvalm	Matrix polynomial evaluation
residue	Convert partial fraction expansion and polynomial coefficients
roots	Polynomial roots

Table A.11.2. Data Interpolation

convhull	Convex hull
convhulln	Multidimensional convex hull
delaunay	Delaunay triangulation
delaunay3	Three-dimensional Delaunay tessellation
delaunayn	Multidimensional Delaunay tessellation
dsearch	Search for nearest point
dsearchn	Multidimensional closest point search
griddata	Data gridding
griddata3	Data gridding and hypersurface fitting for three-dimensional data
griddatan	Data gridding and hypersurface fitting (dimension ≥ 2)
interp1	One-dimensional data interpolation (table lookup)
interp2	Two-dimensional data interpolation (table lookup)

`interp3`	Three-dimensional data interpolation (table lookup)
`interpft`	One-dimensional interpolation using the fast Fourier transform
`interpn`	Multidimensional data interpolation (table lookup)
`meshgrid`	Generate X and Y matrices for three-dimensional plots
`ndgrid`	Generate arrays for multidimensional functions and interpolation
`pchip`	Piecewise Cubic Hermite Interpolating Polynomial (PCHIP)
`ppval`	Piecewise polynomial evaluation
`spline`	Cubic spline data interpolation
`tsearch`	Search for enclosing Delaunay triangle
`tsearchn`	Multidimensional closest simplex search
`voronoi`	Voronoi diagram
`voronoin`	Multidimensional Voronoi diagrams

Table A.12. Functions: Nonlinear Numerical Methods

`bvp4c`	Solve two-point boundry value problems (BVPs) for ordinary differential equations (ODEs)
`Bvpget`	Extract parameters from BVP options structure
`Bvpinit`	Form the initial guess for the bvp4c solver
`bvpset`	Create/alter BVP options structure
`bvpval`	Evaluate the solution computed by the bvp4c solver
`dblquad`	Numerical evaluation of double integrals
`fminbnd`	Minimize a function of one variable
`fminsearch`	Minimize a function of several variables
`fzero`	Find zero of a function of one variable
`ode45, ode23, ode113, ode15s, ode23s, ode23t, ode23tb`	Solution of ordinary linear and nonlinear differential equations
`odeget`	Extract parameters from ODE options structure
`odeset`	Create/alter ODE options structure
`optimget`	Get optimization options structure parameter values
`optimset`	Create or edit optimization options parameter structure
`pdepe`	Solve initial-boundary value problems for parabolic-elliptic partial differential equations
`pdeval`	Evaluate the solution computed by the `pdepe` solver
`quad`	Numerical evaluation of integrals, adaptive Simpson quadrature
`quadl`	Numerical evaluation of integrals, adaptive Lobatto quadrature
`vectorize`	Vectorize expression

Table A.13. Matrices and Matrix Manipulation
Table A.13.1. Elementary Matrices and Arrays

`blkdiag`	Construct a block diagonal matrix from input arguments
`eye`	Create an identity matrix
`linspace`	Generate linearly spaced vectors
`logspace`	Generate logarithmically spaced vectors
`numel`	Number of elements in a matrix or cell array
`ones`	Create an array of all ones

rand	Uniformly distributed random numbers and arrays
randn	Normally distributed random numbers and arrays
zeros	Create an array of all zeros
: (colon)	Regularly spaced vector

Table A.13.2. Special Variables and Constants

ans	Recent answer
computer	Identify the computer on which MATLAB is running
eps	Floating-point relative accuracy
i	Imaginary number $\sqrt{-1}$
inf	Infinity
inputname	Input argument name
j	Imaginary number $\sqrt{-1}$
NaN	Not-a-Number
nargin, nargout	Number of function arguments
nargoutchk	Validate number of output arguments
pi	Ratio of a circle's circumference to its diameter (π constant)
realmax	Largest positive floating-point number
realmin	Smallest positive floating-point number
varargin, varargout	Pass or return variable numbers of arguments

Table A.13.3. Time and Dates

calendar	Calendar
clock	Current time as a date vector
cputime	Elapsed CPU time
date	Current date string
datenum	Serial date number
datestr	Date string format
datevec	Date components
eomday	End of month
etime	Elapsed time
now	Current date and time
tic, toc	Stopwatch timer
weekday	Day of the week

Table A.13.4. Matrix Manipulation

cat	Concatenate arrays
diag	Create diagonal matrices and diagonals of a matrix
fliplr	Flip matrices left - right
flipud	Flip matrices up - down
repmat	Replicate and tile an array
reshape	Reshape array
rot90	Rotate matrix by 90 degrees
tril	Lower triangular part of a matrix
triu	Upper triangular part of a matrix
: (colon)	Index into array, rearrange array

Table A.13.5. Vector Functions

cross	Vector cross product
dot	Vector dot product
intersect	Set intersection of two vectors
ismember	Detect members of a set
setdiff	Return the set difference of two vectors
setxor	Set exclusive or of two vectors
union	Set union of two vectors
unique	Unique elements of a vector

Table A.13.6. Specialized Matrices

company	Companion matrix
gallery	Test matrices
hadamard	Hadamard matrix
hankel	Hankel matrix
hilb	Hilbert matrix
invhilb	Inverse of the Hilbert matrix
magic	Magic square
pascal	Pascal matrix
toeplitz	Toeplitz matrix
wilkinson	Wilkinson's eigenvalue test matrix

Table A.14. Matrix Functions and Linear Algebra

Table A.14.1. Matrix Analysis

cond	Condition number with respect to inversion
condeig	Condition number with respect to eigenvalues
det	Matrix determinant
norm	Vector and matrix norms
null	Null space of a matrix
orth	Range space of a matrix
rank	Rank of a matrix
rcond	Matrix reciprocal condition number estimate
rref, rrefmovie	Reduced row echelon form
subspace	Angle between two subspaces
trace	Sum of diagonal elements

Table A.14.2. Linear Equations

chol	Cholesky factorization
inv	Matrix inverse
lscov	Least squares solution in the presence of known covariance
lu	LU matrix factorization
lsqnonneg	Nonnegative least squares
minres	Minimum residual method
pinv	Moore-Penrose pseudoinverse of a matrix
qr	Orthogonal-triangular decomposition
symmlq	Symmetric LQ method

Table A.14.3. Eigenvalues and Singular Values

balance	Improve accuracy of computed eigenvalues
cdf2rdf	Convert complex diagonal form to real block diagonal form
eig	Eigenvalues and eigenvectors
gsvd	Generalized singular value decomposition
hess	Hessenberg form of a matrix
poly	Polynomial with specified roots
qz	QZ factorization for generalized eigenvalues
rsf2csf	Convert real Schur form to complex Schur form
schur	Schur decomposition
svd	Singular value decomposition

Table A.14.4. Matrix Functions

expm	Matrix exponential
funm	Evaluate general matrix function
logm	Matrix logarithm
sqrtm	Matrix square root

Table A.14.5. Low Level Functions

qrdelete	Delete column from QR factorization
qrinsert	Insert column in QR factorization

Table A.14.6. Sparse Matrix Functions (Elementary Sparse Matrices)

spdiags	Extract and create sparse band and diagonal matrices
speye	Sparse identity matrix
sprand	Sparse uniformly distributed random matrix
sprandn	Sparse normally distributed random matrix
sprandsym	Sparse symmetric random matrix

Table A.14.7. Full-to-Sparse Conversion

find	Find indices and values of nonzero elements
full	Convert sparse matrix to full matrix
sparse	Create sparse matrix
spconvert	Import matrix from sparse matrix external format

Table A.14.8. Sparse Matrices with Nonzero Entries

nnz	Number of nonzero matrix elements
nonzeros	Nonzero matrix elements
nzmax	Amount of storage allocated for nonzero matrix elements
spalloc	Allocate space for sparse matrix
spfun	Apply function to nonzero sparse matrix elements
spones	Replace nonzero sparse matrix elements with ones

Table A.14.9. Visualizing Sparse Matrices

spy	Visualize sparsity pattern

Table A.14.10. Reordering Algorithms

colamd	Column approximate minimum degree permutation
colmmd	Sparse column minimum degree permutation

`colperm`	Sparse column permutation based on nonzero count
`dmperm`	Dulmage-Mendelsohn decomposition
`randperm`	Random permutation
`symamd`	Symmetric approximate minimum degree permutation
`symmmd`	Sparse symmetric minimum degree ordering
`symrcm`	Sparse reverse Cuthill-McKee ordering

Table A.14.11. Norm, Condition Number, and Rank

`condest`	Estimate the matrix first-norm
`normest`	Estimates the matrix second-norm

Table A.14.12. Sparse Systems of Linear Equations

`bicg`	BiConjugate Gradients method
`bicgstab`	BiConjugate Gradients Stabilized method
`cgs`	Conjugate Gradients Squared method
`cholinc`	Sparse Incomplete Cholesky and Cholesky-Infinity factorizations
`cholupdate`	Rank 1 update to Cholesky factorization
`gmres`	Generalized Minimum Residual method (with restarts)
`lsqr`	LSQR implementation of Conjugate Gradients on the normal equations
`luinc`	Incomplete LU matrix factorizations
`pcg`	Preconditioned Conjugate Gradients method
`qmr`	Quasi-Minimal Residual method
`qr`	Orthogonal-triangular decomposition
`qrdelete`	Delete column from QR factorization
`qrinsert`	Insert column in QR factorization
`qrupdate`	Rank 1 update to QR factorization

Table A.14.13. Sparse Eigenvalues and Singular Values

`eigs`	Find eigenvalues and eigenvectors
`svds`	Find singular values

Table A.14.14. Miscellaneous

`spparms`	Set parameters for sparse matrix routines

Table A.15. Coordinate System Conversion

`cart2pol`	Transform Cartesian coordinates to polar or cylindrical
`cart2sph`	Transform Cartesian coordinates to spherical
`pol2cart`	Transform polar or cylindrical coordinates to Cartesian
`sph2cart`	Transform spherical coordinates to Cartesian

Table A.16. Data Analysis and Fourier Transform Functions
Table A.16.1. Basic Operations

`cumprod`	Cumulative product
`cumsum`	Cumulative sum
`cumtrapz`	Cumulative trapezoidal numerical integration
`factor`	Prime factors
`inpolygon`	Detect points inside a polygonal region
`max`	Maximum elements of an array
`mean`	Average or mean value of arrays

median	Median value of arrays
min	Minimum elements of an array
perms	All possible permutations
polyarea	Area of polygon
primes	Generate list of prime numbers
prod	Product of array elements
rectint	Rectangle intersection area
sort	Sort elements in ascending order
sortrows	Sort rows in ascending order
std	Standard deviation
sum	Sum of array elements
trapz	Trapezoidal numerical integration
var	Variance

Table A.16.2. Finite Differences

del2	Discrete Laplacian
diff	Differences and approximate derivatives
gradient	Numerical gradient

Table A.16.3. Correlation

corrcoef	Correlation coefficients
cov	Covariance matrix

Table A.16.4. Filtering and Convolution

conv	Convolution and polynomial multiplication
conv2	Two-dimensional convolution
deconv	Deconvolution and polynomial division
filter	Filter data with an infinite impulse response or finite impulse response filter
filter2	Two-dimensional digital filtering

Table A.16.5. Fourier Transforms

abs	Absolute value and complex magnitude
angle	Phase angle
cplxpair	Sort complex numbers into complex conjugate pairs
fft	One-dimensional fast Fourier transform
fft2	Two-dimensional fast Fourier transform
fftshift	Shift dc component of fast Fourier transform to center of spectrum
ifft	Inverse one-dimensional fast Fourier transform
ifft2	Inverse two-dimensional fast Fourier transform
ifftn	Inverse multidimensional fast Fourier transform
ifftshift	Inverse fast Fourier transform shift
nextpow2	Next power of two
unwrap	Correct phase angles

Table A.17. Graphical User Interface

Table A.17.1. Dialog Boxes

dialog	Create a dialog box
errordlg	Create error dialog box
helpdlg	Display help dialog box

`inputdlg`	Create input dialog box
`listdlg`	Create list selection dialog box
`msgbox`	Create message dialog box
`pagedlg`	Display page layout dialog box
`printdlg`	Display print dialog box
`questdlg`	Create question dialog box
`uigetfile`	Display dialog box to retrieve name of file for reading
`uiputfile`	Display dialog box to retrieve name of file for writing
`uisetcolor`	Interactively set a ColorSpec using a dialog box
`uisetfont`	Interactively set a font using a dialog box
`warndlg`	Create warning dialog box

Table A.17.2. User Interface Deployment

`guidata`	Store or retrieve application data
`guihandles`	Create a structure of handles
`movegui`	Move GUI figure onscreen
`openfig`	Open or raise GUI figure

Table A.17.3. User Interface Development

`guide`	Open the GUI Layout Editor
`inspect`	Display Property Inspector

Table A.18. External Interfaces: MATLAB Interface to Java

`class`	Create object or return class of object
`import`	Add a package or class to the current Java import list
`isa`	Detect an object of a given class
`isjava`	Test whether an object is a Java object
`javaArray`	Constructs a Java array
`javaMethod`	Invokes a Java method
`javaObject`	Constructs a Java object
`methods`	Display method names
`methodsview`	Displays information on all methods implemented by a class

Table A.19. Serial Port Input-Output
Table A.19.1. Creating a Serial Port Object

`serial`	Create a serial port object

Table A.19.2. Writing and Reading Data

`fgetl`	Read one line of text from the device and discard the terminator
`fgets`	Read one line of text from the device and include the terminator
`fprintf`	Write formatted data to file
`fread`	Read binary data from file
`fscanf`	Read data from file and format as text (read formatted data from file)
`fwrite`	Write binary data to file
`readasync`	Read data asynchronously from file
`stopasync`	Stop asynchronous read and write operations

Table A.19.3. Configuring and Returning Properties

get	Return serial port object properties
set	Configure or display serial port object properties

Table A.19.4. State Change

fclose	Disconnect a serial port object from the device (close file)
fopen	Connect a serial port object to the device (open file)
record	Record data and event information to a file

Table A.19.5. General Purpose

clear	Remove a serial port object from the MATLAB workspace
delete	Remove a serial port object from memory
disp	Display serial port object summary information
instraction	Display event information when an event occurs
instrfind	Return serial port objects from memory to the MATLAB workspace
isvalid	Determine if serial port objects are valid
length	Length of serial port object array
load	Load serial port objects and variables into the MATLAB workspace
save	Save serial port objects and variables to an m-file
serialbreak	Send a break to the device connected to the serial port
size	Size of serial port object array

REFERENCES

1.   *MATLAB 6.5 Release 13,* CD-ROM, MathWorks, Inc., 2002.

Index

Aircraft, 139-141, 162-167
Algebraic equation, 95-97
Arithmetic, 42-48
Arithmetic operators, 65
Array, 51, 52, 211, 218, 218

Basic arithmetic, 42
Block diagram, 170, 179-189, 194, 197, 201
Buttons, 23

Characters, 31
Circuit, 144, 145, 154-157, 159-161, 167-169
Clear, 24
Color operation, 103, 215
Command window, 5, 8, 43-46
Commands, 32-41
Conditions, 73-79
Control flow, 208
Converter, 145-151

Debugging, 209
Demo, 9, 16
Demo window, 17-20, 39
Differential equations, 133-139, 146-170, 218
Dynamic system, 133-151, 163, 190-193

Eigenvalue, 61, 62, 221, 222
Exit, 22

Figure window, 8, 9
File window, 8, 9
Flight servo, 141
Format, 68
Fourier transform, 222, 223
Functions, 27-30

General purpose commands, 14, 15, 37, 38
Graphics, 99-120, 216, 217

Help, 9, 10, 33-36, 39
Helpdesk, 9, 15
Helpwin, 9, 10, 33
Help system, 23, 24
Help topics, 10-13
Help window, 13, 36, 43
Helpdesk window, 16
Helpwin window, 33

Image, 25, 26
Induction motor, 195-199
Interactive input, 208
Interpolation, 72, 73, 217

Kirchhoff law, 145

Linear equation, 220
Logic, 66
Logic functions, 207
Loops, 73-79

Mathematical function, 29, 30, 47, 48, 211-212
Mathematical model, 141-151
MATLAB General, 13
MATLAB Icon, 5
Matrix, 8, 43, 53-64, 67, 83-89, 218-221
Menu bar, 22, 23
Missile, 20
Modeling, 141, 152
Movie, 121-124

Newton law, 141-144
Norm, 67

Object-oriented programming, 208
Ones, 8
Operators, 31, 65-67, 207

Pendulum, 143, 179-181
Permanent-magnet DC motor, 169-171,
                                187-190, 203-205
Permanent-magnet synchronous motor, 200-202
Plot, 27, 45, 46, 60, 99-120, 125-132, 212-214
Polynomial, 69-73, 89, 90, 217
Print, 216

Quit, 22

Save, 24
Saving, 24
Scalar, 50-51
SIMULINK, 1, 2, 172-206
SIMULINK demo window, 174, 175, 185
SIMULINK libraries, 182
SIMULINK librarary browser, 183-185
SIMULINK window, 173

Single phase reluctance motor, 193, 194
Special characters, 207
Start, 5
String, 25, 42, 68, 209, 210
Symbolic Math Toolbox, 157-161
Symbols, 31, 65

Toolboxes, 7, 18, 20-22
Tool bar, 22, 23

Three-dimensional graphics, 113-120, 124, 125
Trigonometric functions, 20

Variable, 49
Vector, 51, 52
Van der Pol equation, 134-137, 176-179

Workspace window, 5, 8, 25, 43-46